REGARDING THE MATTER OF
OSWALD'S BODY

Published by

[redacted]

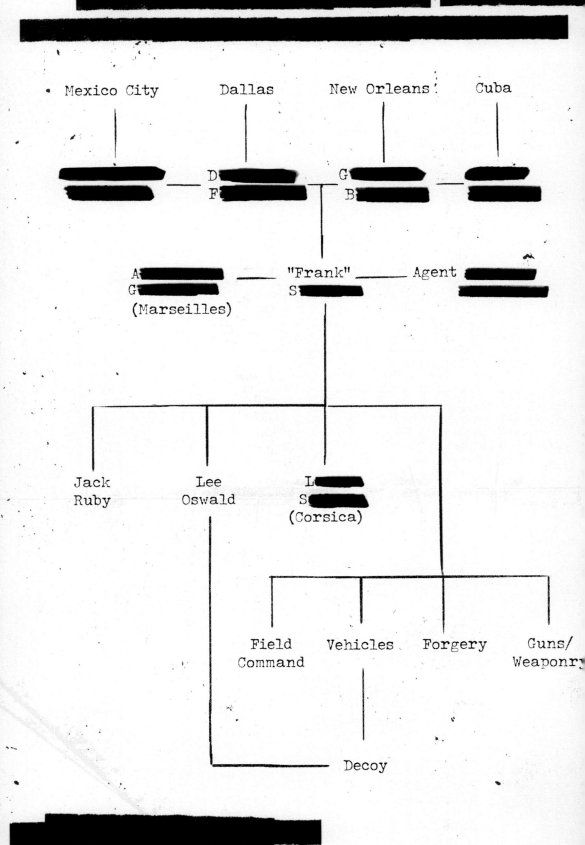

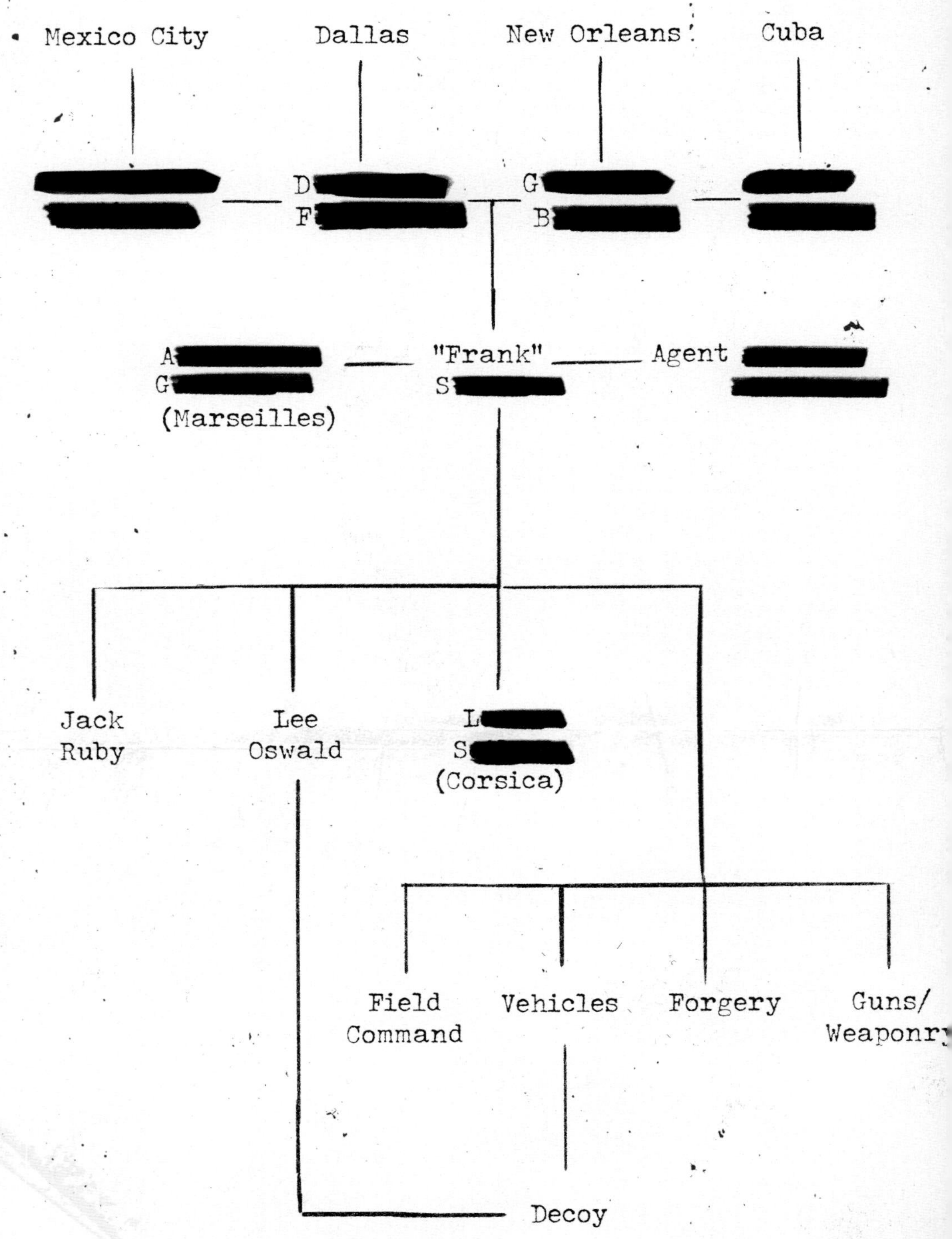
Mexico City
Dallas
New Orleans
Cuba
[redacted]
D[redacted]
F[redacted]
G[redacted]
B[redacted]
[redacted]
A[redacted]
G[redacted]
(Marseilles)
"Frank"
S[redacted]
Agent [redacted]
Jack
Ruby
Lee
Oswald
L[redacted]
S[redacted]
(Corsica)
Field
Command
Vehicles
Forgery
Guns/
Weaponr
Decoy

[redacted]

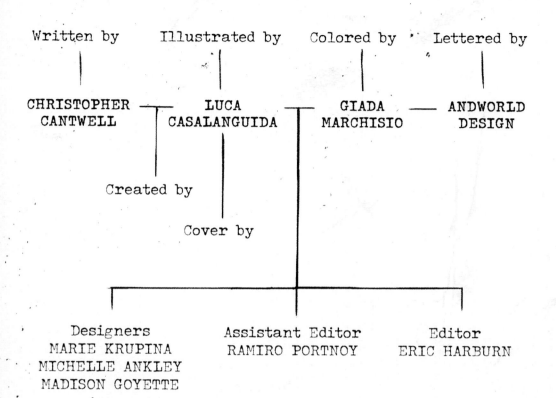

REGARDING THE MATTER OF OSWALD'S BODY

Written by
CHRISTOPHER CANTWELL

Illustrated by
LUCA CASALANGUIDA

Colored by
GIADA MARCHISIO

Lettered by
ANDWORLD DESIGN

Created by

Cover by

Designers
MARIE KRUPINA
MICHELLE ANKLEY
MADISON GOYETTE

Assistant Editor
RAMIRO PORTNOY

Editor
ERIC HARBURN

Ross Richie Chairman & Founder
Jen Harned CFO
Matt Gagnon Editor-in-Chief
Filip Sablik President, Publishing & Marketing
Stephen Christy President, Development
Lance Kreiter Vice President, Licensing & Merchandising
Bryce Carlson Vice President, Editorial & Creative Strategy
Hunter Gorinson Vice President, Business Development
Josh Hayes Vice President, Sales
Sierra Hahn Executive Editor
Eric Harburn Executive Editor
Ryan Matsunaga Director, Marketing
Stephanie Lazarski Director, Operations
Elyse Strandberg Manager, Finance
Michelle Ankley Manager, Production Design
Cheryl Parker Manager, Human Resources
Dafna Pleban Senior Editor
Elizabeth Brei Editor
Kathleen Wisneski Editor
Sophie Philips-Roberts Editor
Allyson Gronowitz Associate Editor
Gavin Gronenthal Assistant Editor
Gwen Waller Assistant Editor
Ramiro Portnoy Assistant Editor
Kenzie Rzonca Assistant Editor
Rey Netschke Editorial Assistant
Marie Krupina Design Lead
Crystal White Design Lead
Grace Park Design Coordinator
Madison Goyette Production Designer
Veronica Gutierrez Production Designer
Jessy Gould Production Designer
Nancy Mojica Production Designer
Samantha Knapp Production Design Assistant
Esther Kim Marketing Lead
Breanna Sarpy Marketing Lead, Digital
Amanda Lawson Marketing Coordinator
Alex Lorenzen Marketing Coordinator, Copywriter
Grecia Martinez Marketing Assistant, Digital
José Meza Consumer Sales Lead
Ashley Troub Consumer Sales Coordinator
Harley Salbacka Sales Coordinator
Megan Christopher Operations Lead
Rodrigo Hernandez Operations Coordinator
Jason Lee Senior Accountant
Faizah Bashir Business Analyst
Amber Peters Staff Accountant
Sabrina Lesin Accounting Assistant

CHAPTER VIII.
DOPPELGÄNGERS, OR DOUBLES.

In the instances detailed in the last chapter, the apparition has shown itself, as nearly as could be discovered, at the moment of dissolution; but there are many cases in which the wraith is seen at an indefinite period before or after the catastrophe. Of these I could quote a great number; but as they generally resolve themselves into simply seeing a person where they were not, and death ensuing very shortly afterward, a few will suffice.

There is a very remarkable story of this kind, related by Macnish, which he calls "a case of hallucination, arising without the individual being conscious of any physical cause by which it might be occasioned." If this case stood alone, strange as it is, I should think so too; but when similar instances abound, as they do, I can not bring myself to dispose of it so easily. The story is as follows: Mr. H—— was one day walking along the street, apparently in perfect health, when he saw, or supposed he saw, his acquaintance, Mr. C——, walking before him. He called to him aloud; but he did not seem to hear him, and continued moving on. Mr. H—— then quickened his pace for the purpose of overtaking him; but the other increased his, also, as if to keep ahead of his pursuer, and proceeded at such a rate that Mr. H—— found it impossible to make up to him. This continued for some time, till, on Mr. C——'s reaching a gate, he opened it and passed in, slamming it violently in Mr. H——'s face. Confounded at such treatment from a friend, the latter instantly opened the gate, and looked down the long lane into which it led, where, to his astonishment, no one was to be seen. Determined to unravel the mystery, he then went to Mr. C——'s house, and his surprise was great to hear that he was confined to his bed, and had been so for several days. A week or two afterward, these gentlemen met at the house of a common friend, when Mr. H—— related the circumstance, jocularly telling Mr. C—— that, as he had seen his wraith, he of course could not live long. The person addressed laughed heartily, as did the rest of the party; but, in a few days, Mr. C—— was attacked with putrid sore throat and died; and within a short period of his death, Mr. H—— was also in the grave.

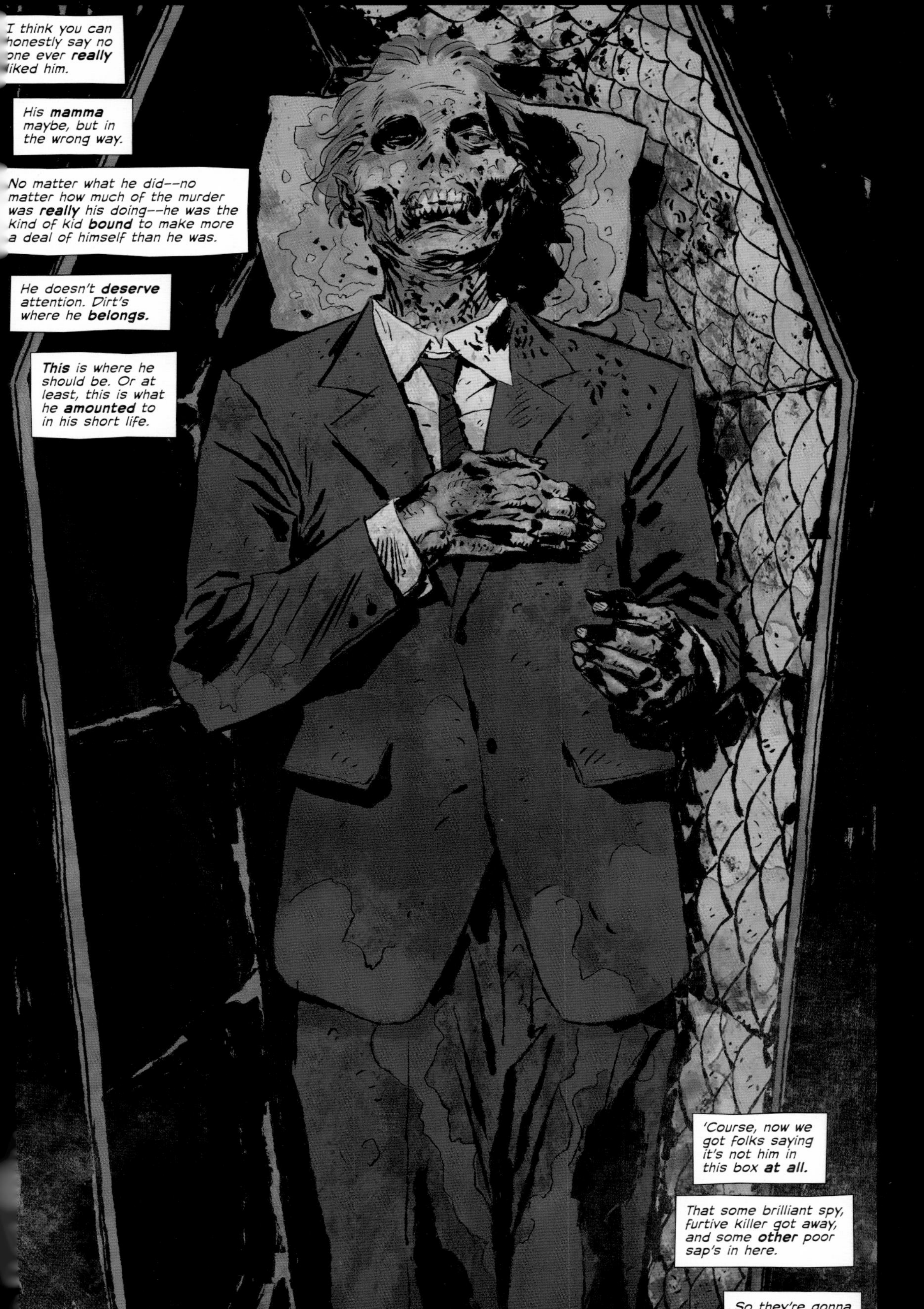
I think you can honestly say no one ever **really** liked him.
His **mamma** maybe, but in the wrong way.
No matter what he did--no matter how much of the murder **was really** his doing--he **was** the kind of kid **bound** to make more a deal of himself than he was.
He doesn't **deserve** attention. Dirt's where he **belongs.**
This is where he should be. Or at least, this is what he **amounted** to in his short life.
'Course, now we got folks saying it's not him in this box **at all.**
That some brilliant spy, furtive killer got away, and some **other** poor sap's in here.
So they're gonna **dig him up.**

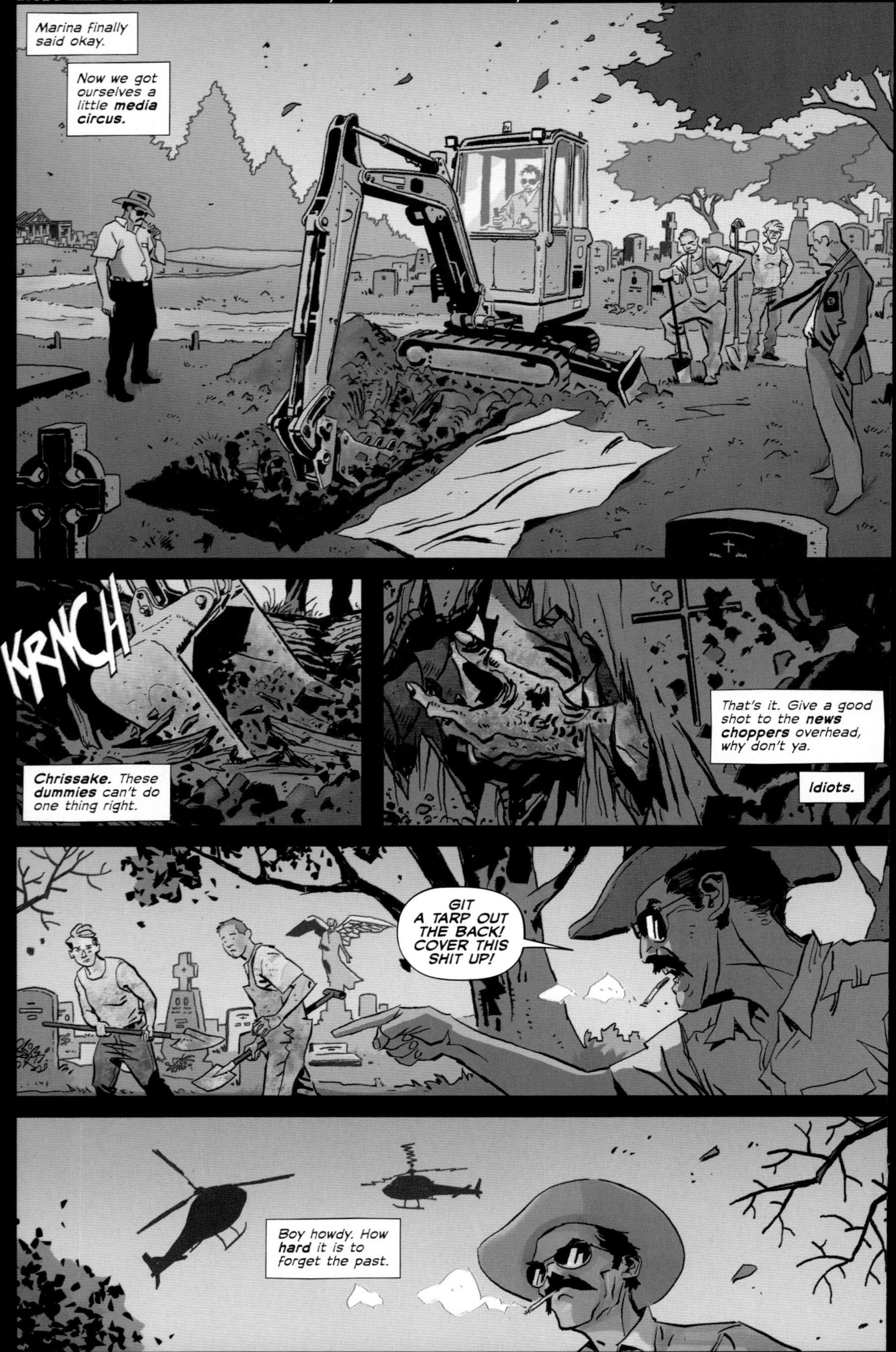

Rose Hill Burial Park. Fort Worth, Texas.
Marina finally said okay.
Now we got ourselves a little **media circus.**
KRNCH
Chrissake. These **dummies** can't do one thing right.
That's it. Give a good shot to the **news choppers** overhead, why don't ya.
Idiots.
GIT A TARP OUT THE BACK! COVER THIS SHIT UP!
Boy howdy. How **hard** it is to forget the past.

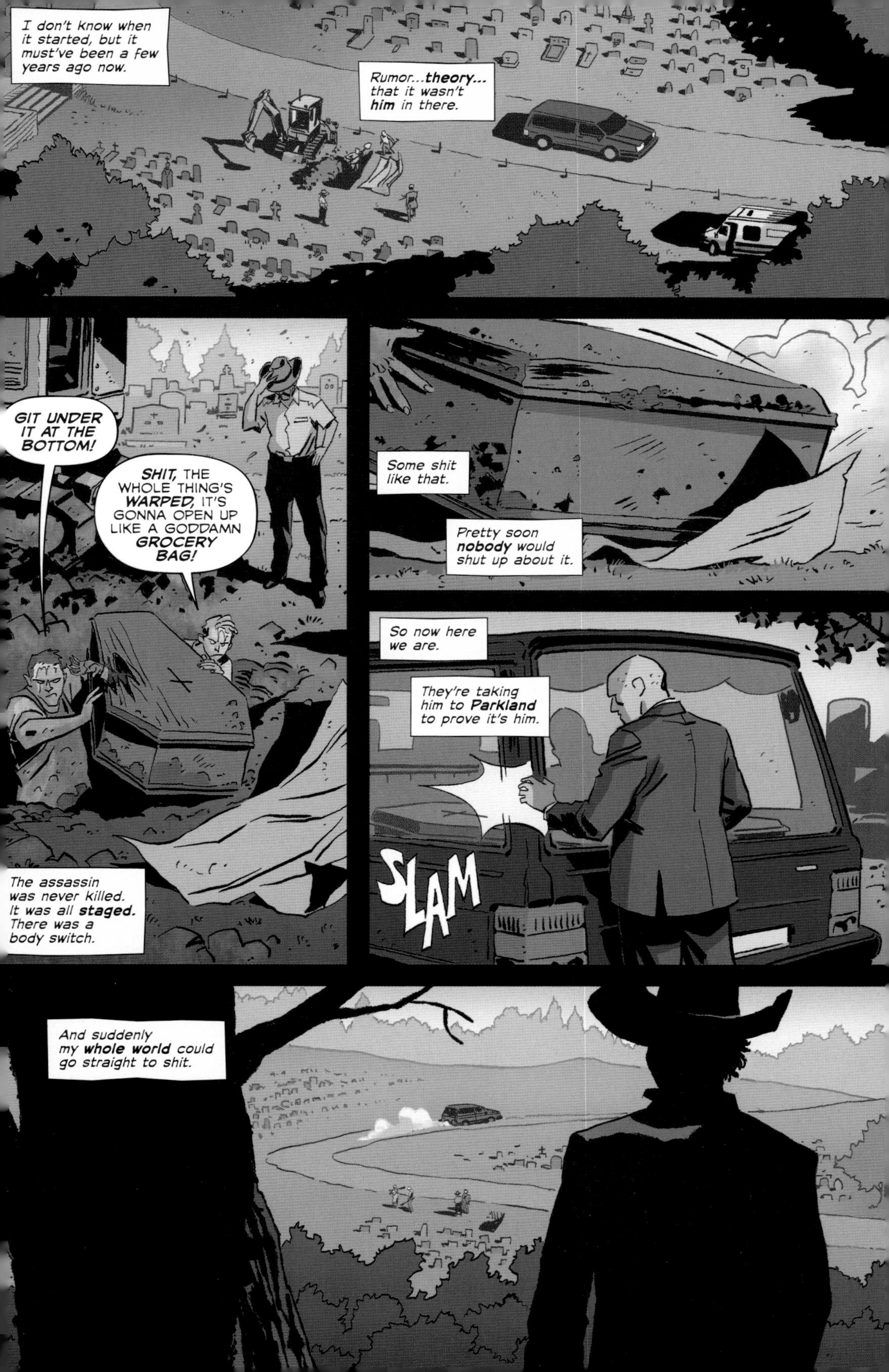
I don't know when it started, but it must've been a few years ago now.
Rumor...theory... that it wasn't him in there.
GIT UNDER IT AT THE BOTTOM!
SHIT, THE WHOLE THING'S WARPED, IT'S GONNA OPEN UP LIKE A GODDAMN GROCERY BAG!
The assassin was never killed. It was all staged. There was a body switch.
Some shit like that.
Pretty soon nobody would shut up about it.
So now here we are.
They're taking him to Parkland to prove it's him.
SLAM
And suddenly my whole world could go straight to shit.

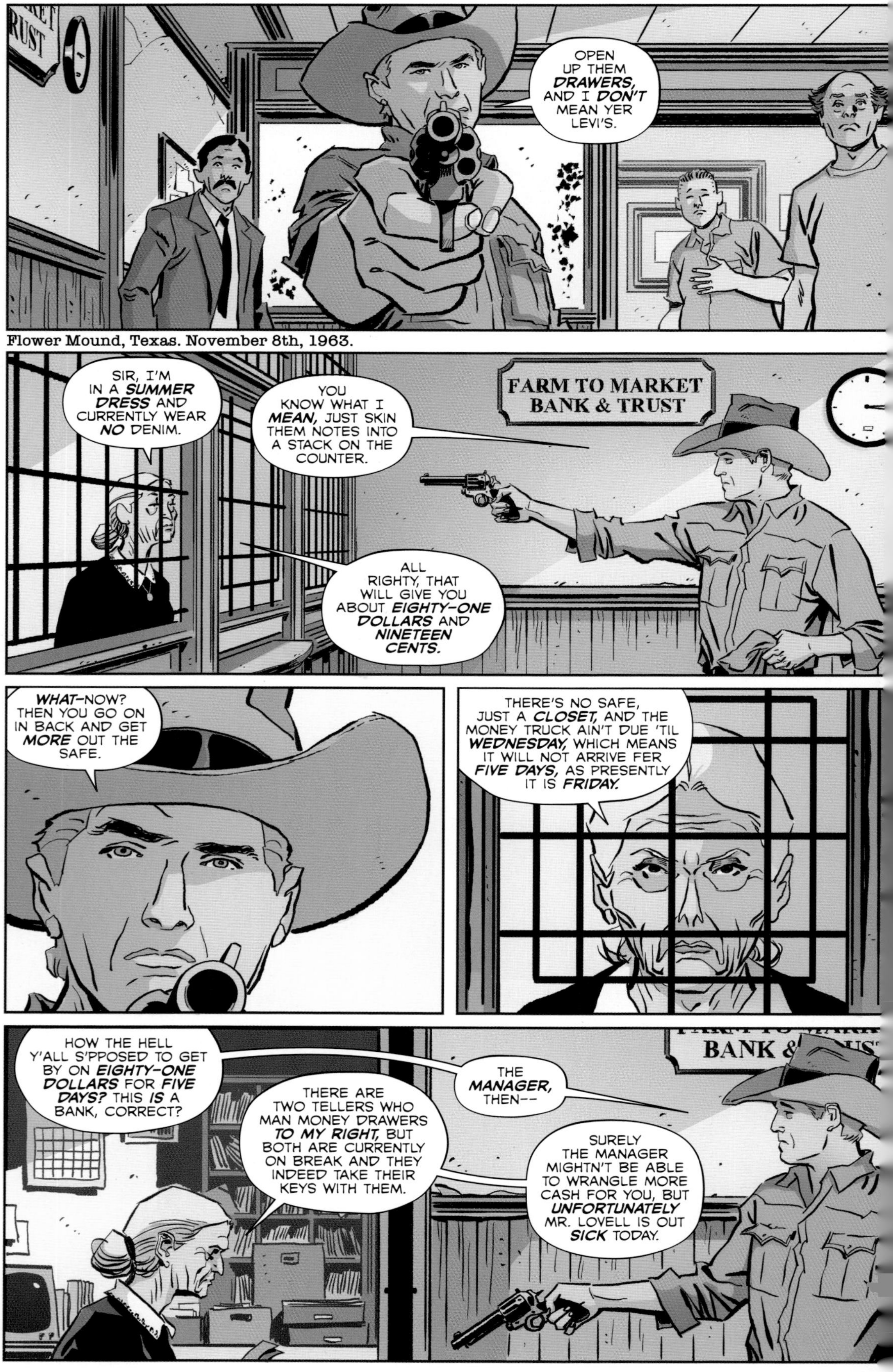

OPEN UP THEM DRAWERS, AND I DON'T MEAN YER LEVI'S.
Flower Mound, Texas. November 8th, 1963.
FARM TO MARKET BANK & TRUST
SIR, I'M IN A SUMMER DRESS AND CURRENTLY WEAR NO DENIM.
YOU KNOW WHAT I MEAN, JUST SKIN THEM NOTES INTO A STACK ON THE COUNTER.
ALL RIGHTY, THAT WILL GIVE YOU ABOUT EIGHTY-ONE DOLLARS AND NINETEEN CENTS.
WHAT-NOW? THEN YOU GO ON IN BACK AND GET MORE OUT THE SAFE.
THERE'S NO SAFE, JUST A CLOSET, AND THE MONEY TRUCK AIN'T DUE 'TIL WEDNESDAY, WHICH MEANS IT WILL NOT ARRIVE FER FIVE DAYS, AS PRESENTLY IT IS FRIDAY.
HOW THE HELL Y'ALL S'PPOSED TO GET BY ON EIGHTY-ONE DOLLARS FOR FIVE DAYS? THIS IS A BANK, CORRECT?
THERE ARE TWO TELLERS WHO MAN MONEY DRAWERS TO MY RIGHT, BUT BOTH ARE CURRENTLY ON BREAK AND THEY INDEED TAKE THEIR KEYS WITH THEM.
THE MANAGER, THEN--
SURELY THE MANAGER MIGHTN'T BE ABLE TO WRANGLE MORE CASH FOR YOU, BUT UNFORTUNATELY MR. LOVELL IS OUT SICK TODAY.

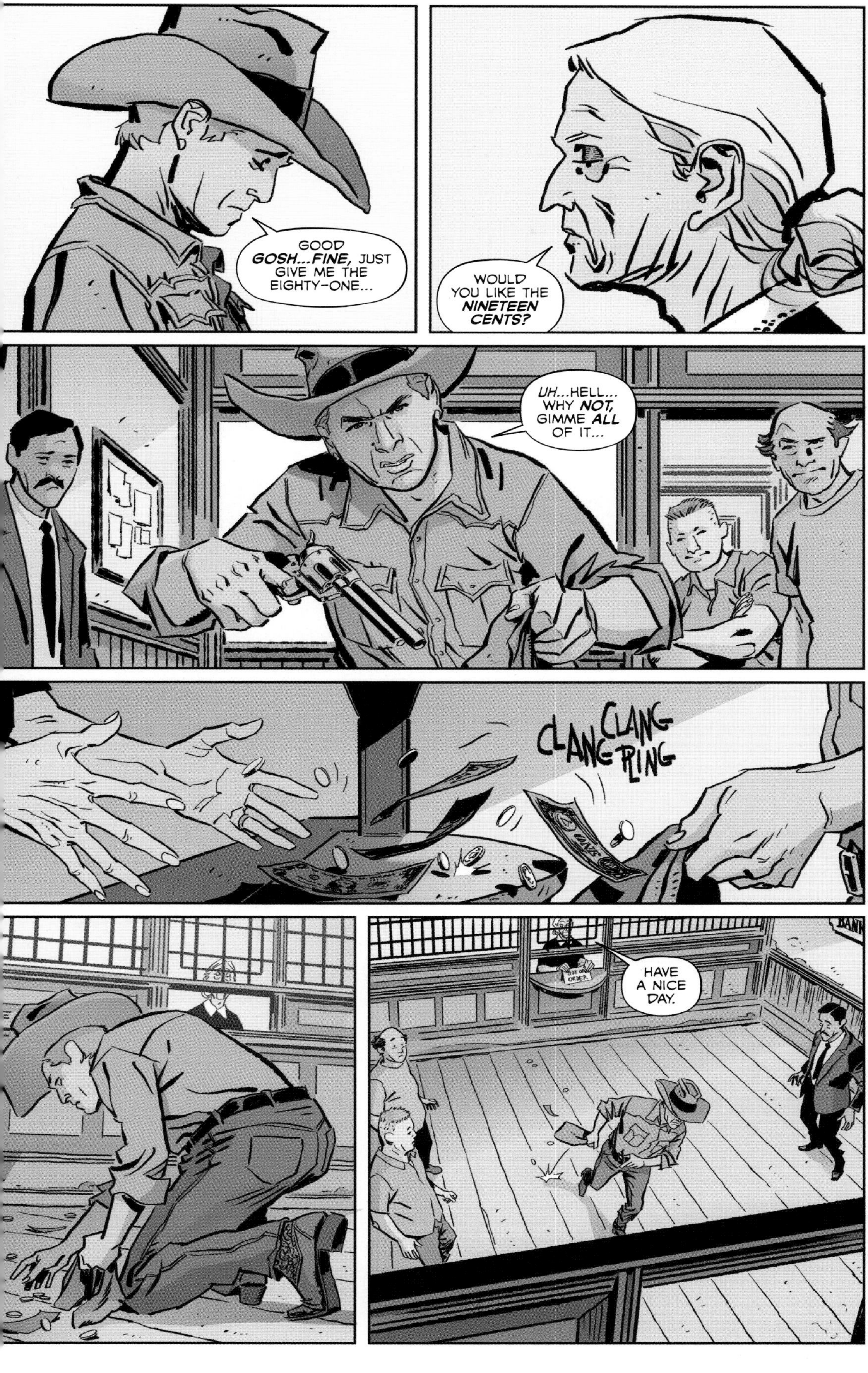
GOOD GOSH...FINE, JUST GIVE ME THE EIGHTY-ONE...
WOULD YOU LIKE THE NINETEEN CENTS?
UH...HELL... WHY NOT, GIMME ALL OF IT...
CLANG CLANG CLANG PLING
OUT OF ORDER
HAVE A NICE DAY.

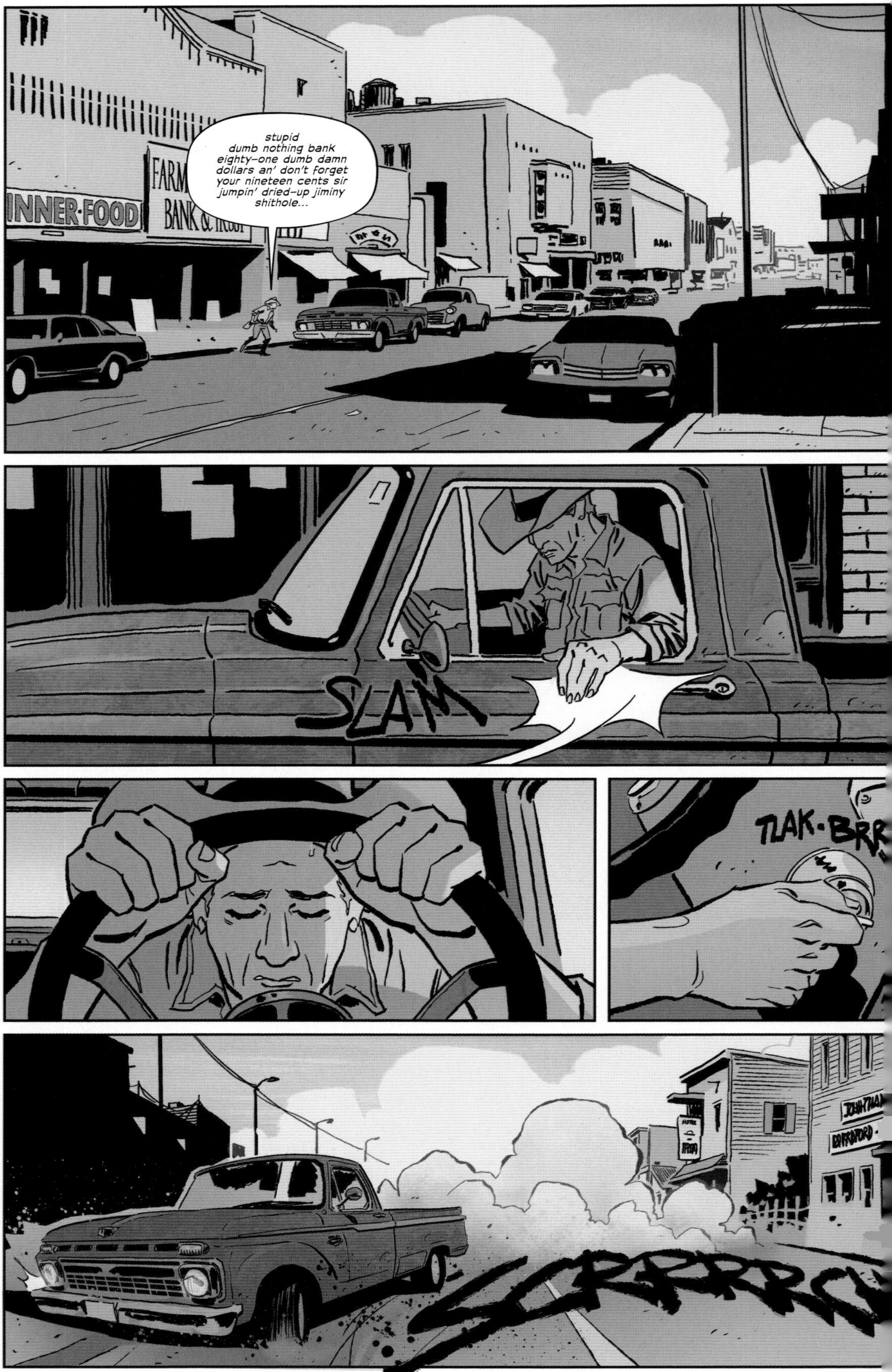
INNER-FOOD
stupid dumb nothing bank eighty-one dumb damn dollars an' don't forget your nineteen cents sir jumpin' dried-up jiminy shithole...
SLAM
TLAK·BRR

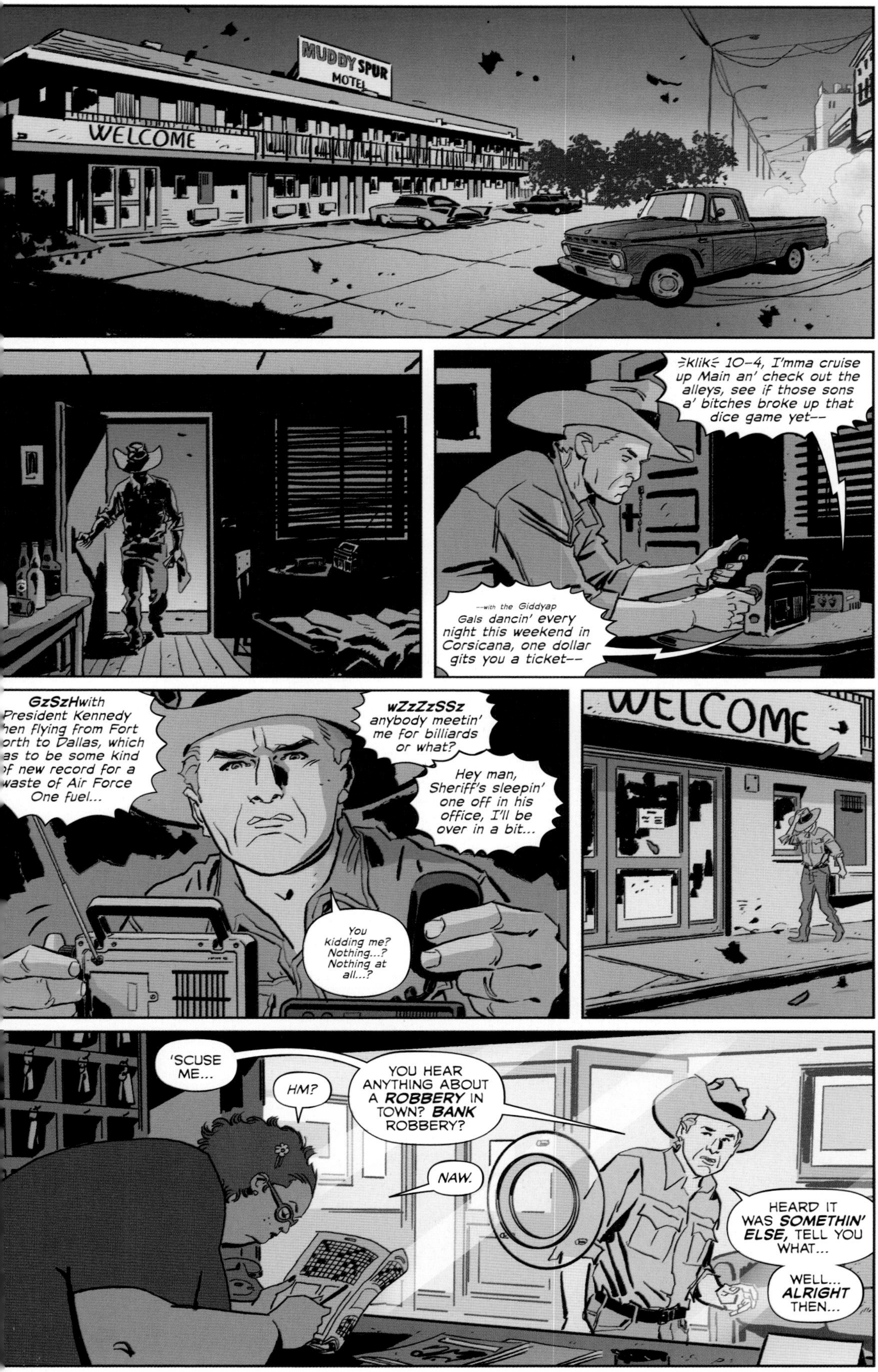
MUDDY SPUR MOTEL
WELCOME
≷klik≶ 10-4, I'mma cruise up Main an' check out the alleys, see if those sons a' bitches broke up that dice game yet--
--with the Giddyap Gals dancin' every night this weekend in Corsicana, one dollar gits you a ticket--
GzSzHwith President Kennedy hen flying from Fort orth to Dallas, which as to be some kind of new record for a waste of Air Force One fuel...
wZzZzSSz anybody meetin' me for billiards or what?
Hey man, Sheriff's sleepin' one off in his office, I'll be over in a bit...
You kidding me? Nothing...? Nothing at all...?
WELCOME
'SCUSE ME...
HM?
YOU HEAR ANYTHING ABOUT A ROBBERY IN TOWN? BANK ROBBERY?
NAW.
HEARD IT WAS SOMETHIN' ELSE, TELL YOU WHAT...
WELL... ALRIGHT THEN...

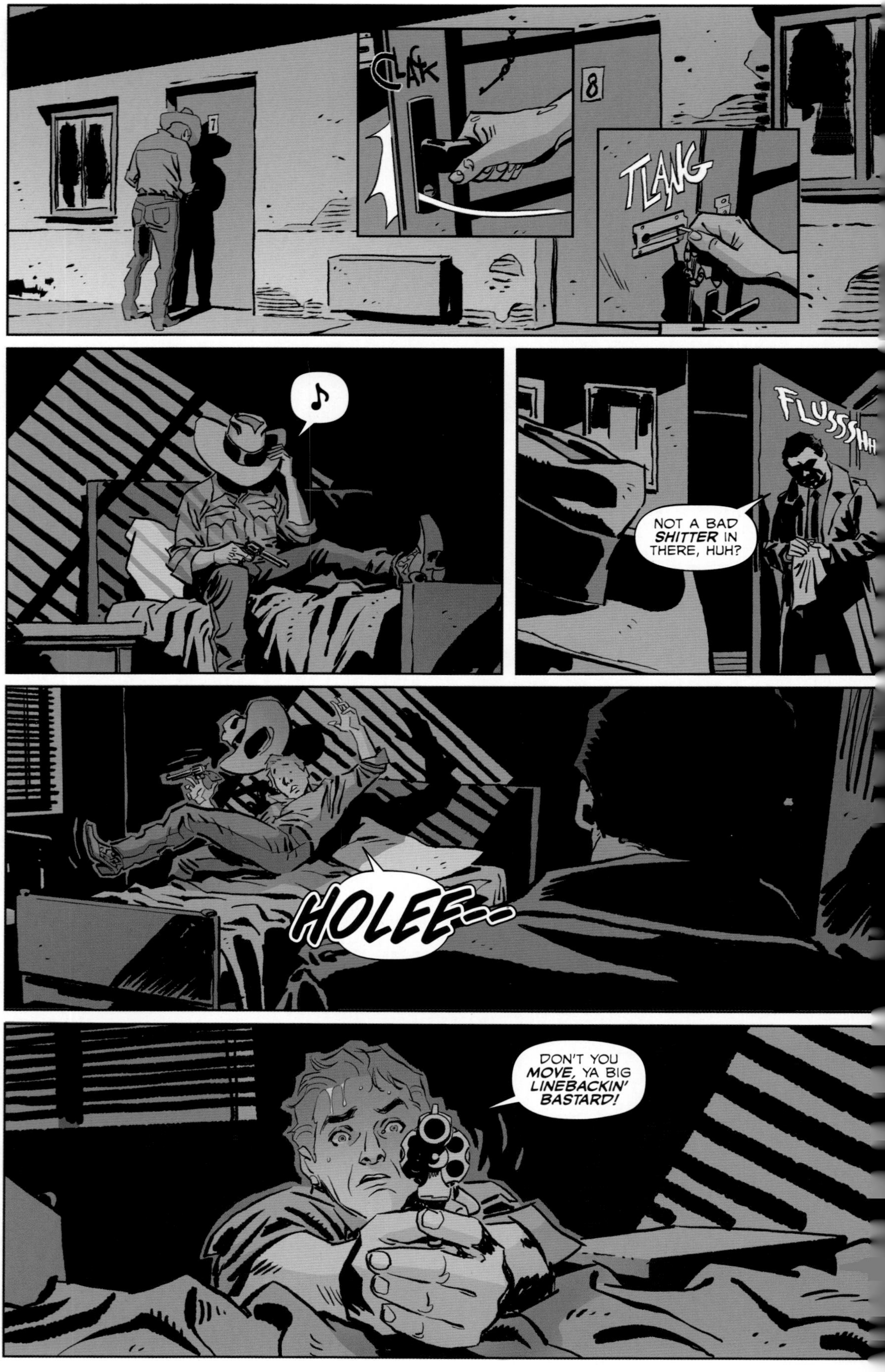
CLAK
TLANG
♪
FLUSSSHH
NOT A BAD SHITTER IN THERE, HUH?
HOLEE---
DON'T YOU MOVE, YA BIG LINEBACKIN' BASTARD!

NAME'S *FRANK*. THAT'S SHORT FOR *"FRANK CONVERSATION."* AND *FRANKLY*, WE BOTH KNOW YA GOT *NO BULLETS* IN THAT PISTOL.

AND LOOK. I ALSO GOT *NOTHING* ON ME TO HURT YA WITH.

BUT THAT *DON'T* MEAN I WON'T *ANYWAYS* IF I HAVE TO.

YOUR NAME'S *SHEP*, RIGHT? AT LEAST THAT'S WHAT YOU CALL YOURSELF *DOWN HERE* WHILE YOU PLAY *BANDIT*.

'CUZ YOU'RE REALLY FROM *WISCONSIN*. I'VE NEVER BEEN, HEARD IT'S QUITE *GREEN*.

YOU WORKED AT A GROCERY STORE BEFORE YOUR WIFE NINA RAN OFF WITH SOME *CHEESEMONGER*. RIGHT?

WHAT DO YOU WANT?

WELL, SHEP, I WANNA GIVE YOU A *JOB*. ONE THAT PAYS MORE THAN *EIGHTY-ONE DOLLARS AND NINETEEN CENTS*. MAKE YOU A REAL *COWBOY*, WITH A HAT THAT ACTUALLY *FITS*.

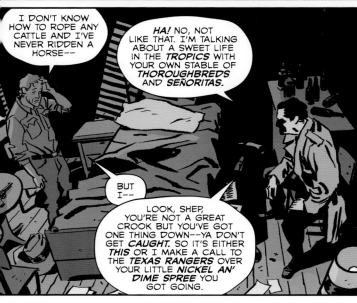

I DON'T KNOW HOW TO ROPE ANY CATTLE AND I'VE NEVER RIDDEN A HORSE--

HA! NO, NOT LIKE THAT. I'M TALKING ABOUT A SWEET LIFE IN THE *TROPICS* WITH YOUR OWN STABLE OF *THOROUGHBREDS* AND *SEÑORITAS*.

BUT I--

LOOK, SHEP, YOU'RE NOT A GREAT CROOK BUT YOU'VE GOT ONE THING DOWN--YA DON'T GET *CAUGHT*. SO IT'S EITHER *THIS* OR I MAKE A CALL TO THE *TEXAS RANGERS* OVER YOUR LITTLE *NICKEL AN' DIME SPREE* YOU GOT GOING.

WHAT DO YA SAY, *JOHN WAYNE?*

Ginger Landing Bar. Garland, Texas. November 9th, 1963.

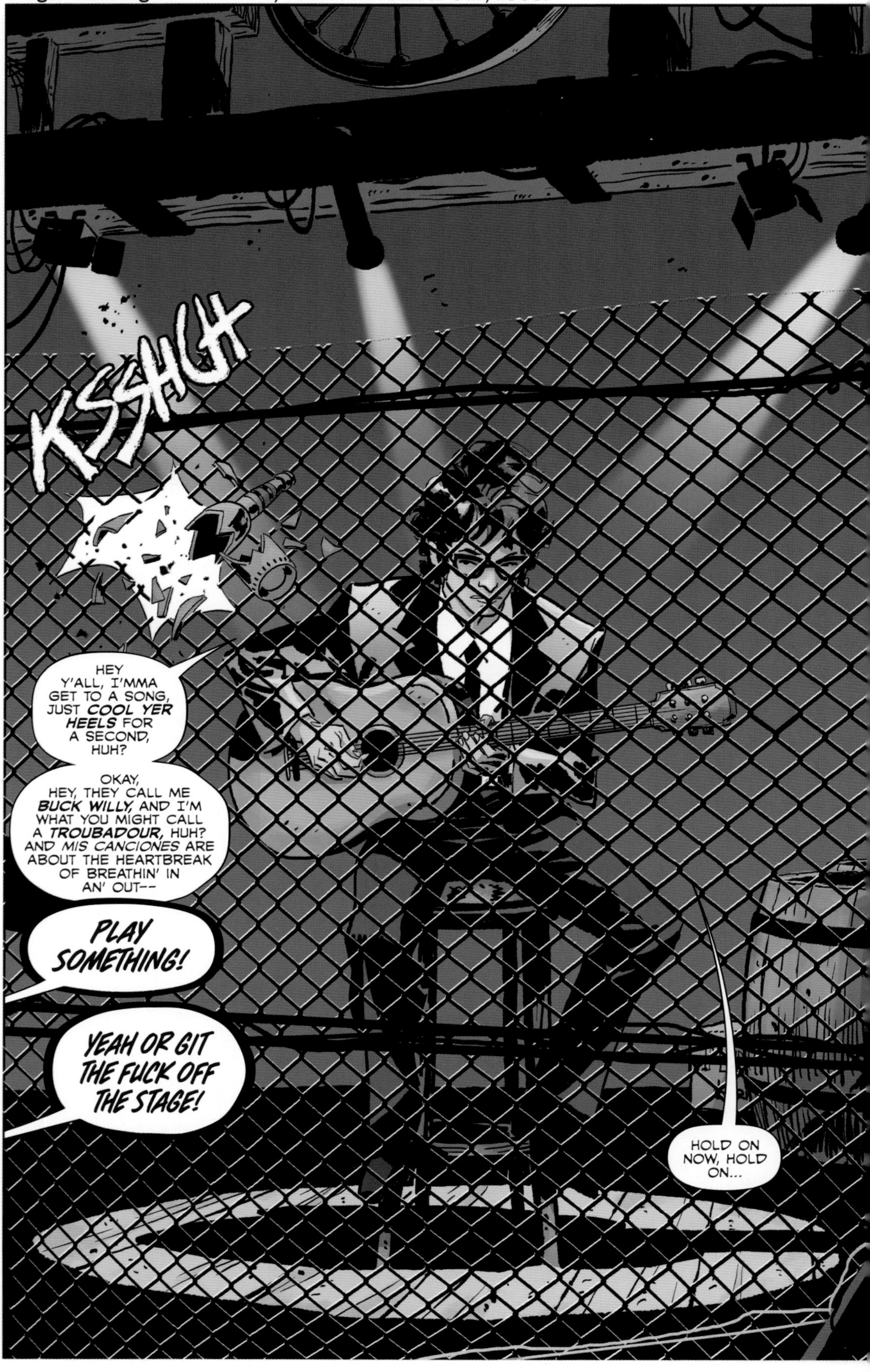
KSSHGH
HEY Y'ALL, I'MMA GET TO A SONG, JUST COOL YER HEELS FOR A SECOND, HUH?
OKAY, HEY, THEY CALL ME BUCK WILLY, AND I'M WHAT YOU MIGHT CALL A TROUBADOUR, HUH? AND MIS CANCIONES ARE ABOUT THE HEARTBREAK OF BREATHIN' IN AN' OUT--
PLAY SOMETHING!
YEAH OR GIT THE FUCK OFF THE STAGE!
HOLD ON NOW, HOLD ON...

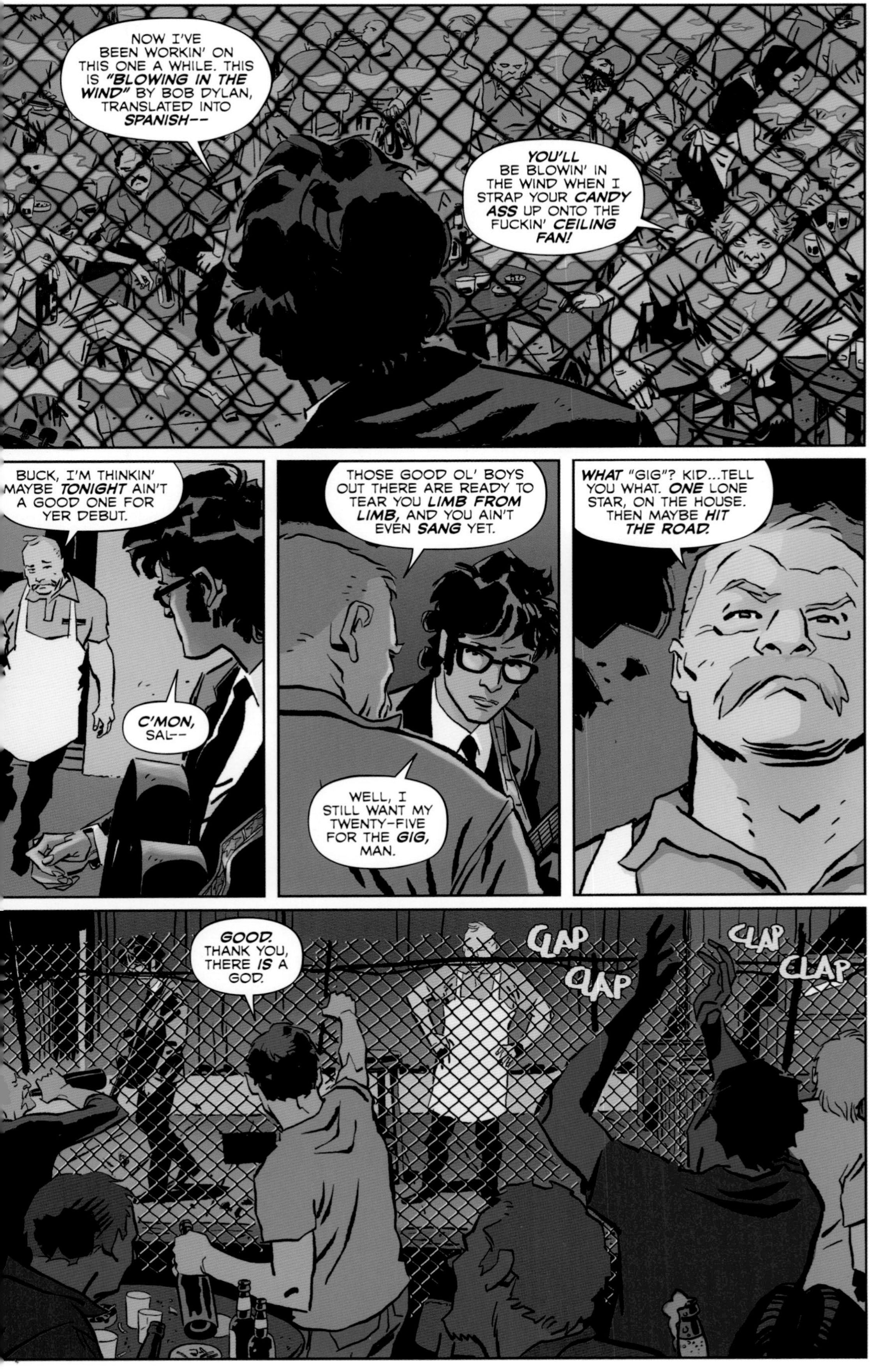
NOW I'VE BEEN WORKIN' ON THIS ONE A WHILE. THIS IS "BLOWING IN THE WIND" BY BOB DYLAN, TRANSLATED INTO SPANISH--
YOU'LL BE BLOWIN' IN THE WIND WHEN I STRAP YOUR CANDY ASS UP ONTO THE FUCKIN' CEILING FAN!
BUCK, I'M THINKIN' MAYBE TONIGHT AIN'T A GOOD ONE FOR YER DEBUT.
C'MON, SAL--
THOSE GOOD OL' BOYS OUT THERE ARE READY TO TEAR YOU LIMB FROM LIMB, AND YOU AIN'T EVEN SANG YET.
WELL, I STILL WANT MY TWENTY-FIVE FOR THE GIG, MAN.
WHAT "GIG"? KID...TELL YOU WHAT. ONE LONE STAR, ON THE HOUSE. THEN MAYBE HIT THE ROAD.
GOOD. THANK YOU, THERE IS A GOD.
CLAP
CLAP
CLAP
CLAP

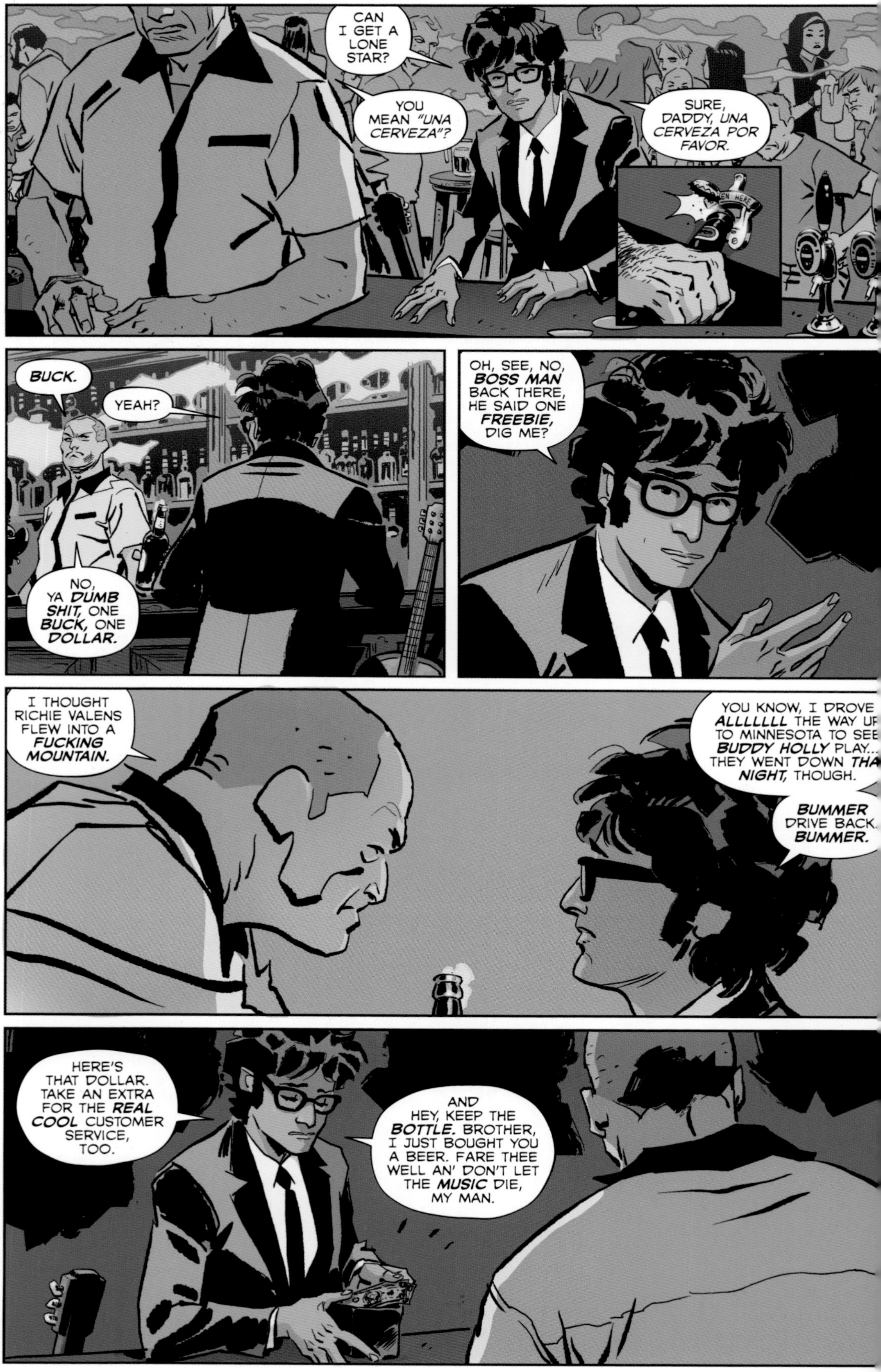
CAN I GET A LONE STAR?
YOU MEAN "UNA CERVEZA"?
SURE, DADDY, UNA CERVEZA POR FAVOR.
BUCK.
YEAH?
NO, YA DUMB SHIT, ONE BUCK, ONE DOLLAR.
OH, SEE, NO, BOSS MAN BACK THERE, HE SAID ONE FREEBIE, DIG ME?
I THOUGHT RICHIE VALENS FLEW INTO A FUCKING MOUNTAIN.
YOU KNOW, I DROVE ALLLLLLL THE WAY UP TO MINNESOTA TO SEE BUDDY HOLLY PLAY... THEY WENT DOWN THAT NIGHT, THOUGH.
BUMMER DRIVE BACK. BUMMER.
HERE'S THAT DOLLAR. TAKE AN EXTRA FOR THE REAL COOL CUSTOMER SERVICE, TOO.
AND HEY, KEEP THE BOTTLE. BROTHER, I JUST BOUGHT YOU A BEER. FARE THEE WELL AN' DON'T LET THE MUSIC DIE, MY MAN.

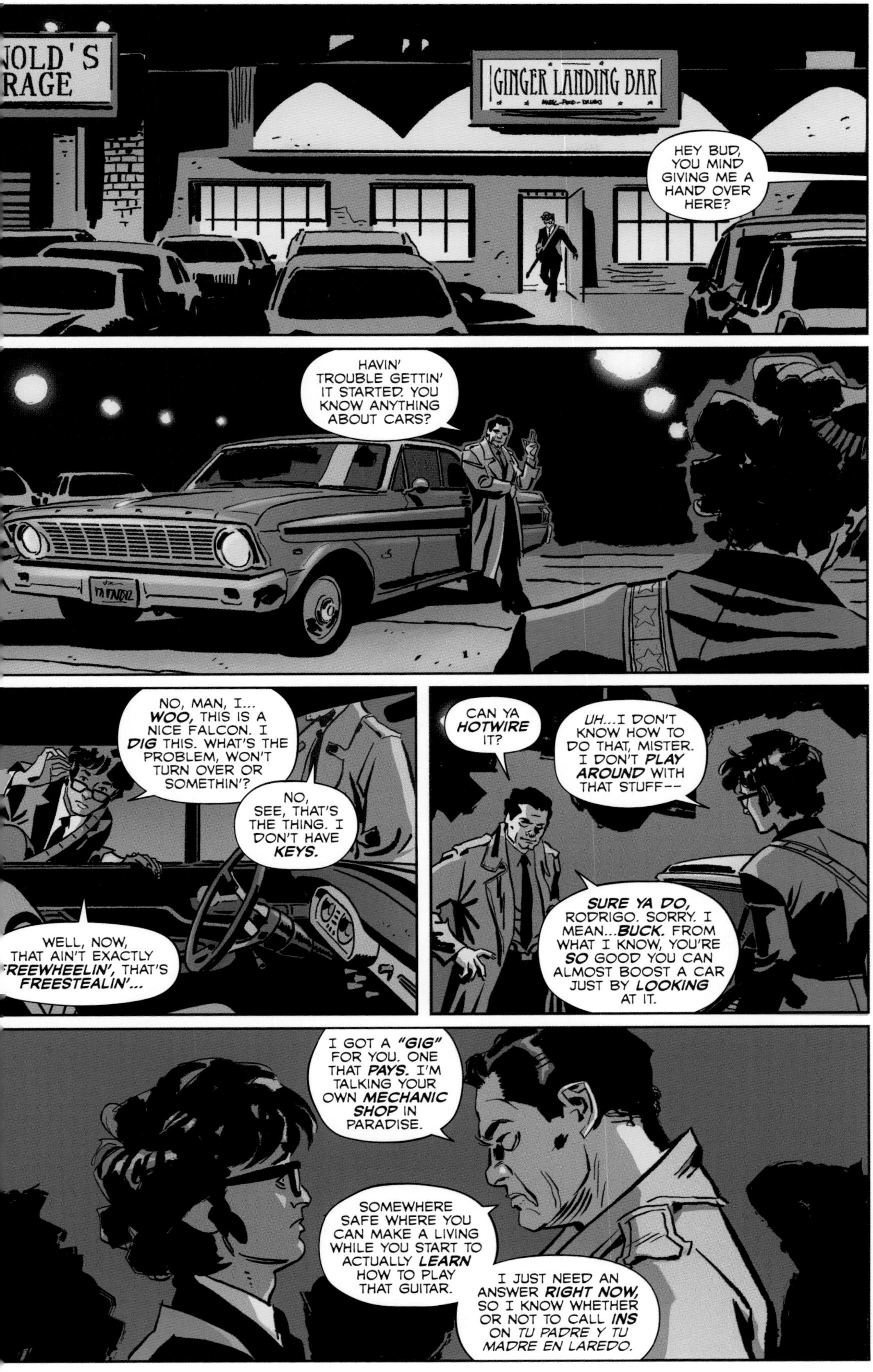

NOLD'S
RAGE
GINGER LANDING BAR
HEY BUD, YOU MIND GIVING ME A HAND OVER HERE?
HAVIN' TROUBLE GETTIN' IT STARTED. YOU KNOW ANYTHING ABOUT CARS?
NO, MAN, I... WOO, THIS IS A NICE FALCON. I DIG THIS. WHAT'S THE PROBLEM, WON'T TURN OVER OR SOMETHIN'?
NO, SEE, THAT'S THE THING. I DON'T HAVE KEYS.
WELL, NOW, THAT AIN'T EXACTLY FREEWHEELIN', THAT'S FREESTEALIN'...
CAN YA HOTWIRE IT?
UH...I DON'T KNOW HOW TO DO THAT, MISTER. I DON'T PLAY AROUND WITH THAT STUFF--
SURE YA DO, RODRIGO. SORRY. I MEAN...BUCK. FROM WHAT I KNOW, YOU'RE SO GOOD YOU CAN ALMOST BOOST A CAR JUST BY LOOKING AT IT.
I GOT A "GIG" FOR YOU. ONE THAT PAYS. I'M TALKING YOUR OWN MECHANIC SHOP IN PARADISE.
SOMEWHERE SAFE WHERE YOU CAN MAKE A LIVING WHILE YOU START TO ACTUALLY LEARN HOW TO PLAY THAT GUITAR.
I JUST NEED AN ANSWER RIGHT NOW, SO I KNOW WHETHER OR NOT TO CALL INS ON TU PADRE Y TU MADRE EN LAREDO.

PCHOCK PCHOW PCHEOF PCHEWM

What do ya think of that, Mr. **Khrushchev?** I got you on the run now...

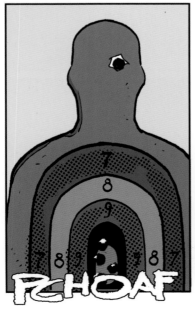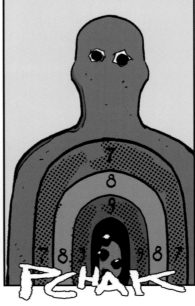

PCHOAF PCHAK PCHAOC

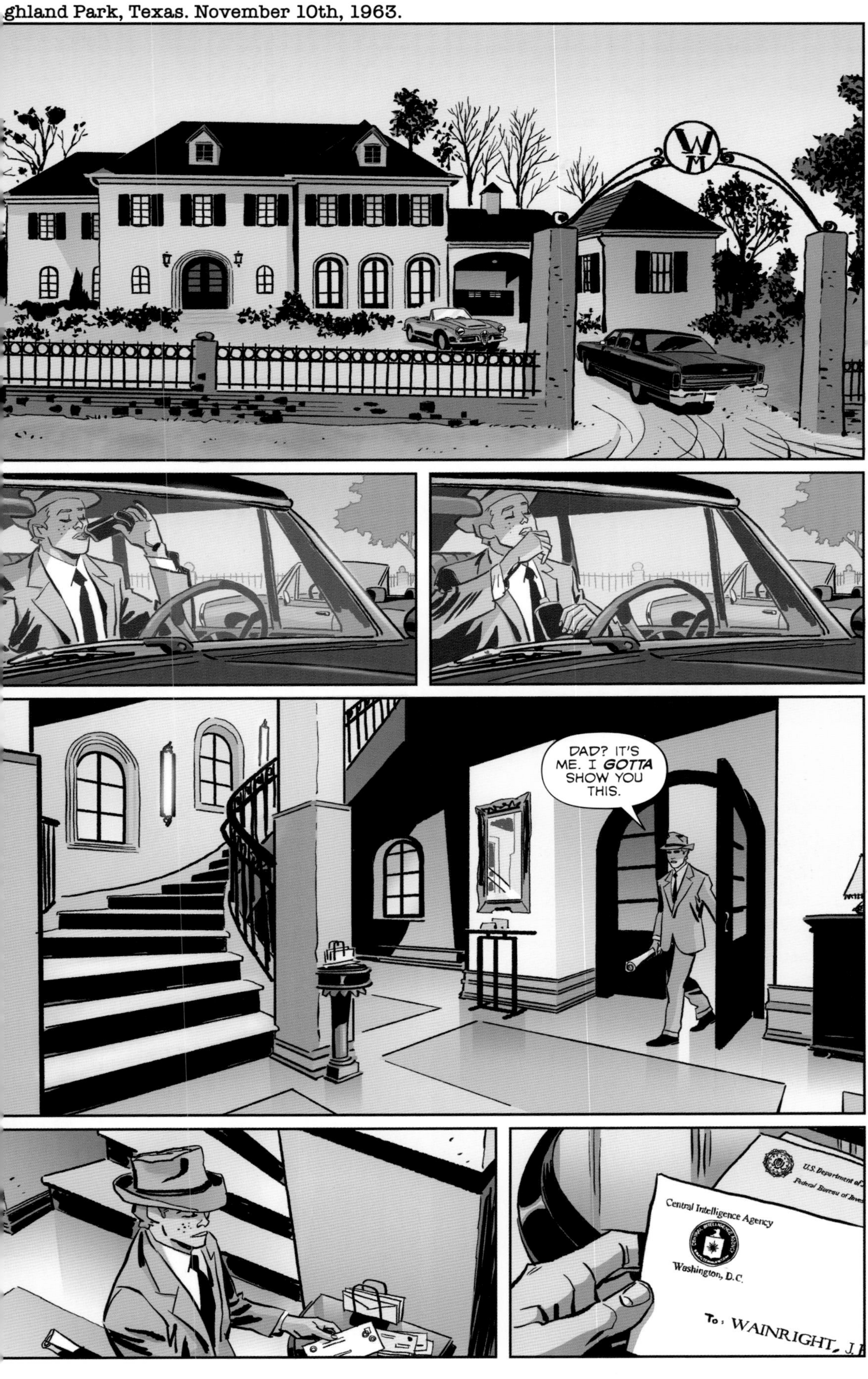
ghland Park, Texas. November 10th, 1963.
DAD? IT'S ME. I *GOTTA* SHOW YOU THIS.
U.S. Department of
Federal Bureau of Inves
Central Intelligence Agency
Washington, D.C.
To: WAINRIGHT, J.

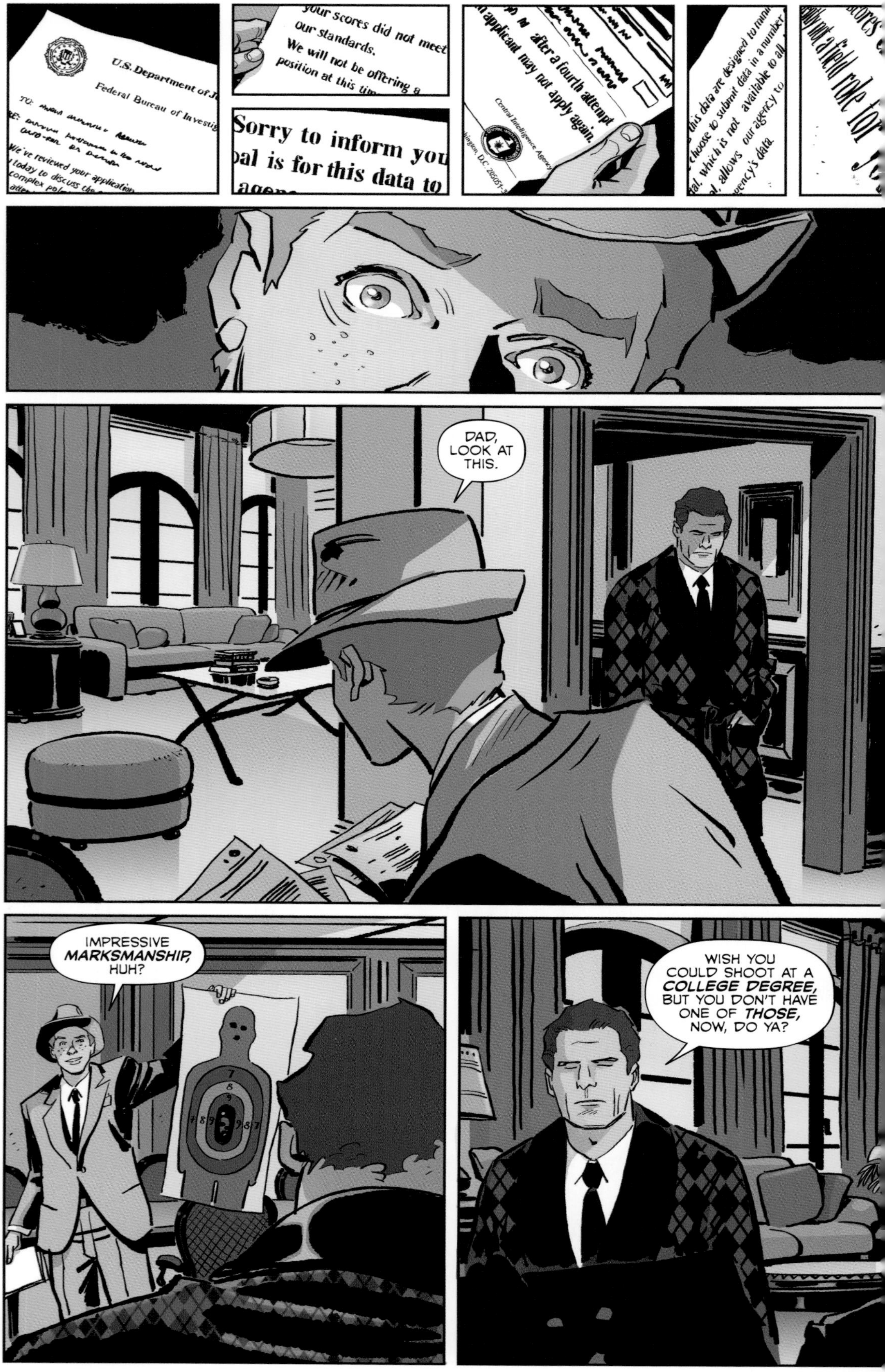
U.S. Department of J
Federal Bureau of Investig
We've reviewed your application
today to discuss the
complex pol
your scores did not meet
our standards.
We will not be offering a
position at this tim
Sorry to inform you
al is for this data to
after a fourth attempt
applicant may not apply again.
Central Intelligence Agency
this data are designed to
choose to submit data in a number
al, which is not available to all
al, allows our agency to
agency's data.
DAD, LOOK AT THIS.
IMPRESSIVE *MARKSMANSHIP,* HUH?
WISH YOU COULD SHOOT AT A *COLLEGE DEGREE,* BUT YOU DON'T HAVE ONE OF *THOSE,* NOW, DO YA?

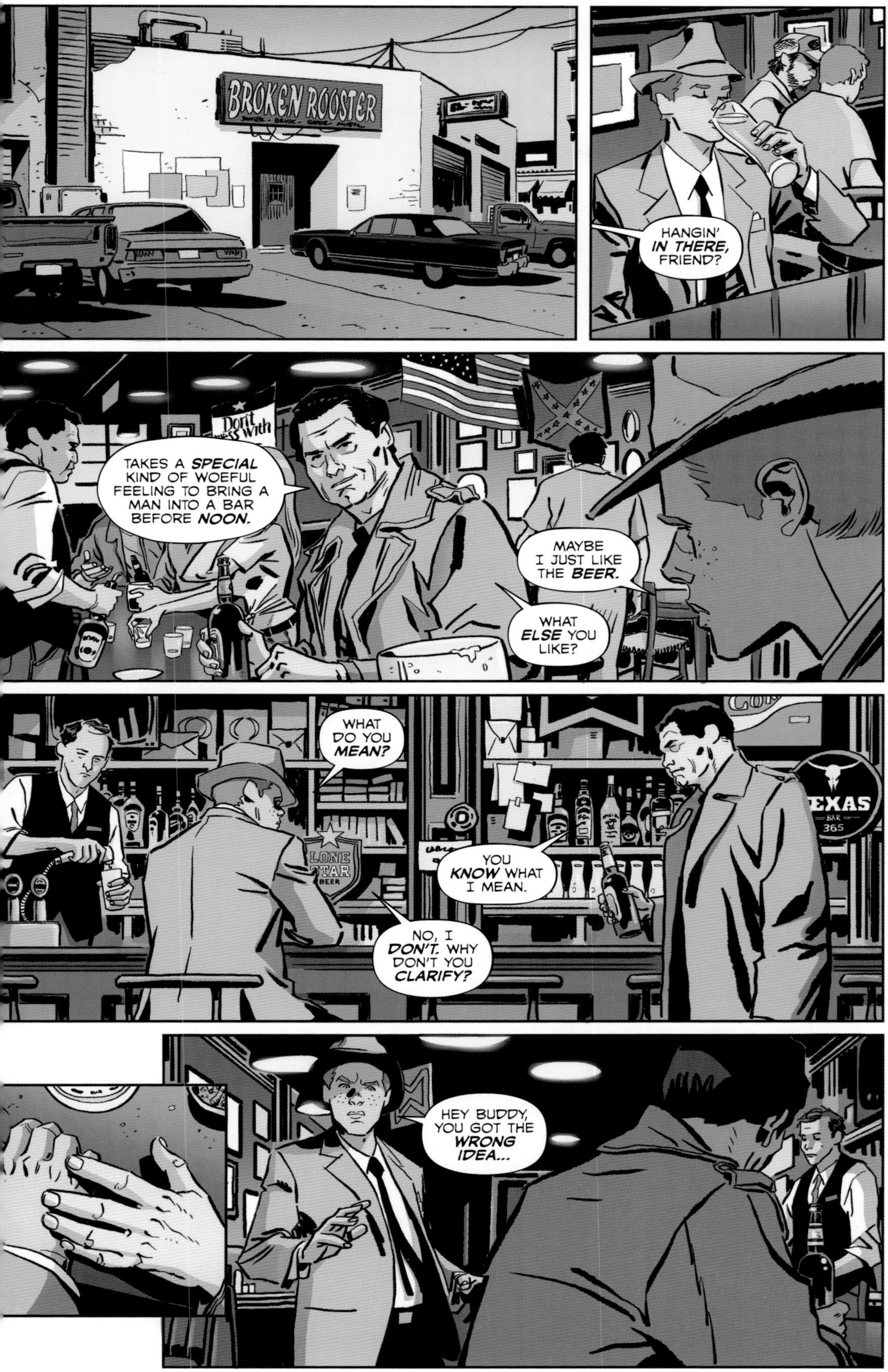
BROKEN ROOSTER
HANGIN' IN THERE, FRIEND?
TAKES A SPECIAL KIND OF WOEFUL FEELING TO BRING A MAN INTO A BAR BEFORE NOON.
MAYBE I JUST LIKE THE BEER.
WHAT ELSE YOU LIKE?
WHAT DO YOU MEAN?
YOU KNOW WHAT I MEAN.
NO, I DON'T. WHY DON'T YOU CLARIFY?
HEY BUDDY, YOU GOT THE WRONG IDEA...

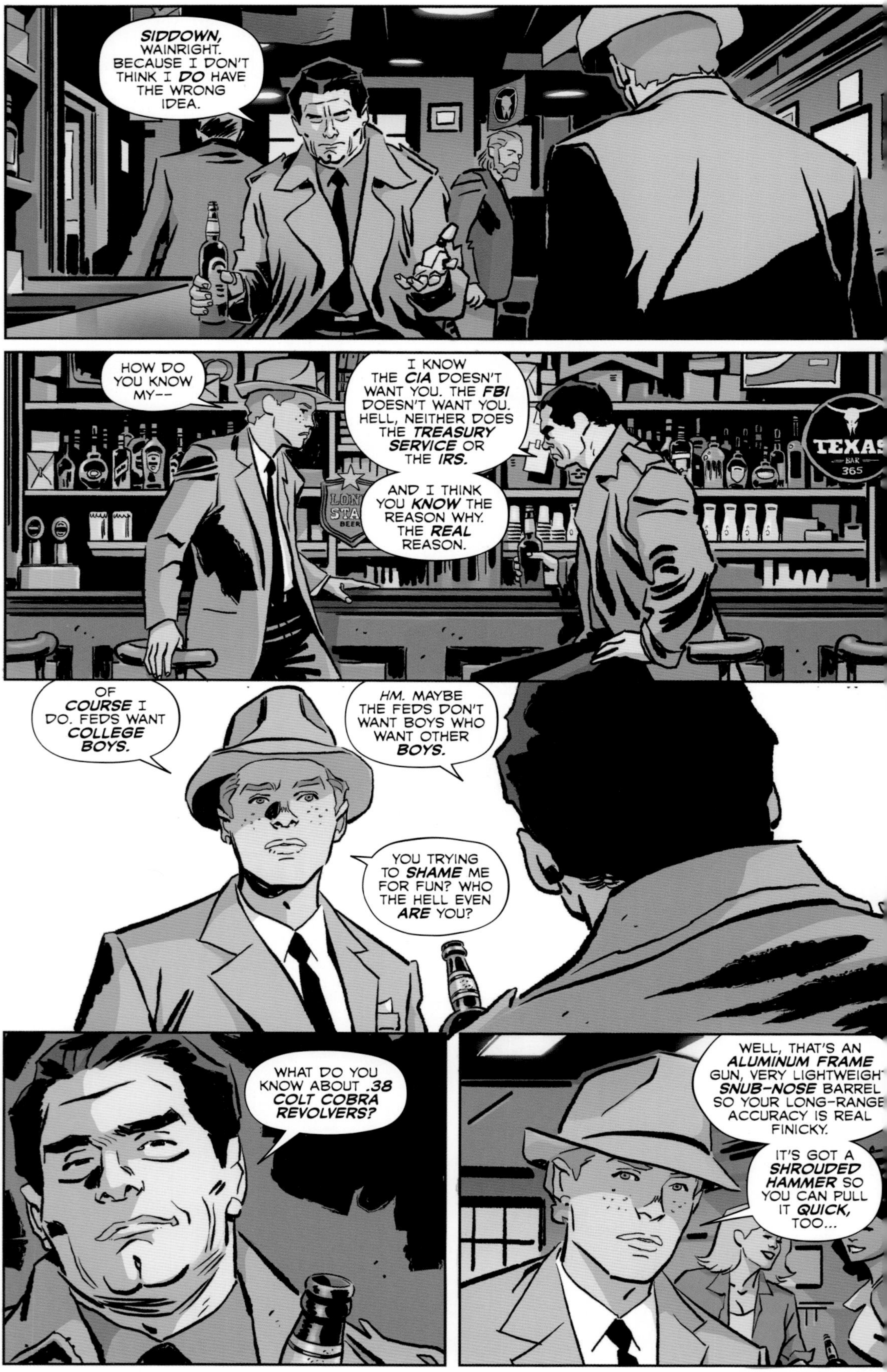
SIDDOWN, WAINRIGHT. BECAUSE I DON'T THINK I DO HAVE THE WRONG IDEA.
HOW DO YOU KNOW MY--
I KNOW THE CIA DOESN'T WANT YOU. THE FBI DOESN'T WANT YOU. HELL, NEITHER DOES THE TREASURY SERVICE OR THE IRS.
AND I THINK YOU KNOW THE REASON WHY. THE REAL REASON.
TEXAS BAR 365
OF COURSE I DO. FEDS WANT COLLEGE BOYS.
HM. MAYBE THE FEDS DON'T WANT BOYS WHO WANT OTHER BOYS.
YOU TRYING TO SHAME ME FOR FUN? WHO THE HELL EVEN ARE YOU?
WHAT DO YOU KNOW ABOUT .38 COLT COBRA REVOLVERS?
WELL, THAT'S AN ALUMINUM FRAME GUN, VERY LIGHTWEIGHT SNUB-NOSE BARREL SO YOUR LONG-RANGE ACCURACY IS REAL FINICKY.
IT'S GOT A SHROUDED HAMMER SO YOU CAN PULL IT QUICK, TOO...

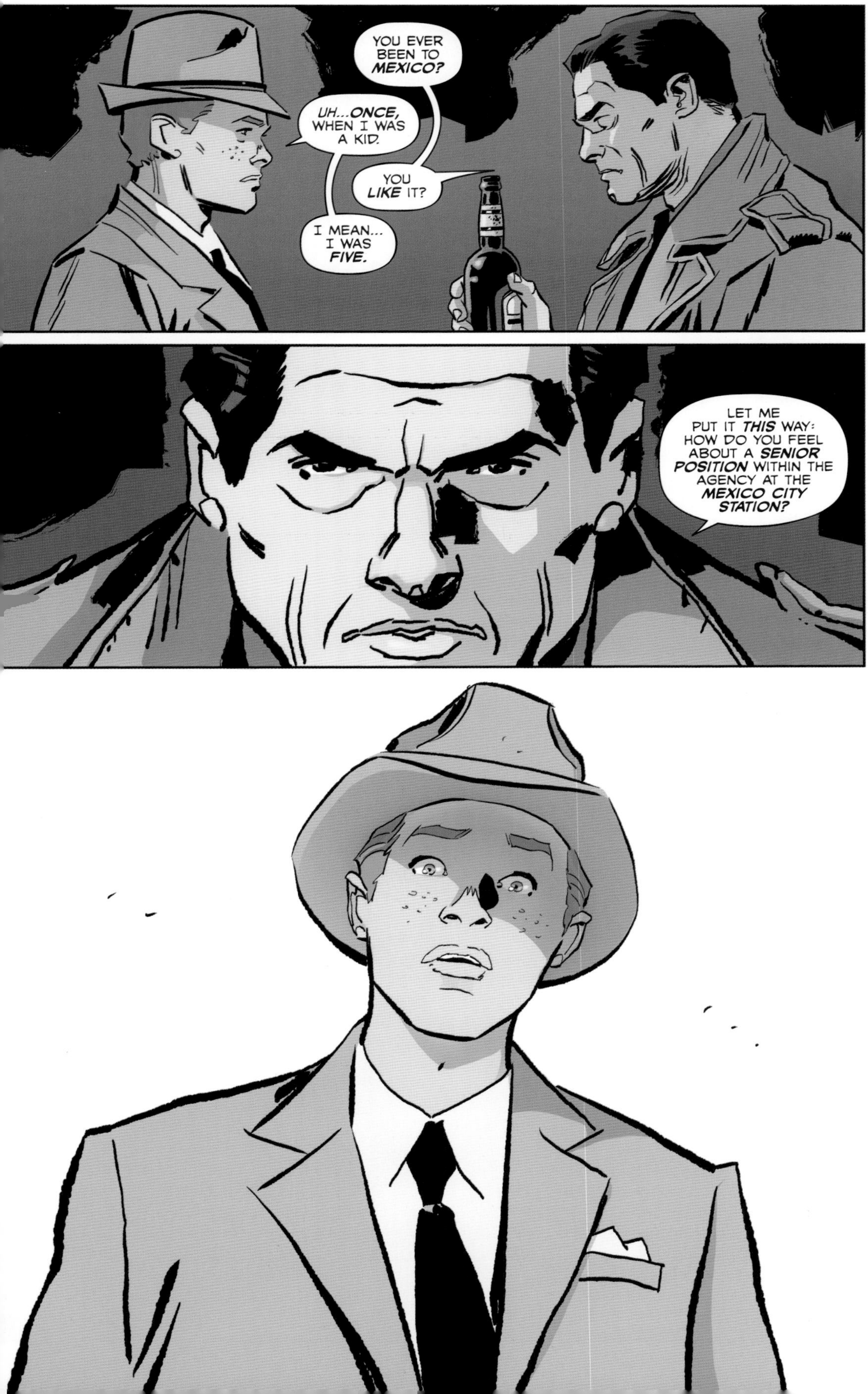

YOU EVER BEEN TO MEXICO?
UH...ONCE, WHEN I WAS A KID.
YOU LIKE IT?
I MEAN... I WAS FIVE.
LET ME PUT IT THIS WAY: HOW DO YOU FEEL ABOUT A SENIOR POSITION WITHIN THE AGENCY AT THE MEXICO CITY STATION?

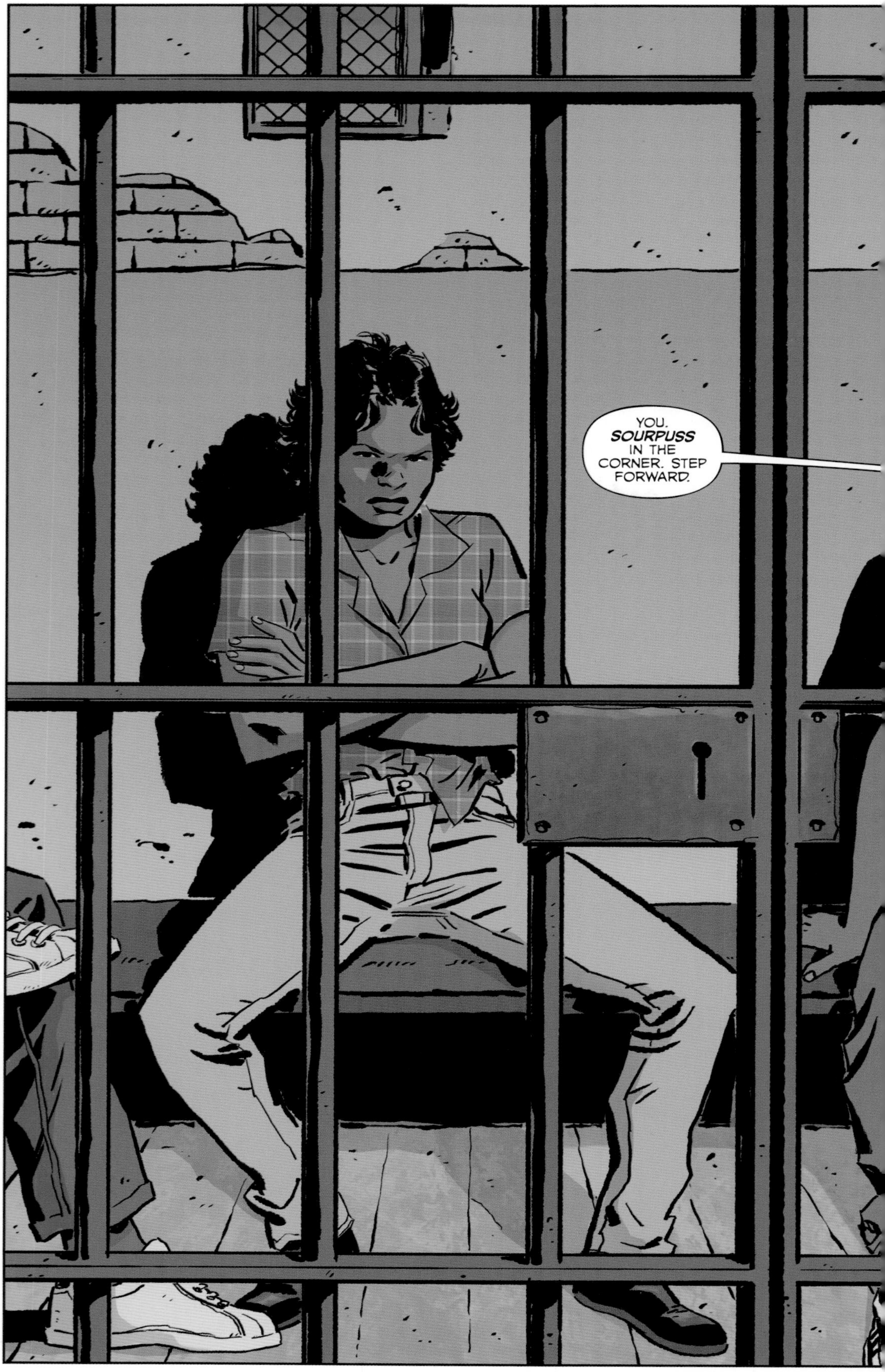
YOU. SOURPUSS IN THE CORNER. STEP FORWARD.

llas County Jail. Later that night.

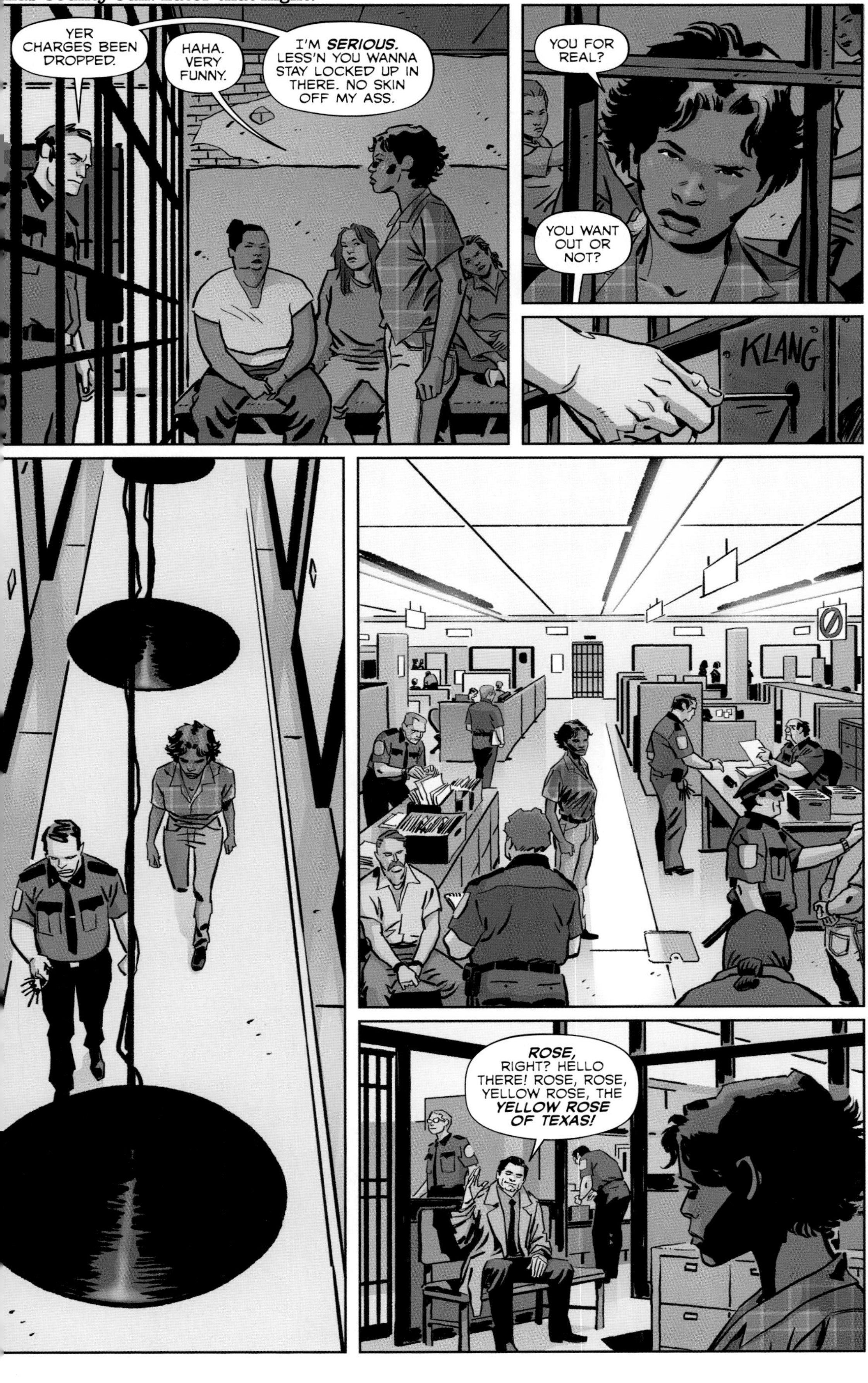
YER CHARGES BEEN DROPPED.
HAHA. VERY FUNNY.
I'M SERIOUS. LESS'N YOU WANNA STAY LOCKED UP IN THERE. NO SKIN OFF MY ASS.
YOU FOR REAL?
YOU WANT OUT OR NOT?
KLANG
ROSE, RIGHT? HELLO THERE! ROSE, ROSE, YELLOW ROSE, THE YELLOW ROSE OF TEXAS!

I DON'T KNOW YOU.

WELL, MY NAME'S *FRANK.* SO *NOW* YOU KNOW ME.

THANKS FOR THE HELP, I GUESS--

NO, NO, YELLOW ROSE, YOU'RE SMART ENOUGH TO KNOW HOW THESE THINGS *WORK.*

'K, FINE. WHAT'S THE *SHOE?*

SHOE?

YOU KNOW, THE OTHER ONE THAT'S ABOUT TO *DROP.*

TAKE A RIDE WITH ME AND I'LL EXPLAIN.

I'M NOT GOING ON A *RIDE* WITH SOME *STRANGE WHITE MAN,* I DON'T CARE IF YOUR NAME IS *FRANK* OR *JERRY* OR *JESUS OF NAZARETH.*

EITHER I CAN DRIVE YOU BACK HOME TO YO GRANDMA'S HOU OR SHE CAN SEE PULL UP *CUFFED* THE BACK OF SQUAD CAR.

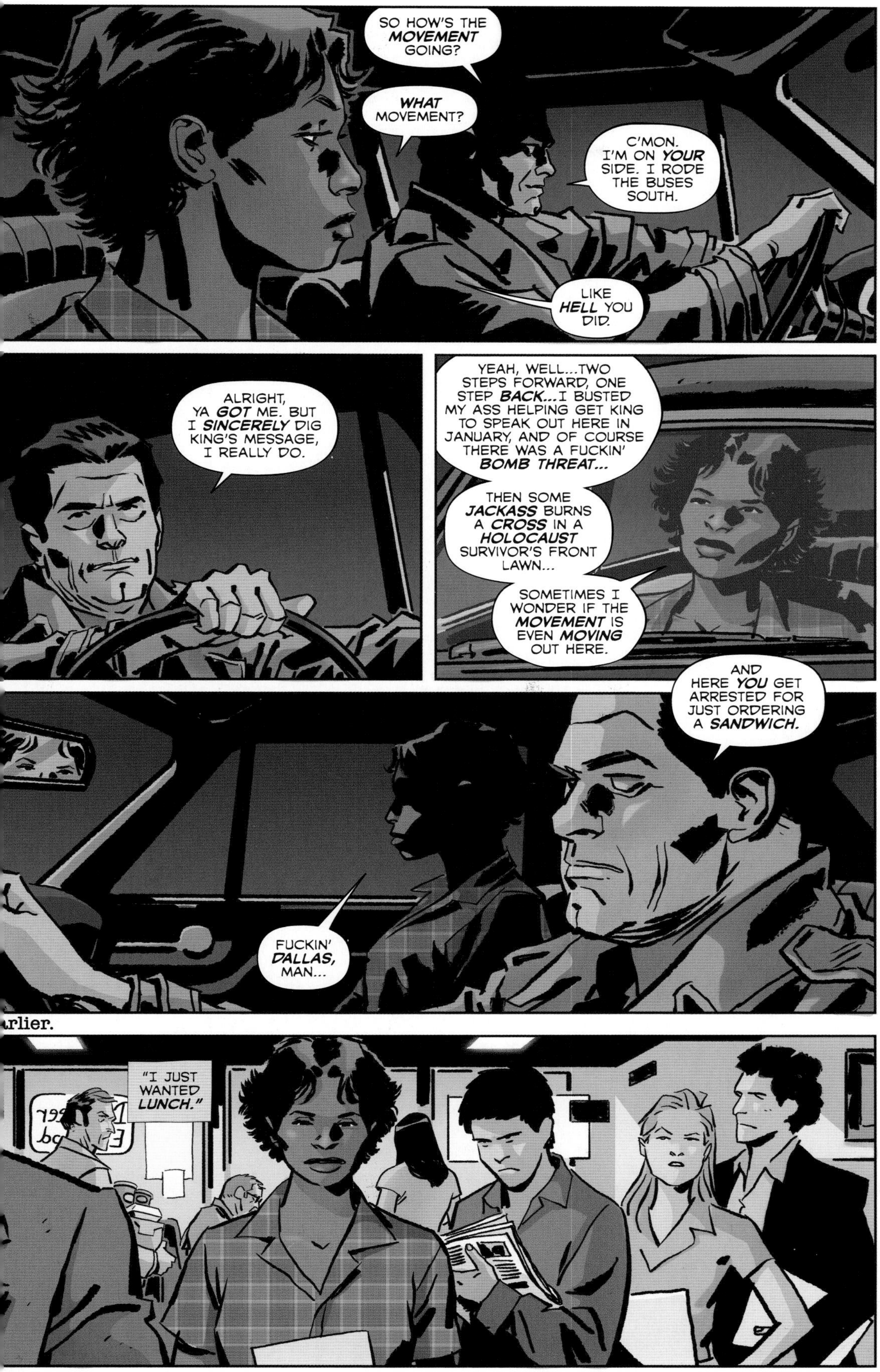
SO HOW'S THE MOVEMENT GOING?
WHAT MOVEMENT?
C'MON. I'M ON YOUR SIDE. I RODE THE BUSES SOUTH.
LIKE HELL YOU DID.
ALRIGHT, YA GOT ME. BUT I SINCERELY DIG KING'S MESSAGE, I REALLY DO.
YEAH, WELL...TWO STEPS FORWARD, ONE STEP BACK...I BUSTED MY ASS HELPING GET KING TO SPEAK OUT HERE IN JANUARY, AND OF COURSE THERE WAS A FUCKIN' BOMB THREAT...
THEN SOME JACKASS BURNS A CROSS IN A HOLOCAUST SURVIVOR'S FRONT LAWN...
SOMETIMES I WONDER IF THE MOVEMENT IS EVEN MOVING OUT HERE.
AND HERE YOU GET ARRESTED FOR JUST ORDERING A SANDWICH.
FUCKIN' DALLAS, MAN...
rlier.
"I JUST WANTED LUNCH."

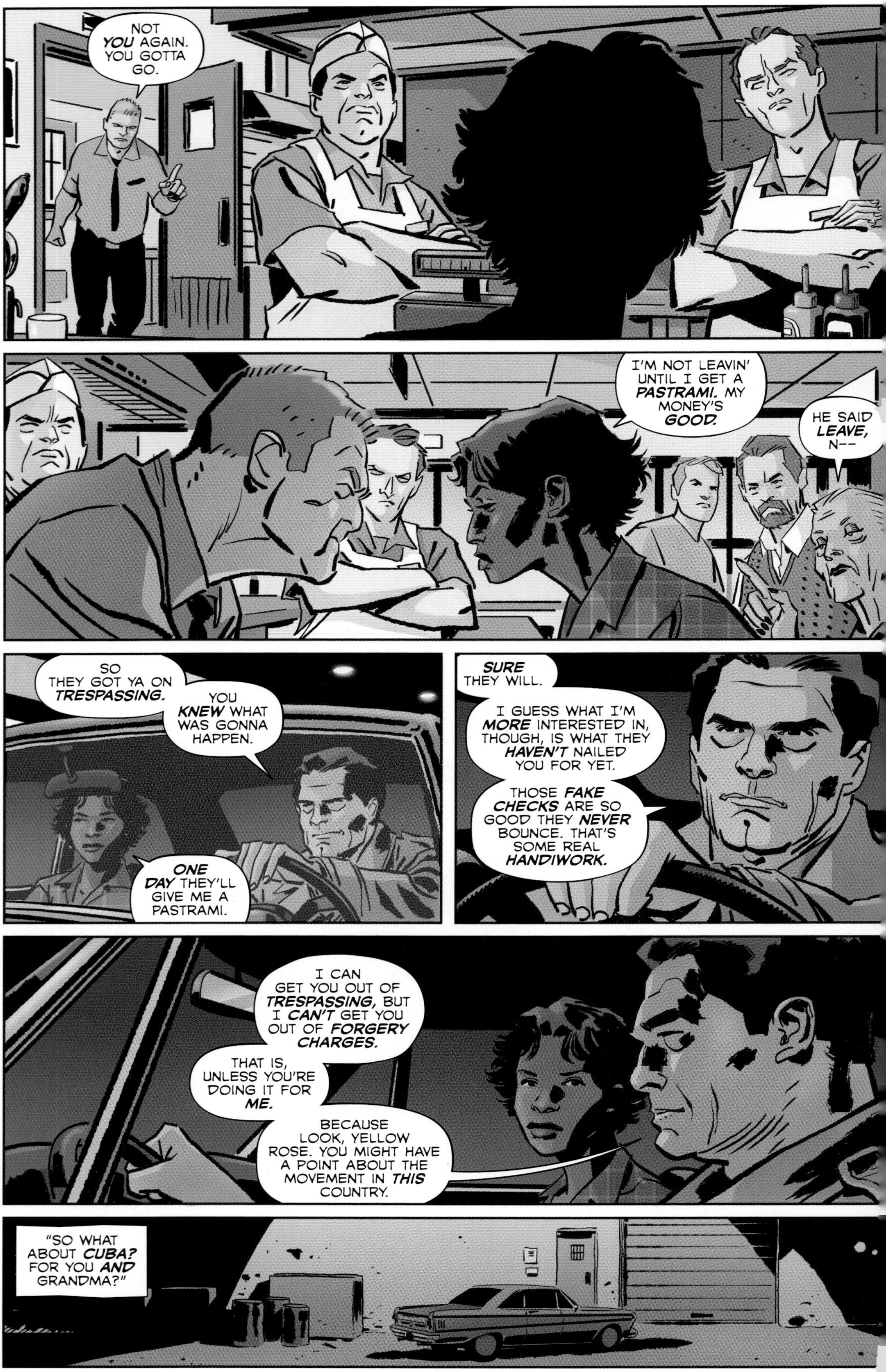
NOT YOU AGAIN. YOU GOTTA GO.
I'M NOT LEAVIN' UNTIL I GET A PASTRAMI. MY MONEY'S GOOD.
HE SAID LEAVE, N--
SO THEY GOT YA ON TRESPASSING.
YOU KNEW WHAT WAS GONNA HAPPEN.
ONE DAY THEY'LL GIVE ME A PASTRAMI.
SURE THEY WILL.
I GUESS WHAT I'M MORE INTERESTED IN, THOUGH, IS WHAT THEY HAVEN'T NAILED YOU FOR YET.
THOSE FAKE CHECKS ARE SO GOOD THEY NEVER BOUNCE. THAT'S SOME REAL HANDIWORK.
I CAN GET YOU OUT OF TRESPASSING, BUT I CAN'T GET YOU OUT OF FORGERY CHARGES.
THAT IS, UNLESS YOU'RE DOING IT FOR ME.
BECAUSE LOOK, YELLOW ROSE. YOU MIGHT HAVE A POINT ABOUT THE MOVEMENT IN THIS COUNTRY.
"SO WHAT ABOUT CUBA? FOR YOU AND GRANDMA?"

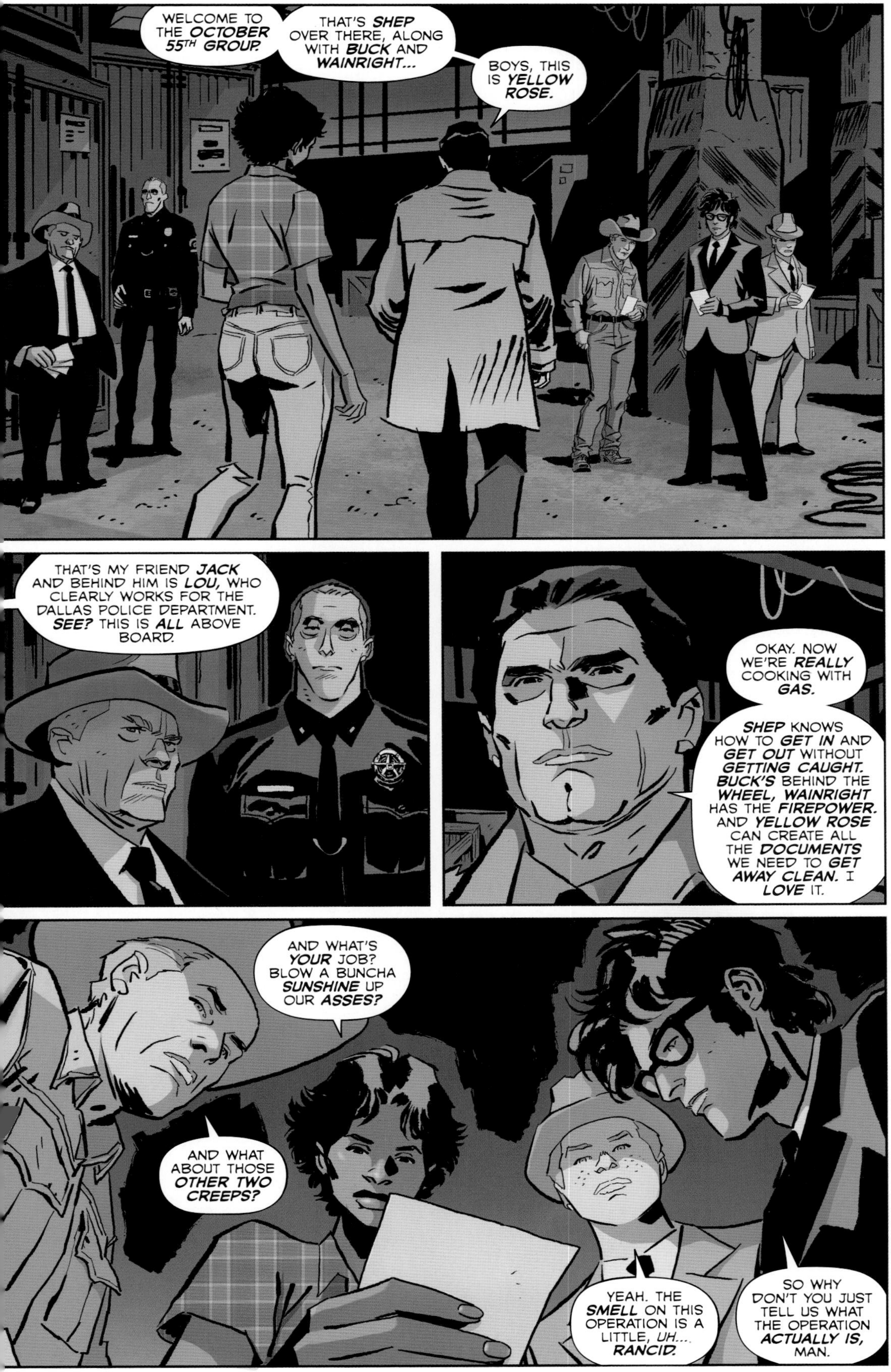
WELCOME TO THE OCTOBER 55TH GROUP.
THAT'S SHEP OVER THERE, ALONG WITH BUCK AND WAINRIGHT...
BOYS, THIS IS YELLOW ROSE.
THAT'S MY FRIEND JACK AND BEHIND HIM IS LOU, WHO CLEARLY WORKS FOR THE DALLAS POLICE DEPARTMENT. SEE? THIS IS ALL ABOVE BOARD.
OKAY. NOW WE'RE REALLY COOKING WITH GAS.
SHEP KNOWS HOW TO GET IN AND GET OUT WITHOUT GETTING CAUGHT. BUCK'S BEHIND THE WHEEL, WAINRIGHT HAS THE FIREPOWER. AND YELLOW ROSE CAN CREATE ALL THE DOCUMENTS WE NEED TO GET AWAY CLEAN. I LOVE IT.
AND WHAT'S YOUR JOB? BLOW A BUNCHA SUNSHINE UP OUR ASSES?
AND WHAT ABOUT THOSE OTHER TWO CREEPS?
YEAH. THE SMELL ON THIS OPERATION IS A LITTLE, UH... RANCID.
SO WHY DON'T YOU JUST TELL US WHAT THE OPERATION ACTUALLY IS, MAN.

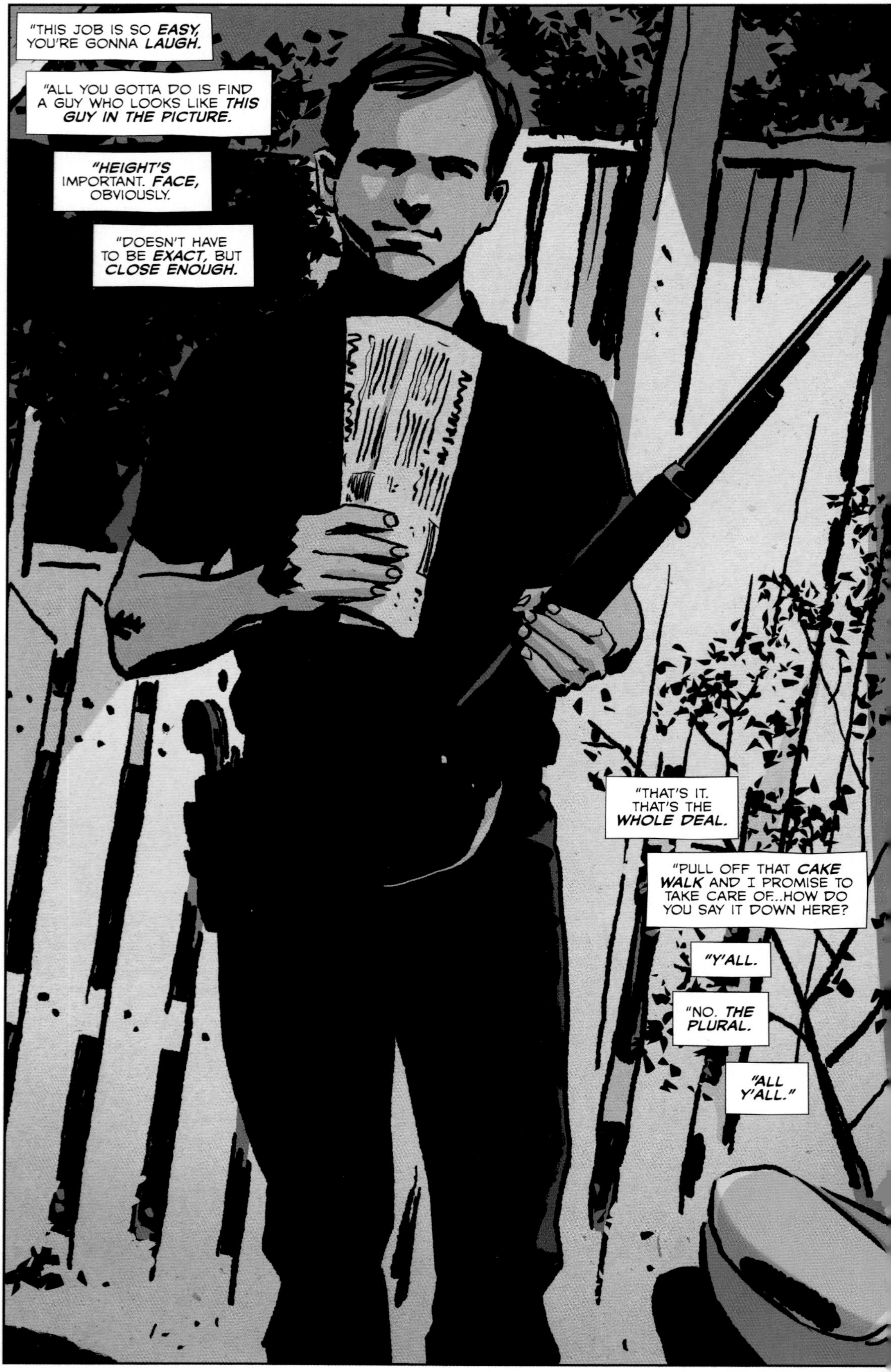
"THIS JOB IS SO EASY, YOU'RE GONNA LAUGH.
"ALL YOU GOTTA DO IS FIND A GUY WHO LOOKS LIKE THIS GUY IN THE PICTURE.
"HEIGHT'S IMPORTANT. FACE, OBVIOUSLY.
"DOESN'T HAVE TO BE EXACT, BUT CLOSE ENOUGH.
"THAT'S IT. THAT'S THE WHOLE DEAL.
"PULL OFF THAT CAKE WALK AND I PROMISE TO TAKE CARE OF...HOW DO YOU SAY IT DOWN HERE?
"Y'ALL.
"NO. THE PLURAL.
"ALL Y'ALL."

The only other theory I have met with, which pretends to explain the mode of this double appearance, is that of the spirit leaving the body, as we have supposed it to do in cases of dreams and catalepsy; in which instances the nerve-spirit, which seems to be the archæus or astral spirit of the ancient philosophers, has the power of projecting a visible body out of the imponderable matter of the atmosphere. According to this theory, this nerve-spirit, which seems to be an embodiment of—or rather, a body constructed out of the nervous fluid, or ether—in short, the spiritual body of St. Paul, is the bond of union between the body and the soul, or spirit; and has the plastic force of raising up an aerial form. Being the highest organic power, it can not by any other, physical or chemical, be destroyed; and when the body is cast off, it follows the soul; and as, during life, it is the means by which the soul acts upon the body, and is thus enabled to communicate with the external world, so when the spirit is disembodied, it is through this nerve-spirit that it can make itself visible, and even exercise mechanical powers.

It is certain that not only somnambules, but sick persons, are occasionally sensible of a feeling that seems to lend some countenance to this latter theory.

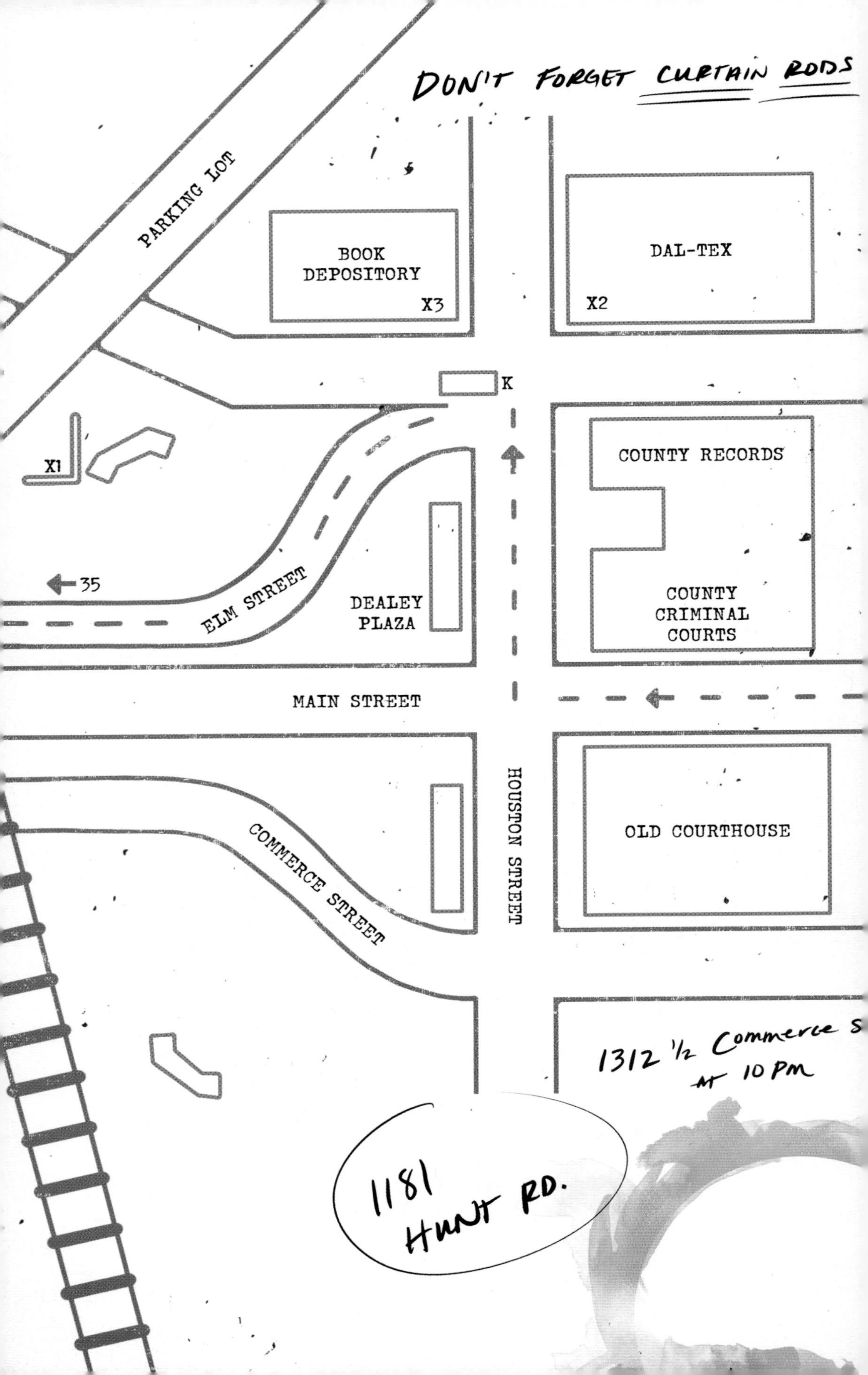
DON'T FORGET CURTAIN RODS
PARKING LOT
BOOK DEPOSITORY
X3
DAL-TEX
X2
K
X1
COUNTY RECORDS
35
ELM STREET
DEALEY PLAZA
COUNTY CRIMINAL COURTS
MAIN STREET
HOUSTON STREET
COMMERCE STREET
OLD COURTHOUSE
1312 ½ Commerce S
AT 10 PM
1181 HUNT RD.

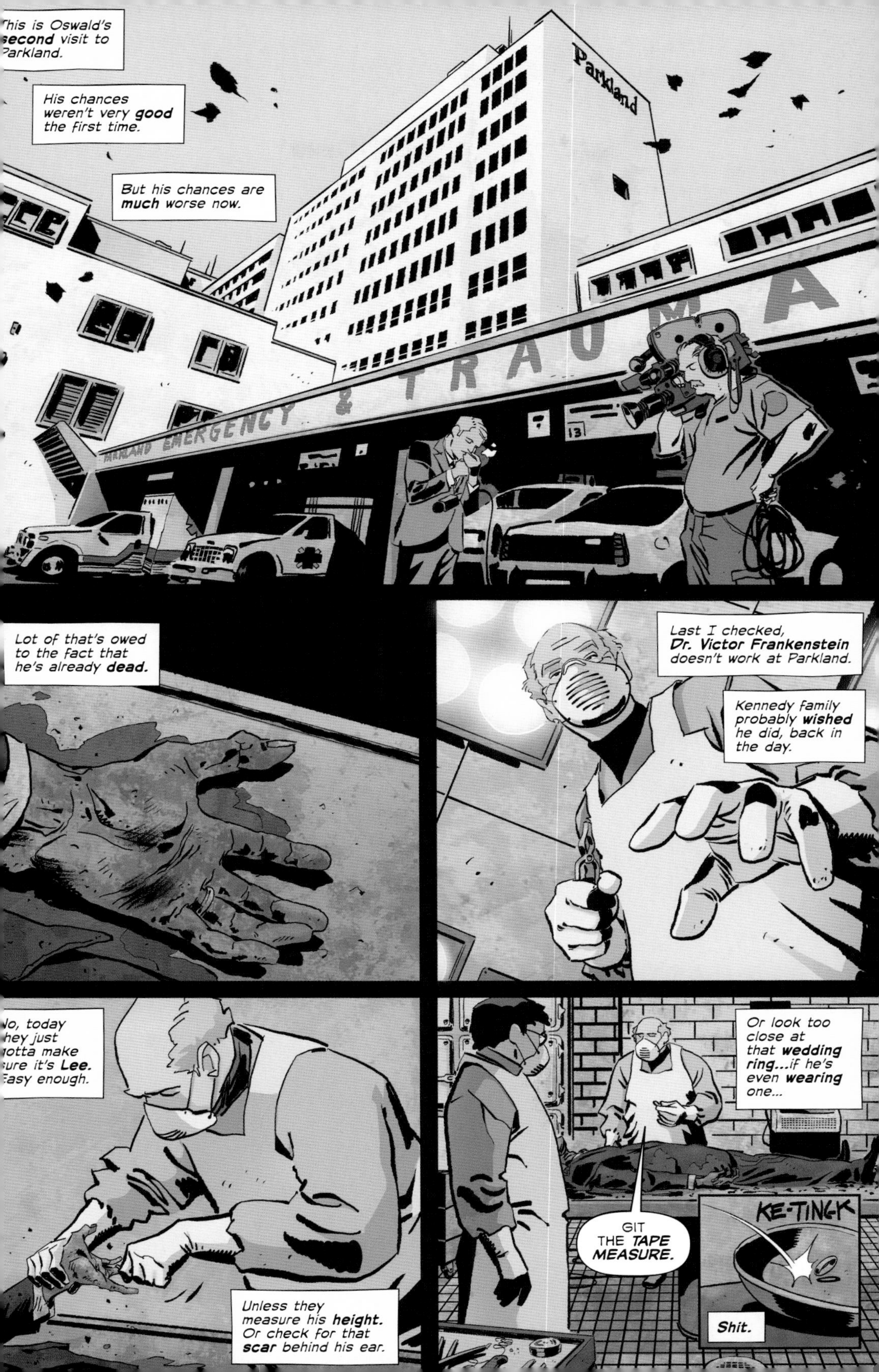

This is Oswald's second visit to Parkland.
His chances weren't very good the first time.
But his chances are much worse now.
Parkland
PARKLAND EMERGENCY & TRAUMA
Lot of that's owed to the fact that he's already dead.
Last I checked, Dr. Victor Frankenstein doesn't work at Parkland.
Kennedy family probably wished he did, back in the day.
No, today they just gotta make sure it's Lee. Easy enough.
Unless they measure his height. Or check for that scar behind his ear.
Or look too close at that wedding ring...if he's even wearing one...
GIT THE TAPE MEASURE.
KE-TINGK
Shit.

East Dallas. November 21st, 1963.

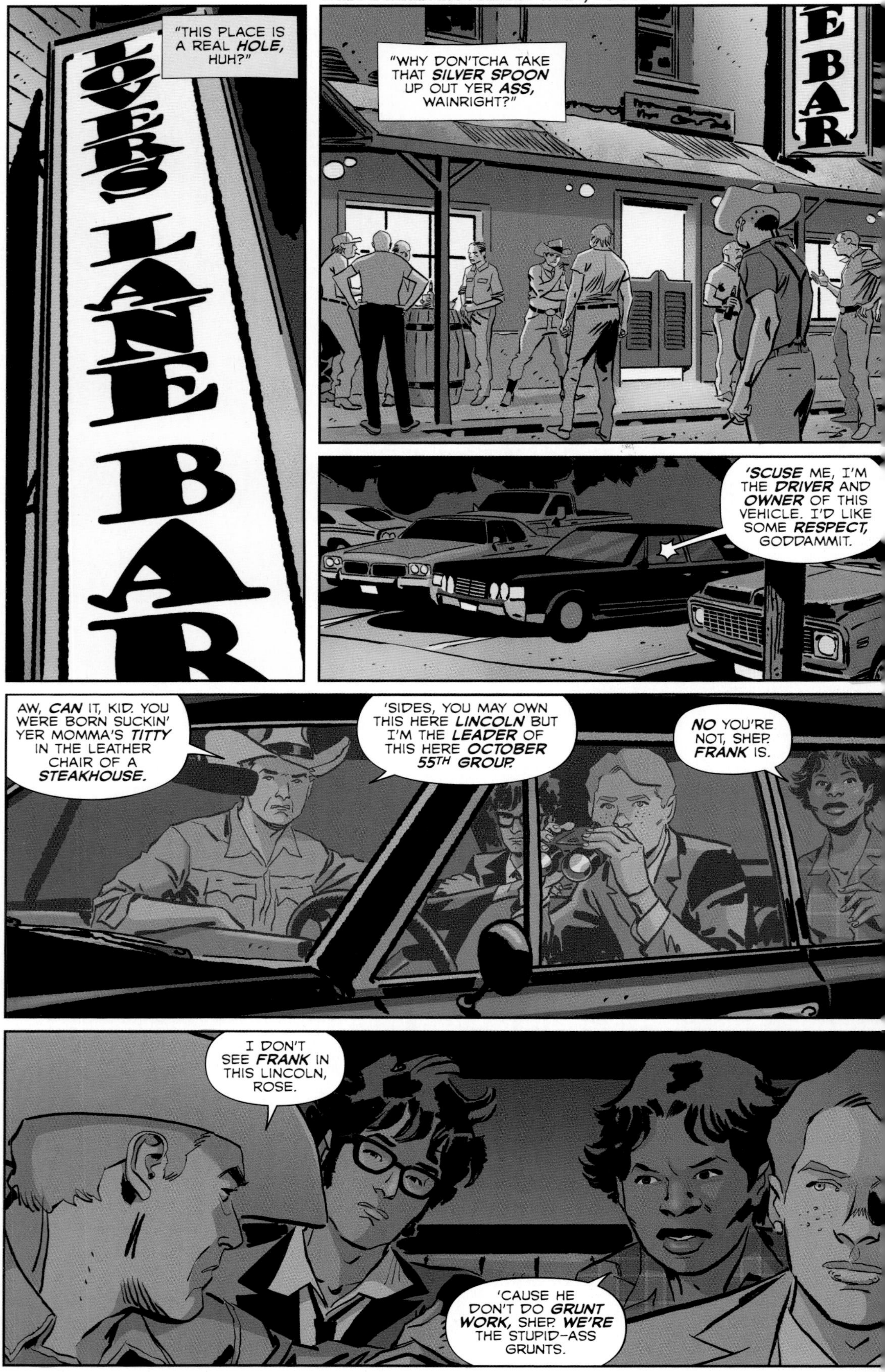

LOVERS LANE BAR
"THIS PLACE IS A REAL HOLE, HUH?"
EBAR
"WHY DON'TCHA TAKE THAT SILVER SPOON UP OUT YER ASS, WAINRIGHT?"
'SCUSE ME, I'M THE DRIVER AND OWNER OF THIS VEHICLE. I'D LIKE SOME RESPECT, GODDAMMIT.
AW, CAN IT, KID. YOU WERE BORN SUCKIN' YER MOMMA'S TITTY IN THE LEATHER CHAIR OF A STEAKHOUSE.
'SIDES, YOU MAY OWN THIS HERE LINCOLN BUT I'M THE LEADER OF THIS HERE OCTOBER 55TH GROUP.
NO YOU'RE NOT, SHEP. FRANK IS.
I DON'T SEE FRANK IN THIS LINCOLN, ROSE.
'CAUSE HE DON'T DO GRUNT WORK, SHEP. WE'RE THE STUPID-ASS GRUNTS.

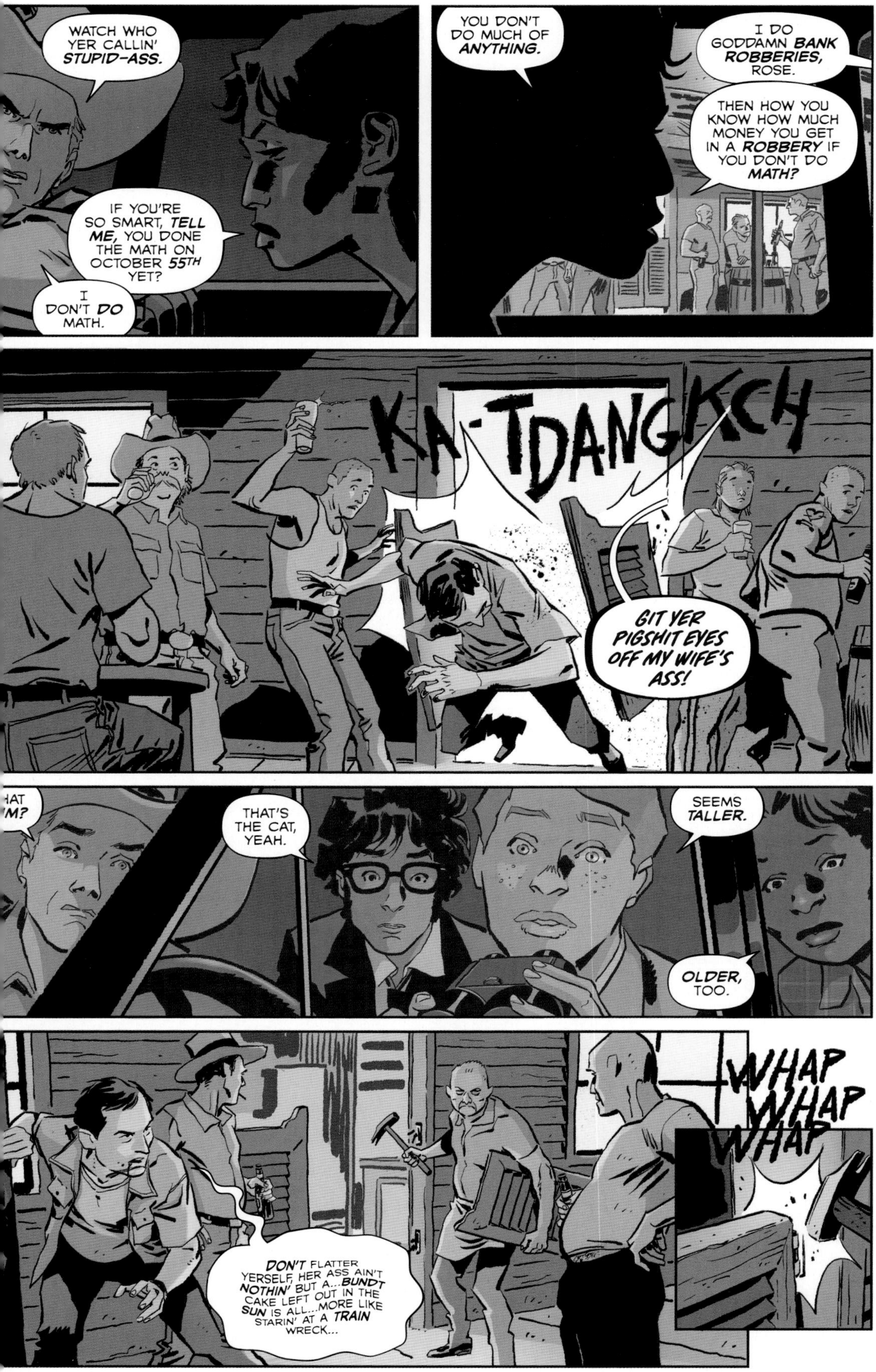
WATCH WHO YER CALLIN' STUPID-ASS.
IF YOU'RE SO SMART, TELL ME, YOU DONE THE MATH ON OCTOBER 55TH YET?
I DON'T DO MATH.
YOU DON'T DO MUCH OF ANYTHING.
I DO GODDAMN BANK ROBBERIES, ROSE.
THEN HOW YOU KNOW HOW MUCH MONEY YOU GET IN A ROBBERY IF YOU DON'T DO MATH?
KA-TDANG KCH
GIT YER PIGSHIT EYES OFF MY WIFE'S ASS!
THAT'S THE CAT, YEAH.
SEEMS TALLER.
OLDER, TOO.
WHAP WHAP WHAP
DON'T FLATTER YERSELF, HER ASS AIN'T NOTHIN' BUT A...BUNDT CAKE LEFT OUT IN THE SUN IS ALL...MORE LIKE STARIN' AT A TRAIN WRECK...

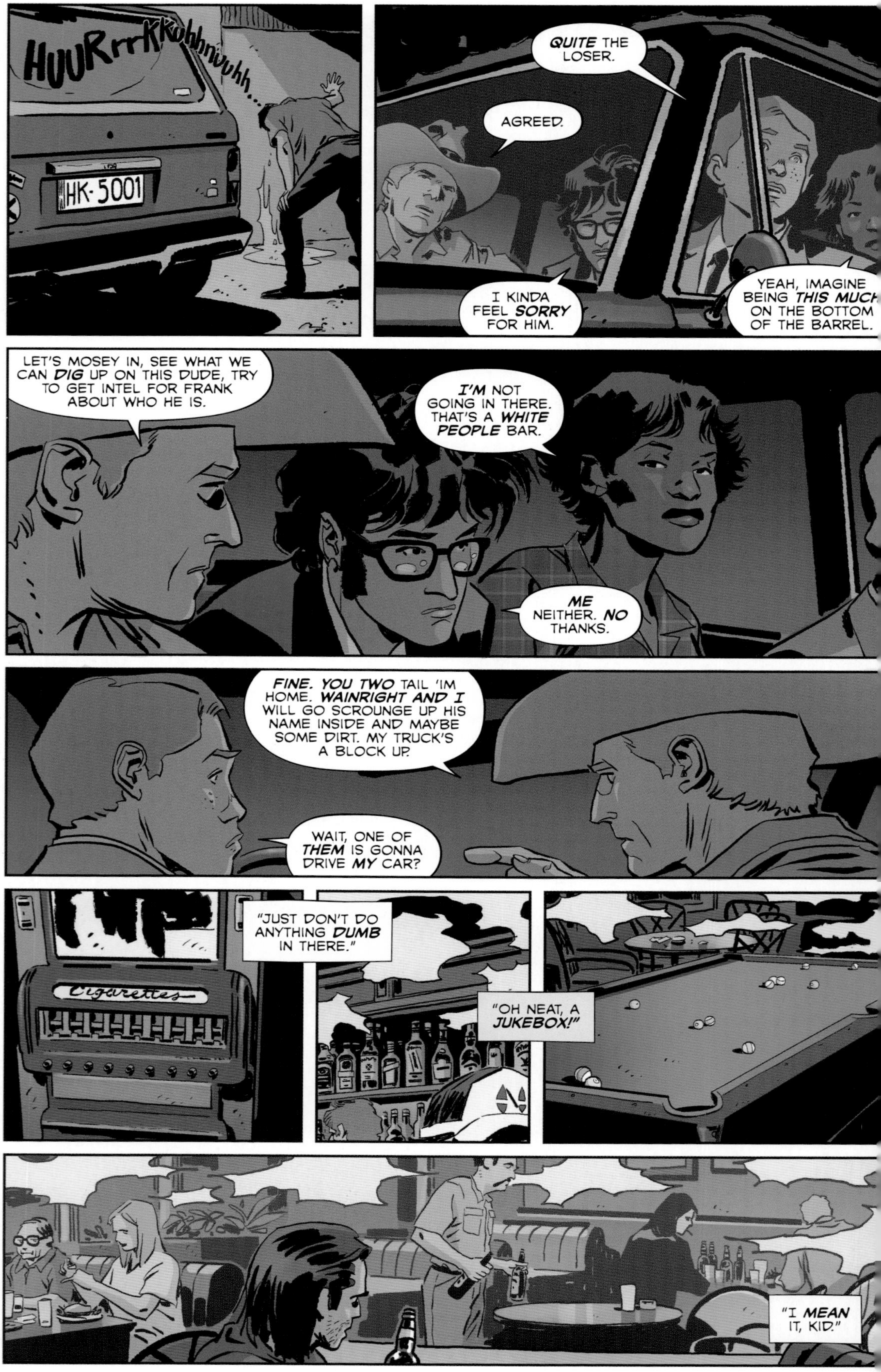
HUURrrKkohhnuuhh...
HK-5001
QUITE THE LOSER.
AGREED.
I KINDA FEEL SORRY FOR HIM.
YEAH, IMAGINE BEING THIS MUCH ON THE BOTTOM OF THE BARREL.
LET'S MOSEY IN, SEE WHAT WE CAN DIG UP ON THIS DUDE, TRY TO GET INTEL FOR FRANK ABOUT WHO HE IS.
I'M NOT GOING IN THERE. THAT'S A WHITE PEOPLE BAR.
ME NEITHER. NO THANKS.
FINE. YOU TWO TAIL 'IM HOME. WAINRIGHT AND I WILL GO SCROUNGE UP HIS NAME INSIDE AND MAYBE SOME DIRT. MY TRUCK'S A BLOCK UP.
WAIT, ONE OF THEM IS GONNA DRIVE MY CAR?
Cigarettes
"JUST DON'T DO ANYTHING DUMB IN THERE."
"OH NEAT, A JUKEBOX!"
"I MEAN IT, KID."

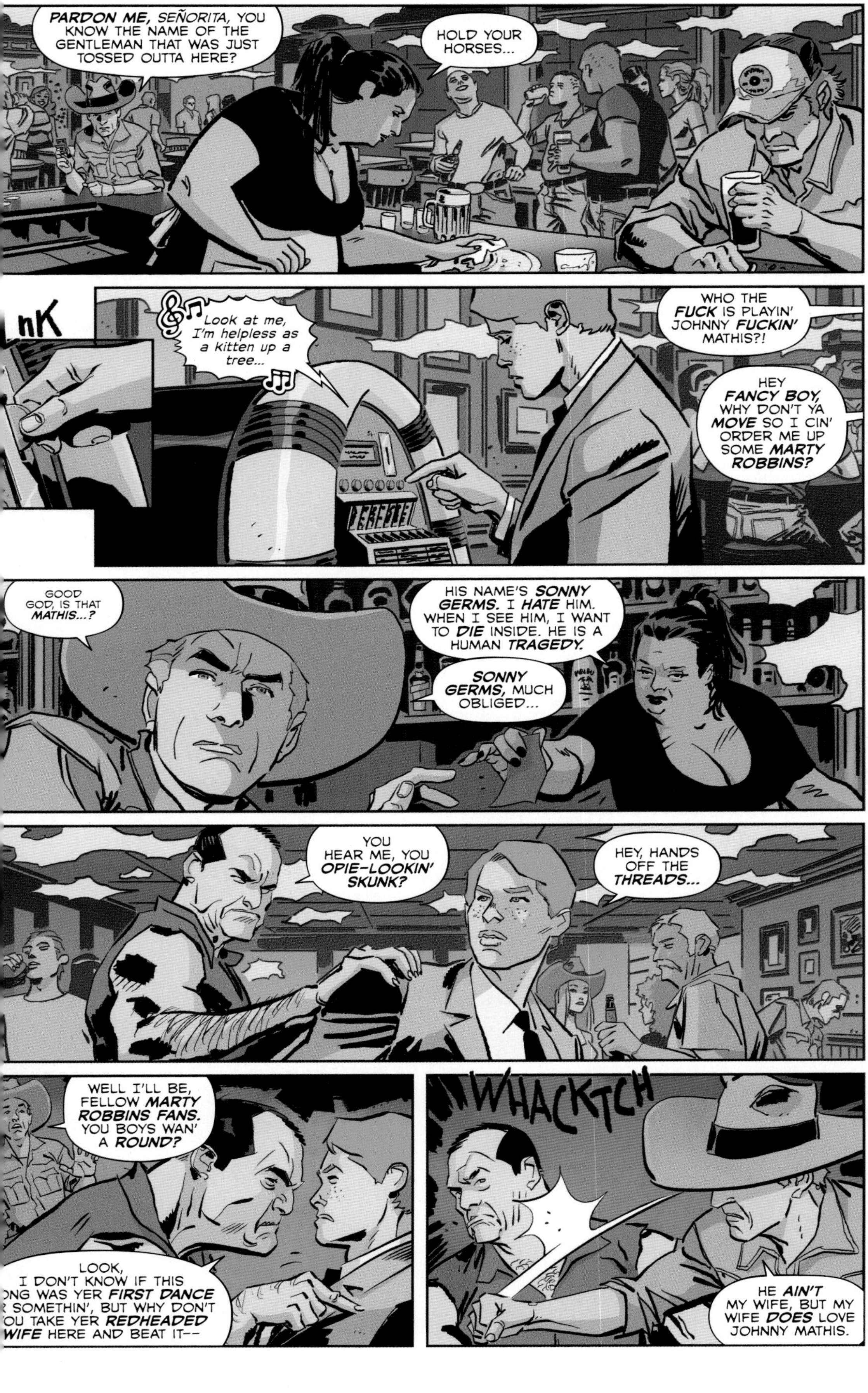
PARDON ME, SEÑORITA, YOU KNOW THE NAME OF THE GENTLEMAN THAT WAS JUST TOSSED OUTTA HERE?
HOLD YOUR HORSES...
Look at me, I'm helpless as a kitten up a tree...
WHO THE FUCK IS PLAYIN' JOHNNY FUCKIN' MATHIS?!
HEY FANCY BOY, WHY DON'T YA MOVE SO I CIN' ORDER ME UP SOME MARTY ROBBINS?
GOOD GOD, IS THAT MATHIS...?
HIS NAME'S SONNY GERMS. I HATE HIM. WHEN I SEE HIM, I WANT TO DIE INSIDE. HE IS A HUMAN TRAGEDY.
SONNY GERMS, MUCH OBLIGED...
YOU HEAR ME, YOU OPIE-LOOKIN' SKUNK?
HEY, HANDS OFF THE THREADS...
WELL I'LL BE, FELLOW MARTY ROBBINS FANS. YOU BOYS WAN' A ROUND?
LOOK, I DON'T KNOW IF THIS ONG WAS YER FIRST DANCE R SOMETHIN', BUT WHY DON'T OU TAKE YER REDHEADED WIFE HERE AND BEAT IT--
WHACKTCH
HE AIN'T MY WIFE, BUT MY WIFE DOES LOVE JOHNNY MATHIS.

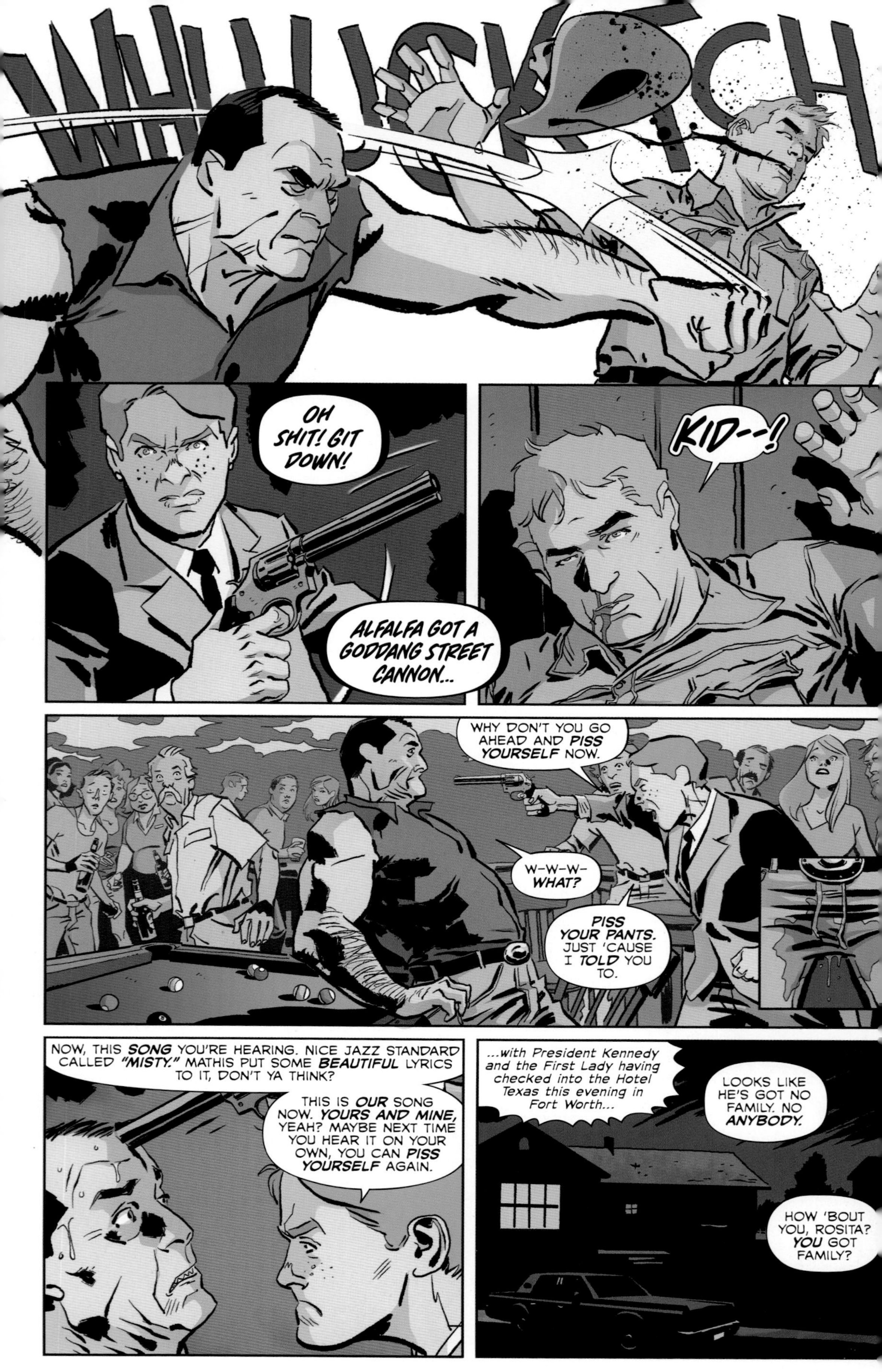
OH SHIT! GIT DOWN!
ALFALFA GOT A GODDANG STREET CANNON...
KID--!
WHY DON'T YOU GO AHEAD AND PISS YOURSELF NOW.
W-W-W- WHAT?
PISS YOUR PANTS. JUST 'CAUSE I TOLD YOU TO.
NOW, THIS SONG YOU'RE HEARING. NICE JAZZ STANDARD CALLED "MISTY." MATHIS PUT SOME BEAUTIFUL LYRICS TO IT, DON'T YA THINK?
THIS IS OUR SONG NOW. YOURS AND MINE, YEAH? MAYBE NEXT TIME YOU HEAR IT ON YOUR OWN, YOU CAN PISS YOURSELF AGAIN.
...with President Kennedy and the First Lady having checked into the Hotel Texas this evening in Fort Worth...
LOOKS LIKE HE'S GOT NO FAMILY. NO ANYBODY.
HOW 'BOUT YOU, ROSITA? YOU GOT FAMILY?

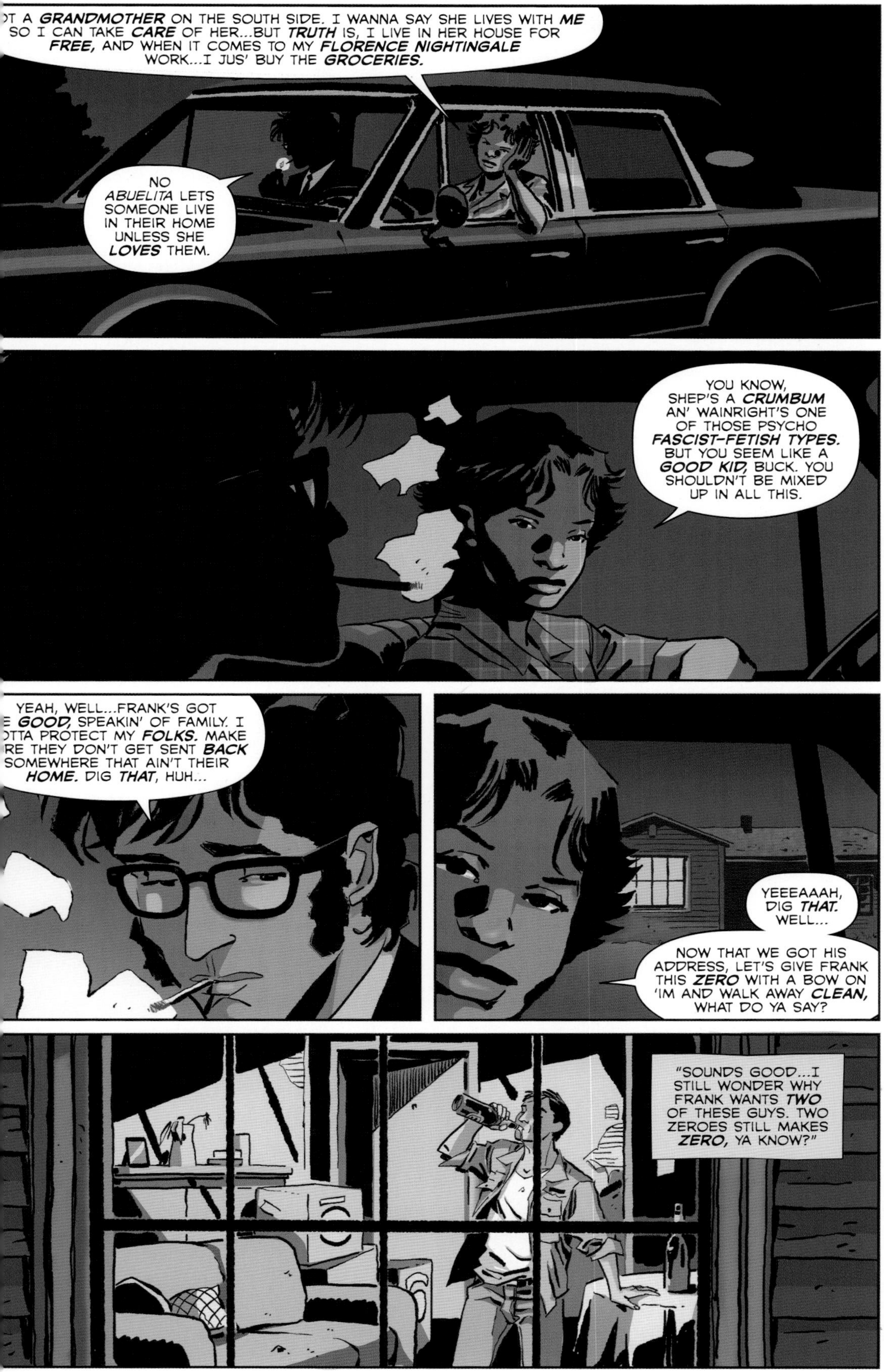
OT A GRANDMOTHER ON THE SOUTH SIDE. I WANNA SAY SHE LIVES WITH ME SO I CAN TAKE CARE OF HER...BUT TRUTH IS, I LIVE IN HER HOUSE FOR FREE, AND WHEN IT COMES TO MY FLORENCE NIGHTINGALE WORK...I JUS' BUY THE GROCERIES.
NO ABUELITA LETS SOMEONE LIVE IN THEIR HOME UNLESS SHE LOVES THEM.
YOU KNOW, SHEP'S A CRUMBUM AN' WAINRIGHT'S ONE OF THOSE PSYCHO FASCIST-FETISH TYPES. BUT YOU SEEM LIKE A GOOD KID, BUCK. YOU SHOULDN'T BE MIXED UP IN ALL THIS.
YEAH, WELL...FRANK'S GOT E GOOD, SPEAKIN' OF FAMILY. I OTTA PROTECT MY FOLKS. MAKE RE THEY DON'T GET SENT BACK SOMEWHERE THAT AIN'T THEIR HOME. DIG THAT, HUH...
YEEEAAAH, DIG THAT. WELL...
NOW THAT WE GOT HIS ADDRESS, LET'S GIVE FRANK THIS ZERO WITH A BOW ON 'IM AND WALK AWAY CLEAN, WHAT DO YA SAY?
"SOUNDS GOOD...I STILL WONDER WHY FRANK WANTS TWO OF THESE GUYS. TWO ZEROES STILL MAKES ZERO, YA KNOW?"

Hours later.

THEN THAT'S *FLOOR SIX* ALL SET. TEAM 2 FROM THE TOP OF THE DAL-TEX WALKS THE *PLAZA* TONIGHT. WITH YOU BEHIND THE FENCE IS *JIMMY,* DONE UP LIKE HIS USUAL THING.

THEY COME.

G'MORNING. I *LIKE* HIM. AND NOT A MOMENT *TOO SOON,* HUH?

BUCK SPOTTED HIM FIRST.

AW, LOOK AT YOU, GIVING HIM CREDIT.

GOES WHERE IT'S *DUE,* FRANK.

GOT A LITTLE BIT OF A *HEIGHT* ISSUE, BUT I'M FINE WITH IT. WHERE'S HE LIVE?

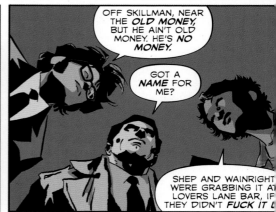

OFF SKILLMAN, NEAR THE *OLD MONEY,* BUT HE AIN'T OLD MONEY. HE'S *NO MONEY.*

GOT A *NAME* FOR ME?

SHEP AND WAINRIGHT WERE GRABBING IT A[T] LOVERS LANE BAR, IF THEY DIDN'T *FUCK IT [U]*

WHERE *ARE* THOSE TWO YOKELS? TO ME, *PUNCTUALITY* IS A TOKEN OF *RESPECT.*

SONNY GERMS.

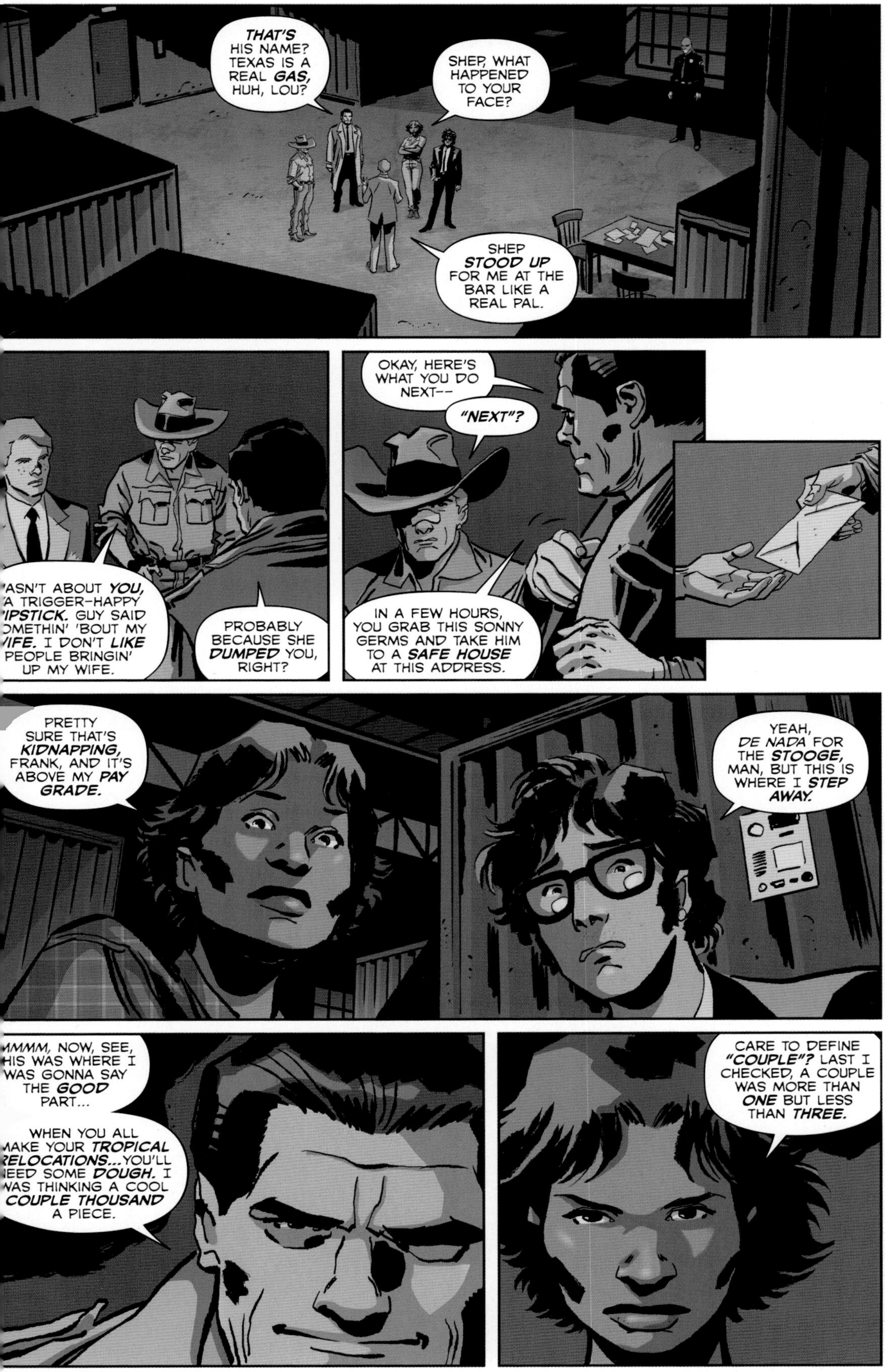
THAT'S HIS NAME? TEXAS IS A REAL GAS, HUH, LOU?
SHEP, WHAT HAPPENED TO YOUR FACE?
SHEP STOOD UP FOR ME AT THE BAR LIKE A REAL PAL.
'ASN'T ABOUT YOU, 'A TRIGGER-HAPPY 'IPSTICK. GUY SAID OMETHIN' 'BOUT MY VIFE. I DON'T LIKE PEOPLE BRINGIN' UP MY WIFE.
PROBABLY BECAUSE SHE DUMPED YOU, RIGHT?
OKAY, HERE'S WHAT YOU DO NEXT--
"NEXT"?
IN A FEW HOURS, YOU GRAB THIS SONNY GERMS AND TAKE HIM TO A SAFE HOUSE AT THIS ADDRESS.
PRETTY SURE THAT'S KIDNAPPING, FRANK, AND IT'S ABOVE MY PAY GRADE.
YEAH, DE NADA FOR THE STOOGE, MAN, BUT THIS IS WHERE I STEP AWAY.
MMMM, NOW, SEE, HIS WAS WHERE I WAS GONNA SAY THE GOOD PART...
WHEN YOU ALL MAKE YOUR TROPICAL RELOCATIONS...YOU'LL NEED SOME DOUGH. I WAS THINKING A COOL COUPLE THOUSAND A PIECE.
CARE TO DEFINE "COUPLE"? LAST I CHECKED, A COUPLE WAS MORE THAN ONE BUT LESS THAN THREE.

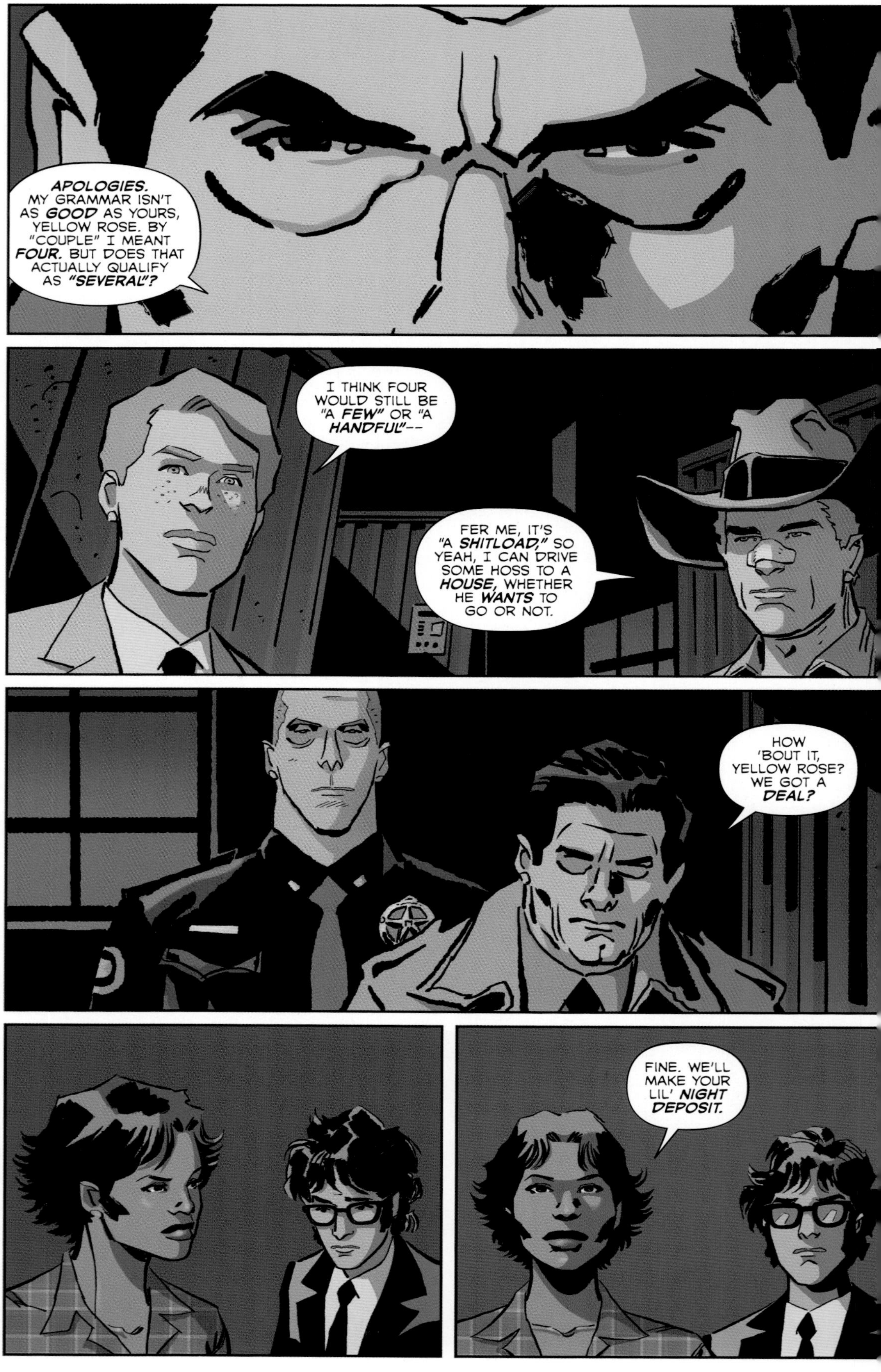
APOLOGIES. MY GRAMMAR ISN'T AS GOOD AS YOURS, YELLOW ROSE. BY "COUPLE" I MEANT FOUR. BUT DOES THAT ACTUALLY QUALIFY AS "SEVERAL"?
I THINK FOUR WOULD STILL BE "A FEW" OR "A HANDFUL"--
FER ME, IT'S "A SHITLOAD," SO YEAH, I CAN DRIVE SOME HOSS TO A HOUSE, WHETHER HE WANTS TO GO OR NOT.
HOW 'BOUT IT, YELLOW ROSE? WE GOT A DEAL?
FINE. WE'LL MAKE YOUR LIL' NIGHT DEPOSIT.

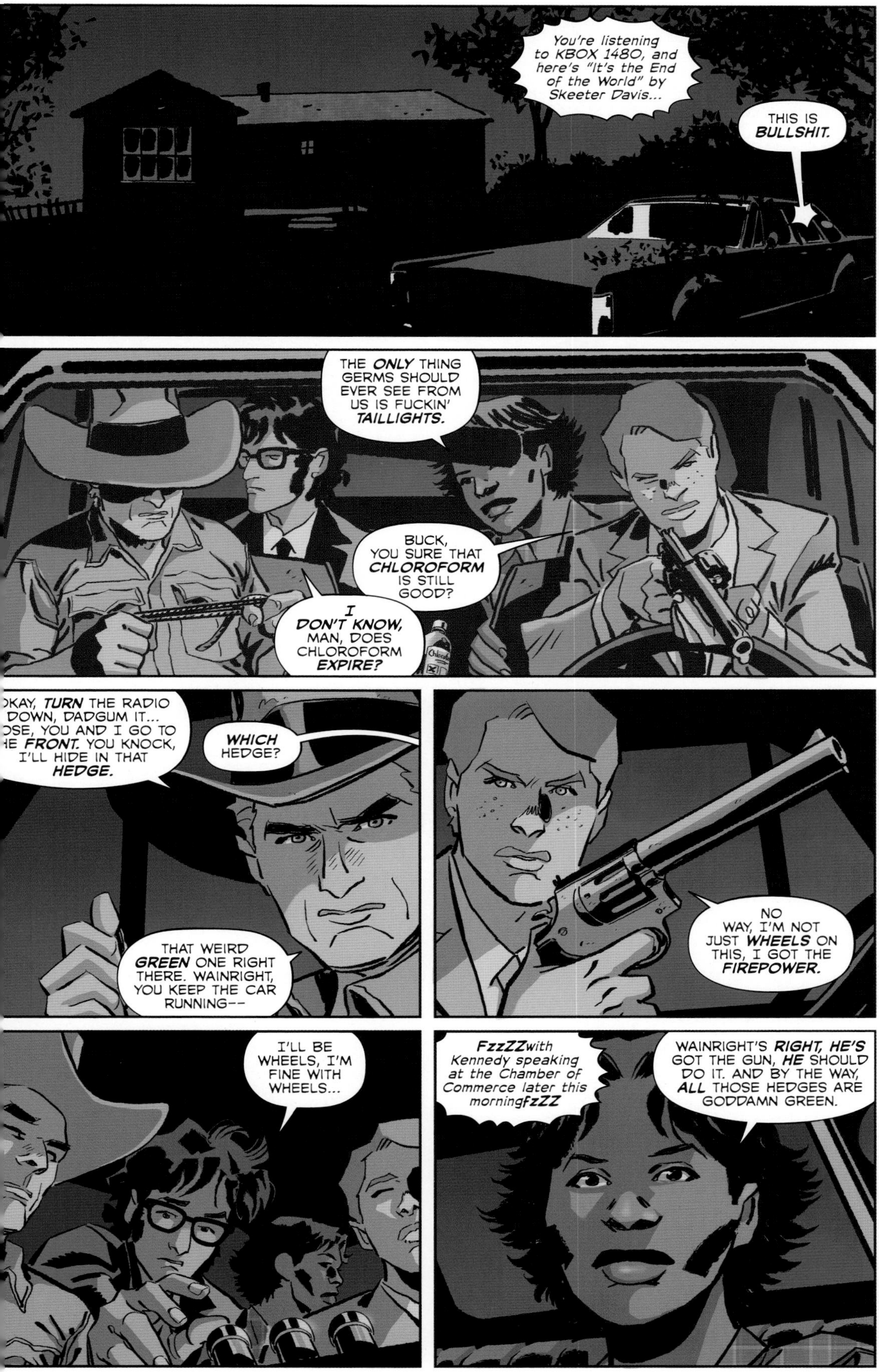
You're listening to KBOX 1480, and here's "It's the End of the World" by Skeeter Davis...
THIS IS BULLSHIT.
THE ONLY THING GERMS SHOULD EVER SEE FROM US IS FUCKIN' TAILLIGHTS.
BUCK, YOU SURE THAT CHLOROFORM IS STILL GOOD?
I DON'T KNOW, MAN, DOES CHLOROFORM EXPIRE?
OKAY, TURN THE RADIO DOWN, DADGUM IT... OSE, YOU AND I GO TO HE FRONT. YOU KNOCK, I'LL HIDE IN THAT HEDGE.
WHICH HEDGE?
THAT WEIRD GREEN ONE RIGHT THERE. WAINRIGHT, YOU KEEP THE CAR RUNNING--
NO WAY, I'M NOT JUST WHEELS ON THIS, I GOT THE FIREPOWER.
I'LL BE WHEELS, I'M FINE WITH WHEELS...
FzzZZwith Kennedy speaking at the Chamber of Commerce later this morningFzZZ
WAINRIGHT'S RIGHT, HE'S GOT THE GUN, HE SHOULD DO IT. AND BY THE WAY, ALL THOSE HEDGES ARE GODDAMN GREEN.

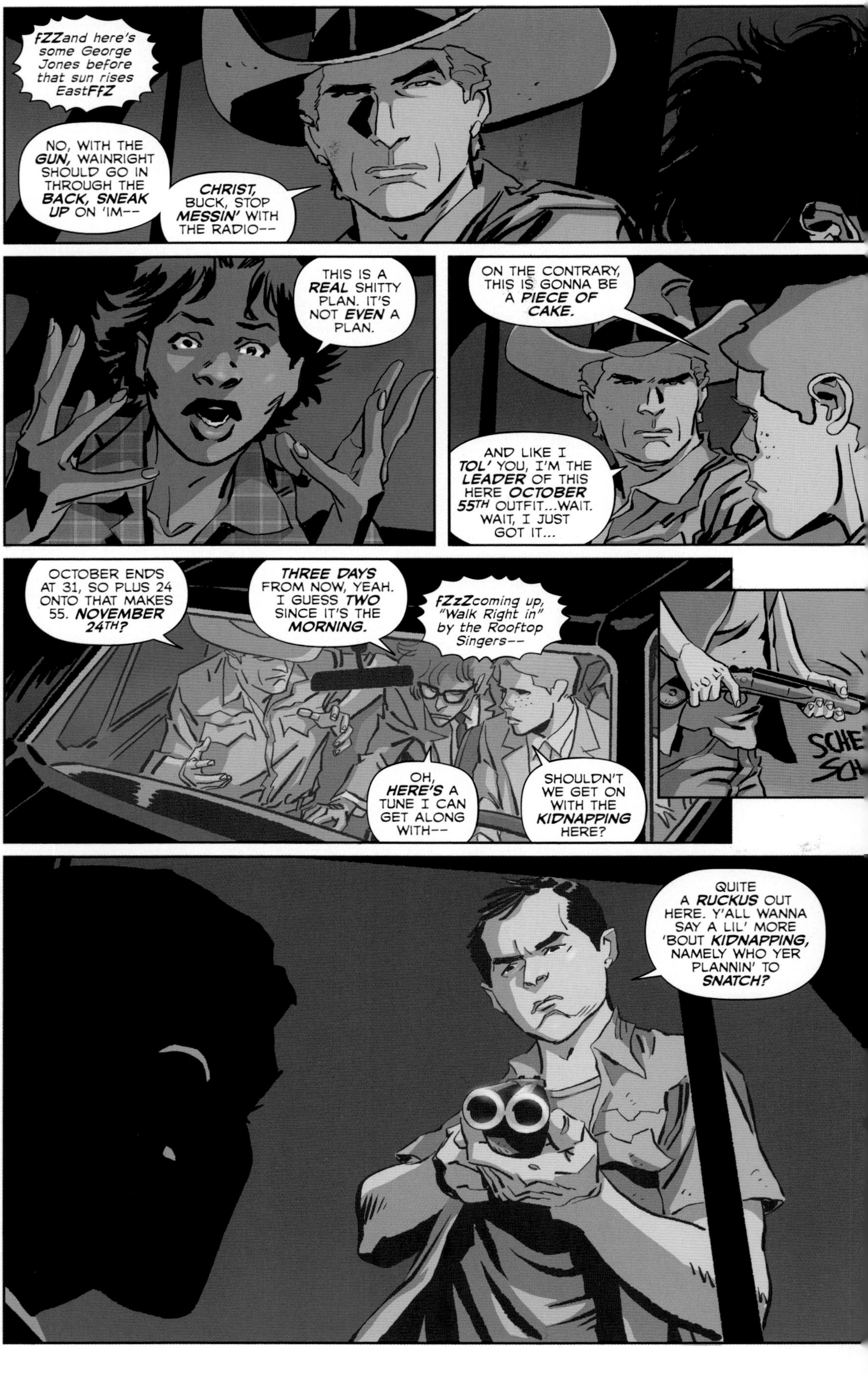
fZZand here's some George Jones before that sun rises EastFfZ
NO, WITH THE GUN, WAINRIGHT SHOULD GO IN THROUGH THE BACK, SNEAK UP ON 'IM--
CHRIST, BUCK, STOP MESSIN' WITH THE RADIO--
THIS IS A REAL SHITTY PLAN. IT'S NOT EVEN A PLAN.
ON THE CONTRARY, THIS IS GONNA BE A PIECE OF CAKE.
AND LIKE I TOL' YOU, I'M THE LEADER OF THIS HERE OCTOBER 55TH OUTFIT...WAIT. WAIT, I JUST GOT IT...
OCTOBER ENDS AT 31, SO PLUS 24 ONTO THAT MAKES 55. NOVEMBER 24TH?
THREE DAYS FROM NOW, YEAH. I GUESS TWO SINCE IT'S THE MORNING.
fZzZcoming up, "Walk Right in" by the Rooftop Singers--
OH, HERE'S A TUNE I CAN GET ALONG WITH--
SHOULDN'T WE GET ON WITH THE KIDNAPPING HERE?
QUITE A RUCKUS OUT HERE. Y'ALL WANNA SAY A LIL' MORE 'BOUT KIDNAPPING, NAMELY WHO YER PLANNIN' TO SNATCH?

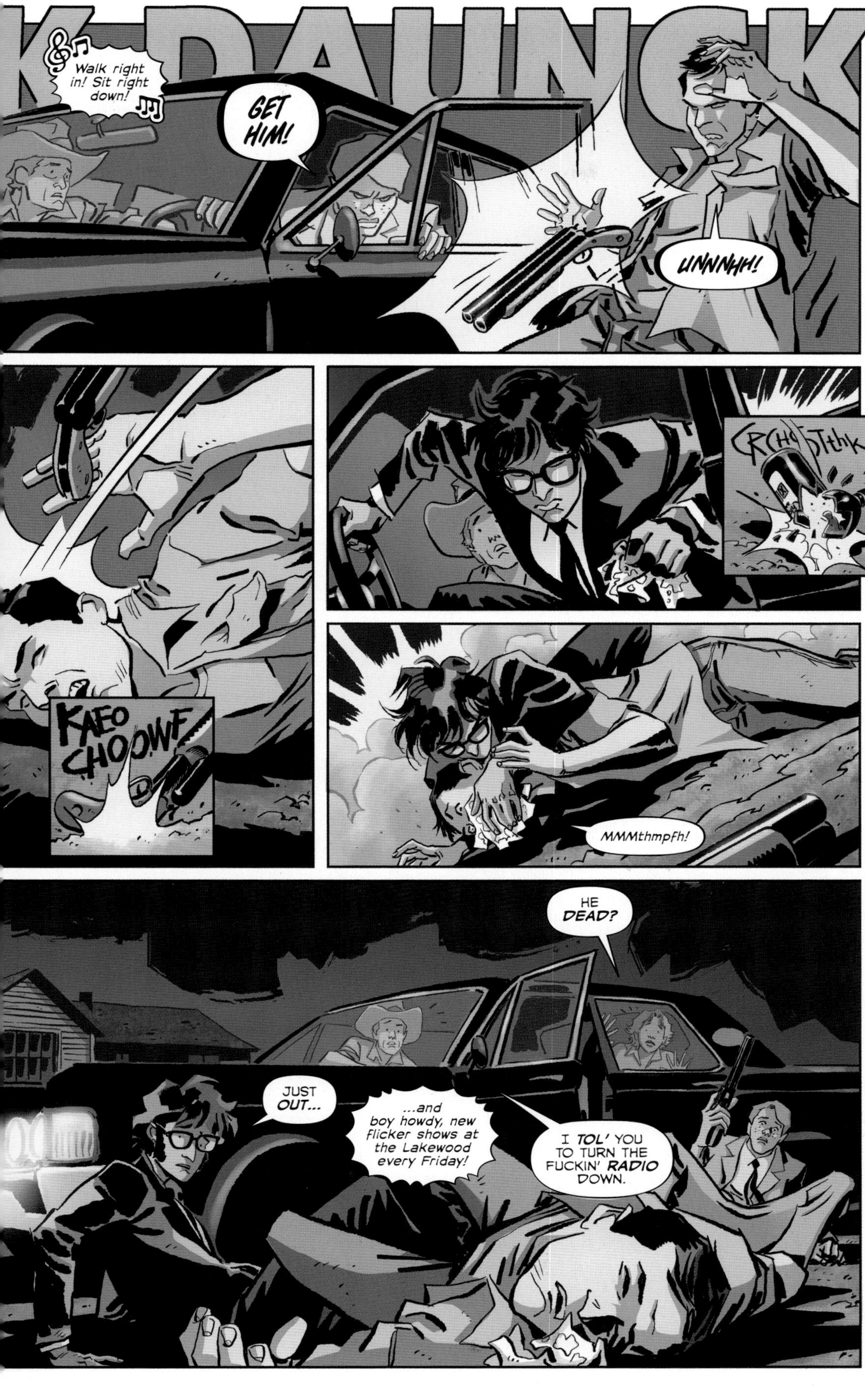

KRAUNCK
Walk right in! Sit right down!
GET HIM!
UNNNHH!
KAEO CHOOWF
CRCHSHTthk
MMMthmpfh!
HE DEAD?
JUST OUT...
...and boy howdy, new flicker shows at the Lakewood every Friday!
I TOL' YOU TO TURN THE FUCKIN' RADIO DOWN.

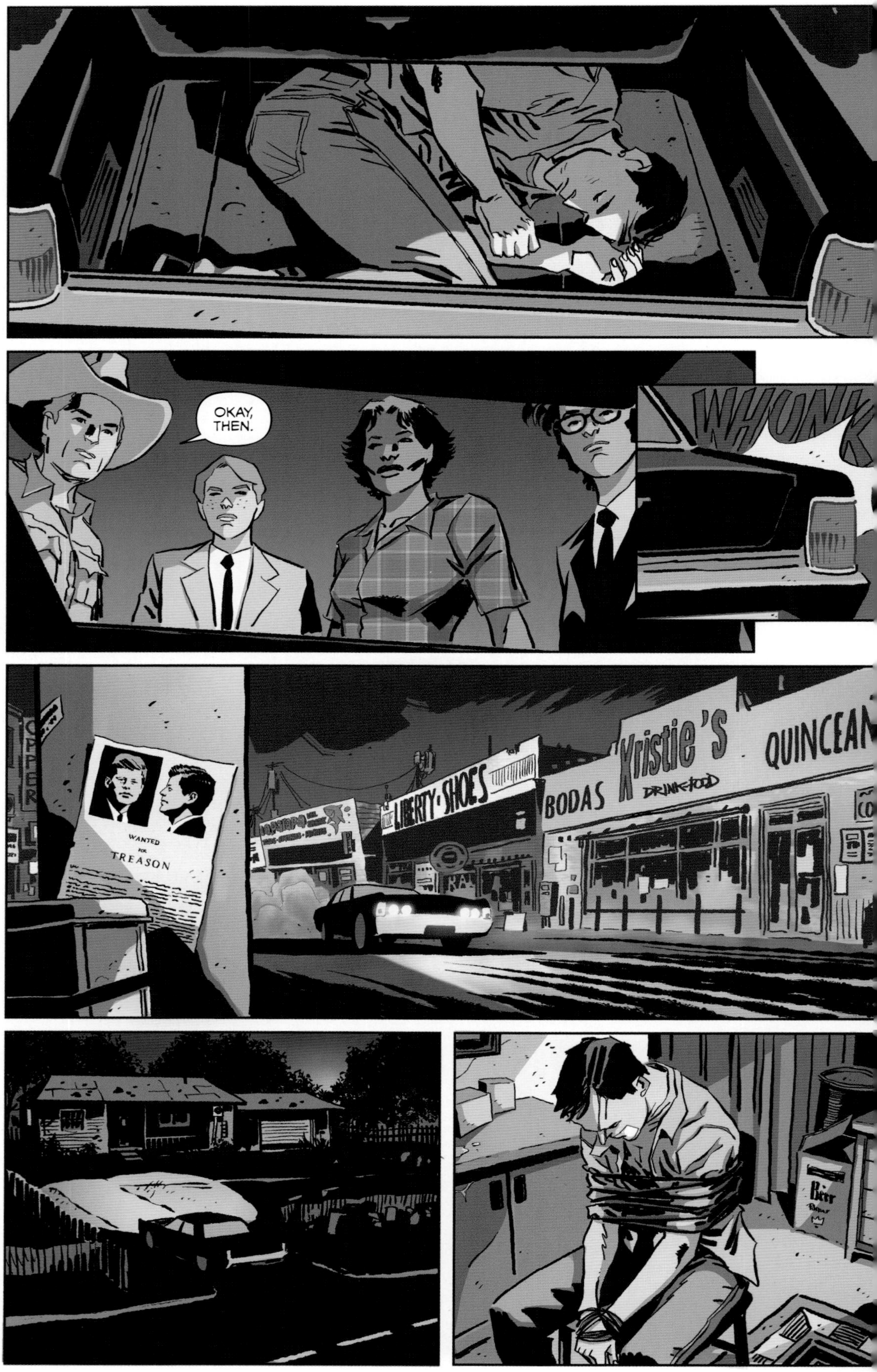
OKAY, THEN.
WANTED FOR TREASON
LIBERTY SHOES
BODAS
Kristie's
DRINK FOOD

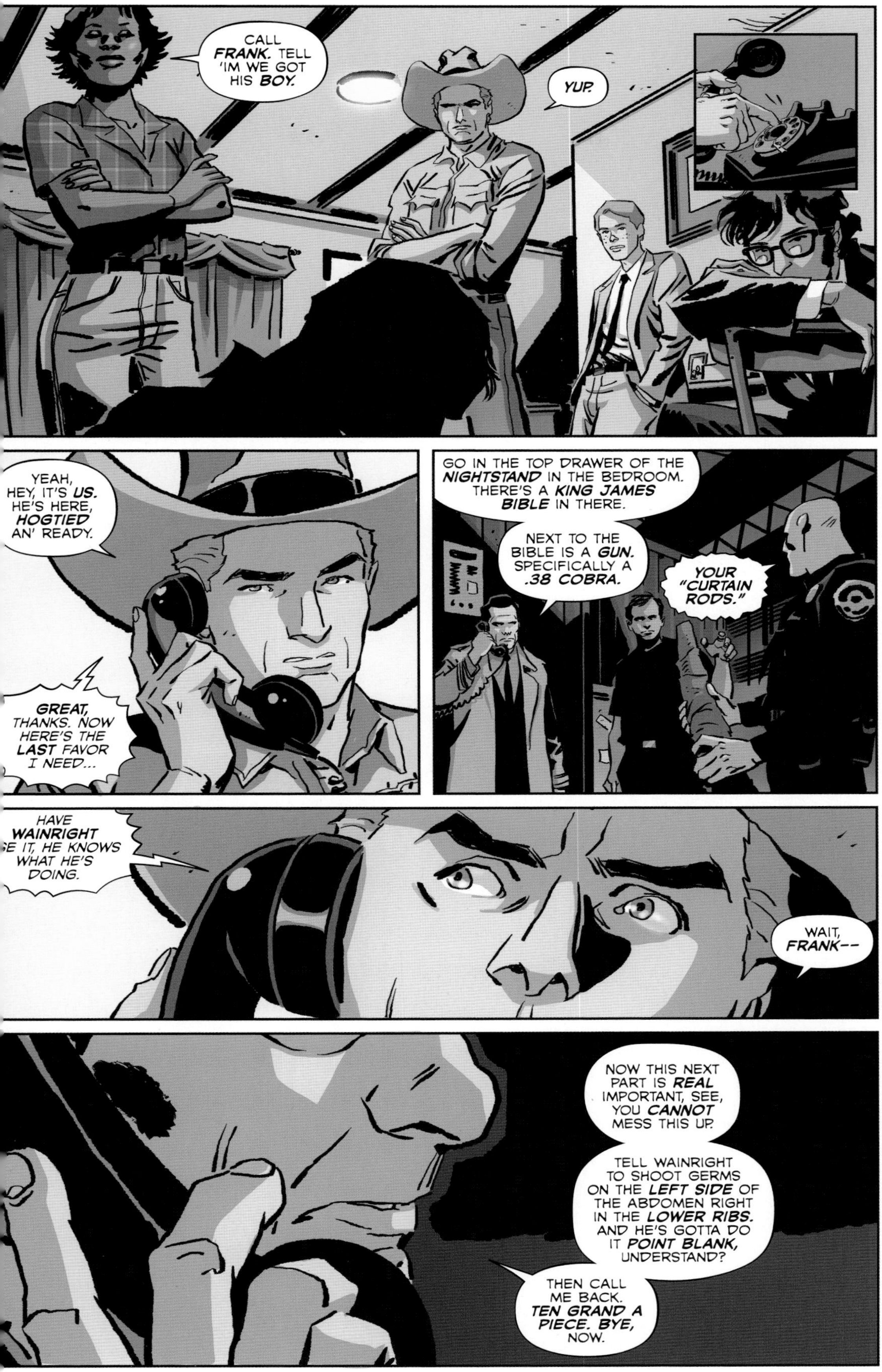
CALL FRANK. TELL 'IM WE GOT HIS BOY.
YUP.
YEAH, HEY, IT'S US. HE'S HERE, HOGTIED AN' READY.
GREAT, THANKS. NOW HERE'S THE LAST FAVOR I NEED...
GO IN THE TOP DRAWER OF THE NIGHTSTAND IN THE BEDROOM. THERE'S A KING JAMES BIBLE IN THERE.
NEXT TO THE BIBLE IS A GUN. SPECIFICALLY A .38 COBRA.
YOUR "CURTAIN RODS."
HAVE WAINRIGHT ...E IT, HE KNOWS WHAT HE'S DOING.
WAIT, FRANK--
NOW THIS NEXT PART IS REAL IMPORTANT, SEE, YOU CANNOT MESS THIS UP.
TELL WAINRIGHT TO SHOOT GERMS ON THE LEFT SIDE OF THE ABDOMEN RIGHT IN THE LOWER RIBS. AND HE'S GOTTA DO IT POINT BLANK, UNDERSTAND?
THEN CALL ME BACK. TEN GRAND A PIECE. BYE, NOW.

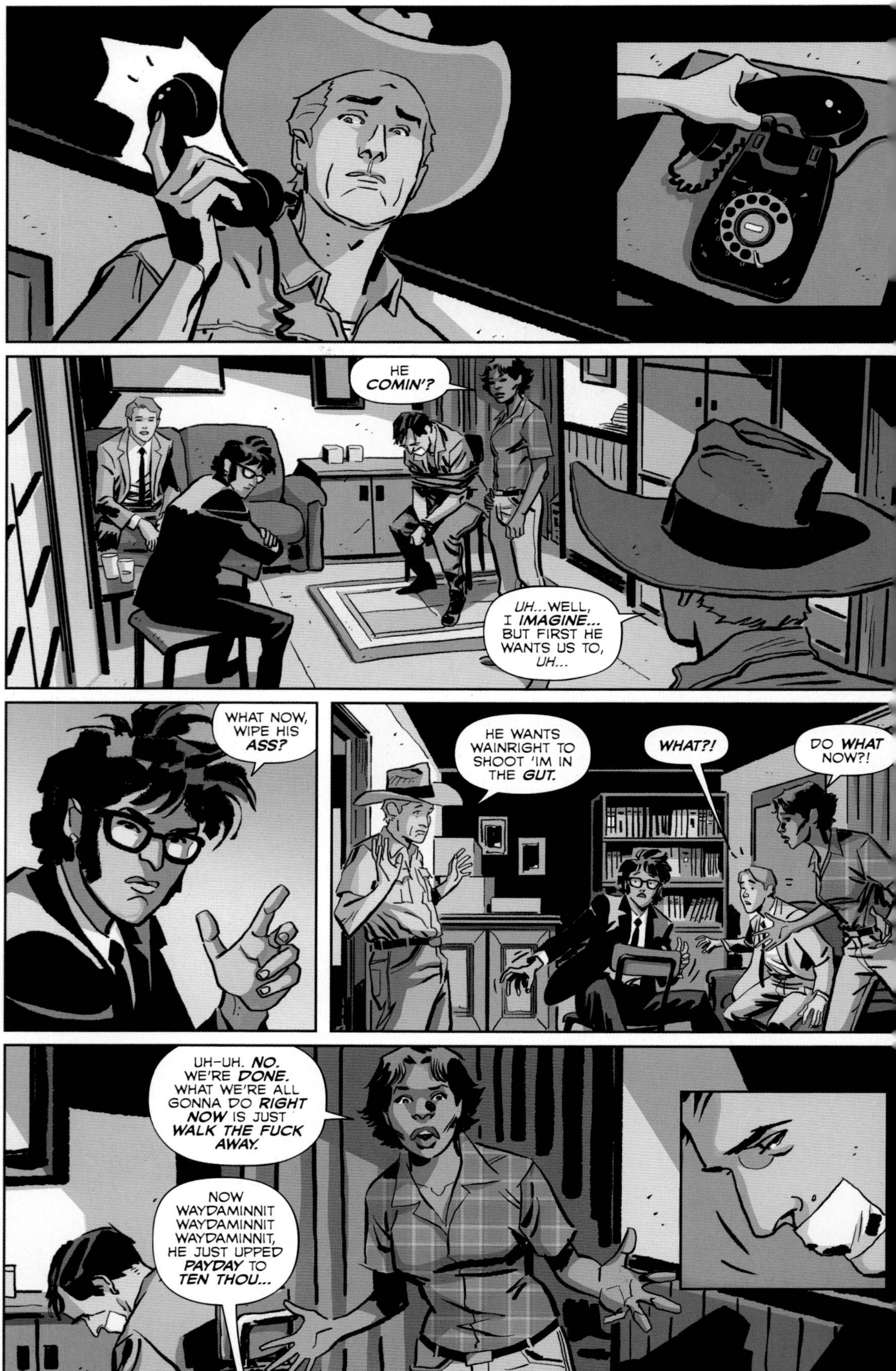
HE COMIN'?
UH... WELL, I IMAGINE... BUT FIRST HE WANTS US TO, UH...
WHAT NOW, WIPE HIS ASS?
HE WANTS WAINRIGHT TO SHOOT 'IM IN THE GUT.
WHAT?!
DO WHAT NOW?!
UH-UH. NO. WE'RE DONE. WHAT WE'RE ALL GONNA DO RIGHT NOW IS JUST WALK THE FUCK AWAY.
NOW WAYDAMINNIT WAYDAMINNIT WAYDAMINNIT, HE JUST UPPED PAYDAY TO TEN THOU...

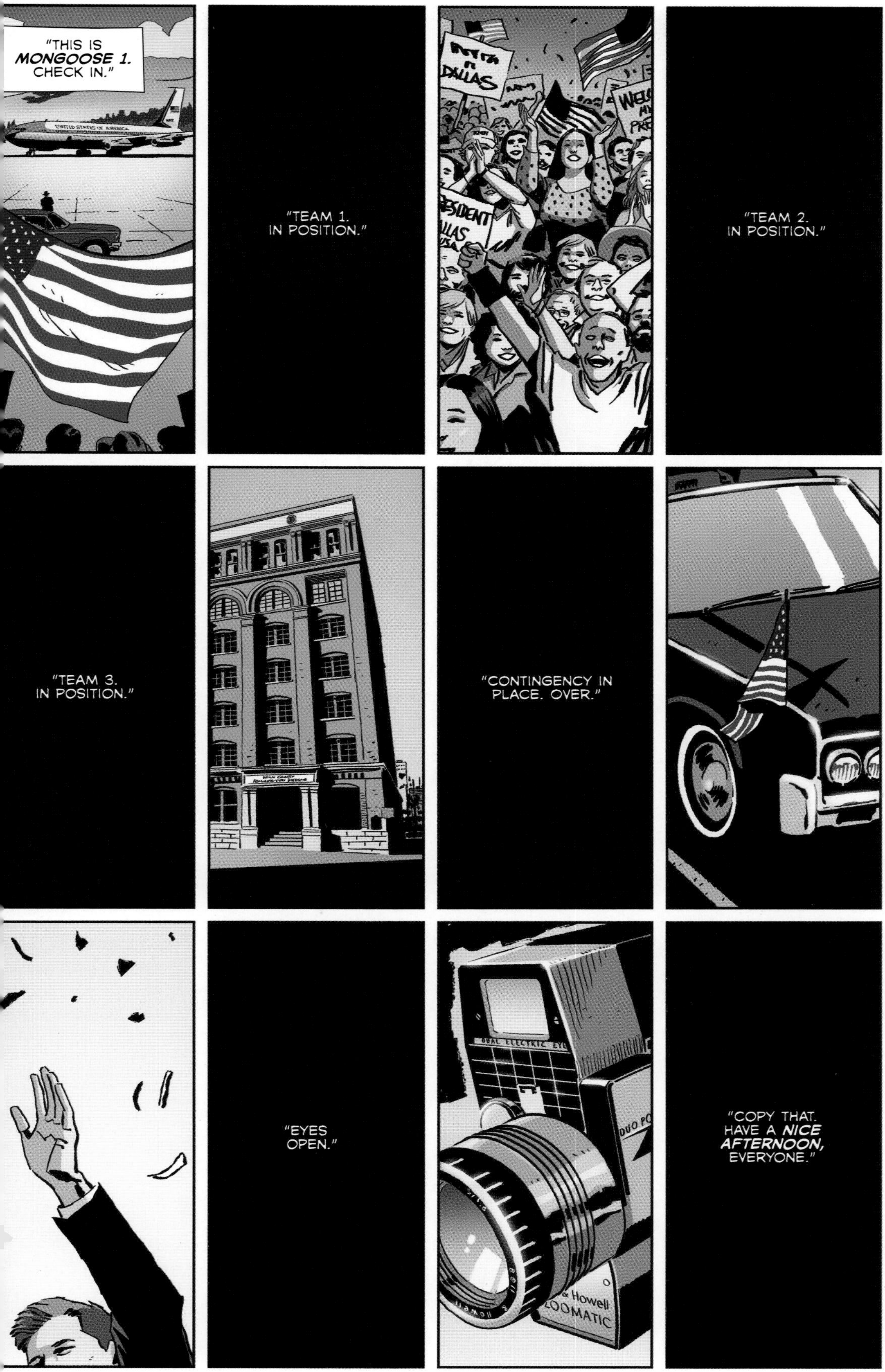
"THIS IS *MONGOOSE 1.* CHECK IN."
"TEAM 1. IN POSITION."
DALLAS
"TEAM 2. IN POSITION."
"TEAM 3. IN POSITION."
"CONTINGENCY IN PLACE. OVER."
"EYES OPEN."
& Howell
ZOOMATIC
"COPY THAT. HAVE A *NICE AFTERNOON,* EVERYONE."

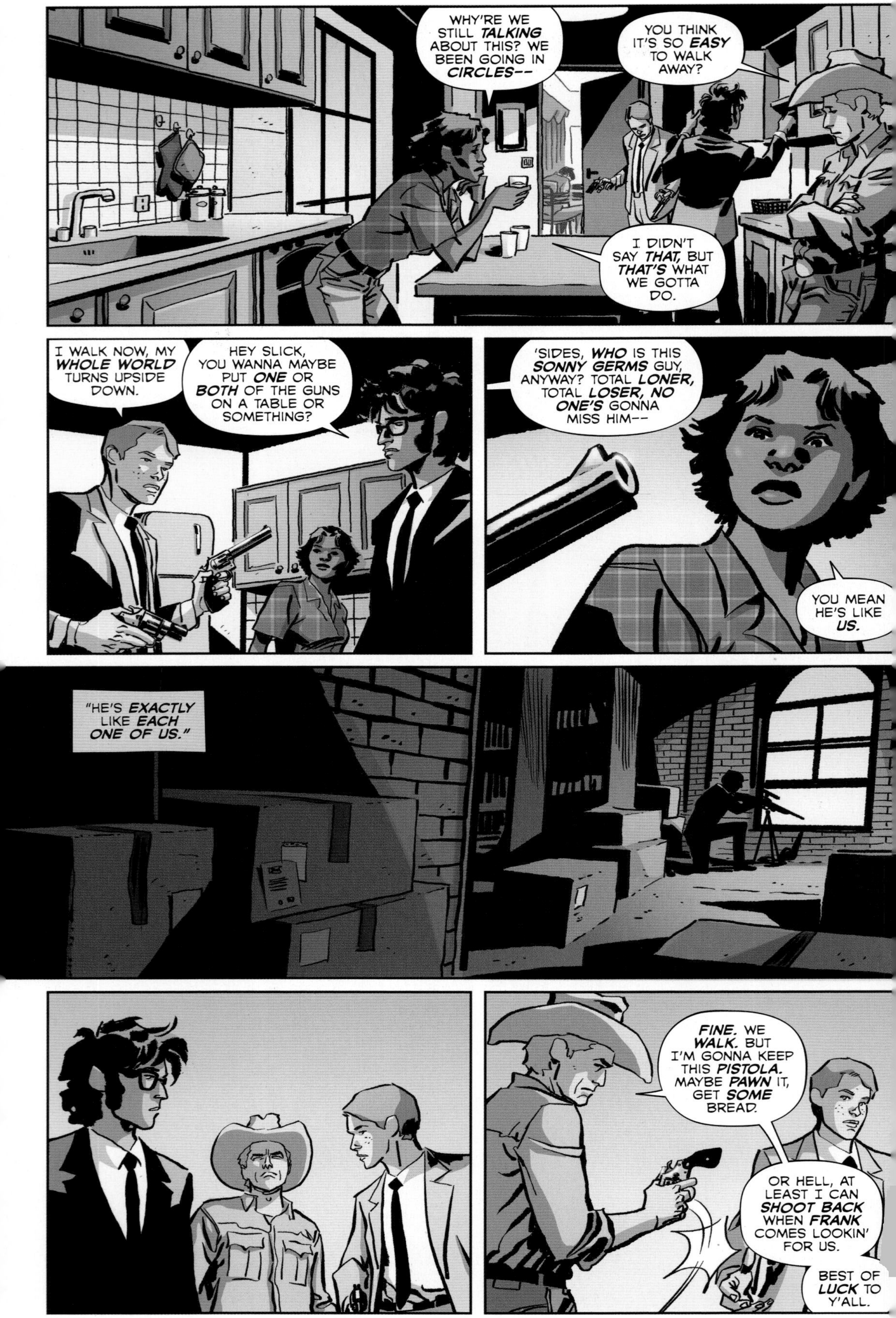
WHY'RE WE STILL TALKING ABOUT THIS? WE BEEN GOING IN CIRCLES--
YOU THINK IT'S SO EASY TO WALK AWAY?
I DIDN'T SAY THAT, BUT THAT'S WHAT WE GOTTA DO.
I WALK NOW, MY WHOLE WORLD TURNS UPSIDE DOWN.
HEY SLICK, YOU WANNA MAYBE PUT ONE OR BOTH OF THE GUNS ON A TABLE OR SOMETHING?
'SIDES, WHO IS THIS SONNY GERMS GUY, ANYWAY? TOTAL LONER, TOTAL LOSER, NO ONE'S GONNA MISS HIM--
YOU MEAN HE'S LIKE US.
"HE'S EXACTLY LIKE EACH ONE OF US."
FINE. WE WALK. BUT I'M GONNA KEEP THIS PISTOLA. MAYBE PAWN IT, GET SOME BREAD.
OR HELL, AT LEAST I CAN SHOOT BACK WHEN FRANK COMES LOOKIN' FOR US.
BEST OF LUCK TO Y'ALL.

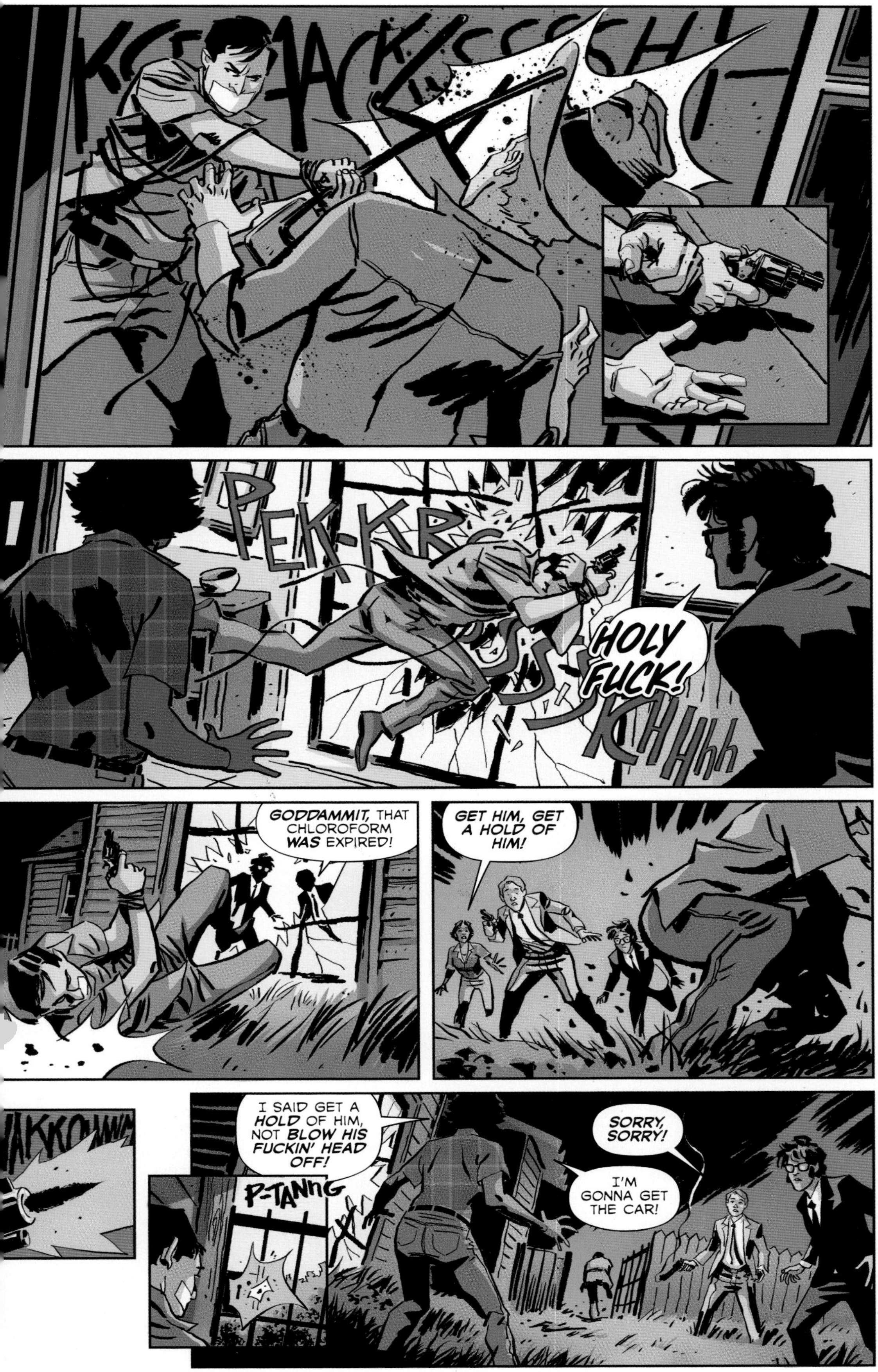

KCRAACK
HOLY FUCK!
GODDAMMIT, THAT CHLOROFORM WAS EXPIRED!
GET HIM, GET A HOLD OF HIM!
I SAID GET A HOLD OF HIM, NOT BLOW HIS FUCKIN' HEAD OFF!
P-TANNG
SORRY, SORRY!
I'M GONNA GET THE CAR!

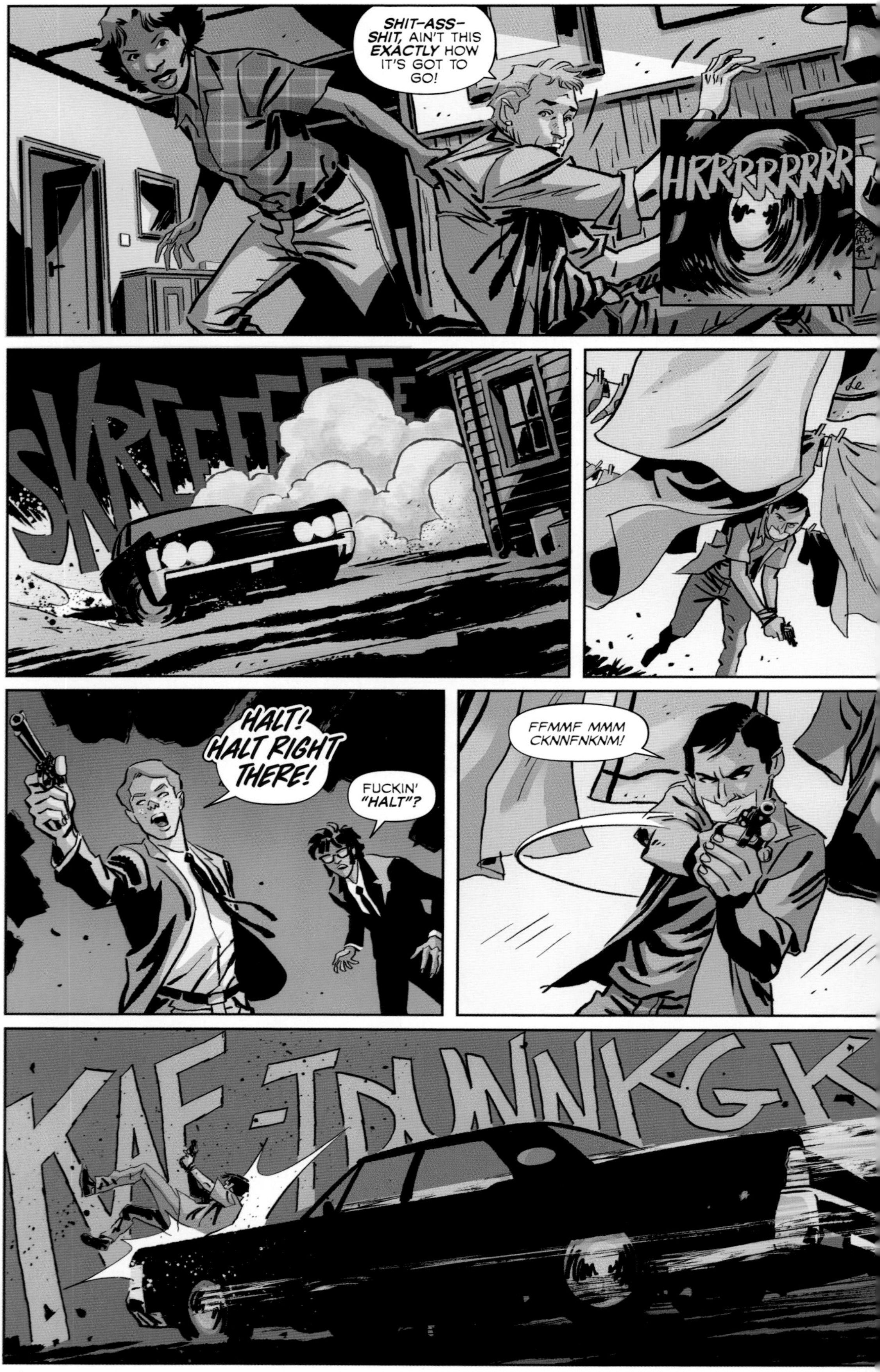
SHIT-ASS-SHIT, AIN'T THIS EXACTLY HOW IT'S GOT TO GO!
HRRRRRRRR
SKREEEEEEE
HALT! HALT RIGHT THERE!
FUCKIN' "HALT"?
FFMMF MMM CKNNFNKNM!
KAF-TDUNNKGK

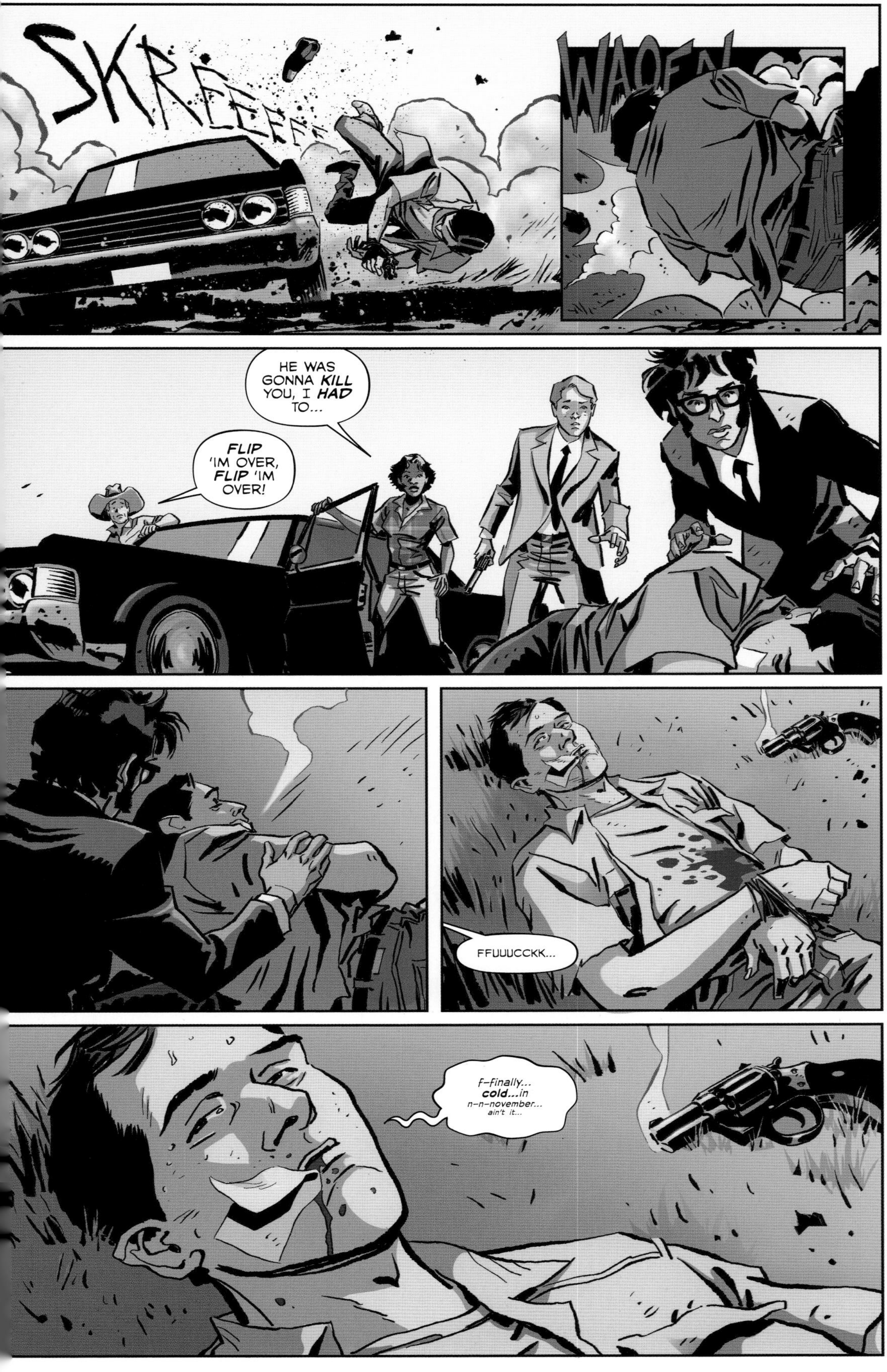
SKREEEFF
HE WAS GONNA **KILL** YOU, I **HAD** TO...
FLIP 'IM OVER, ***FLIP*** 'IM OVER!
FFUUUCCKK...
f–finally... ***cold...****in*
n–n–november...
ain't it...

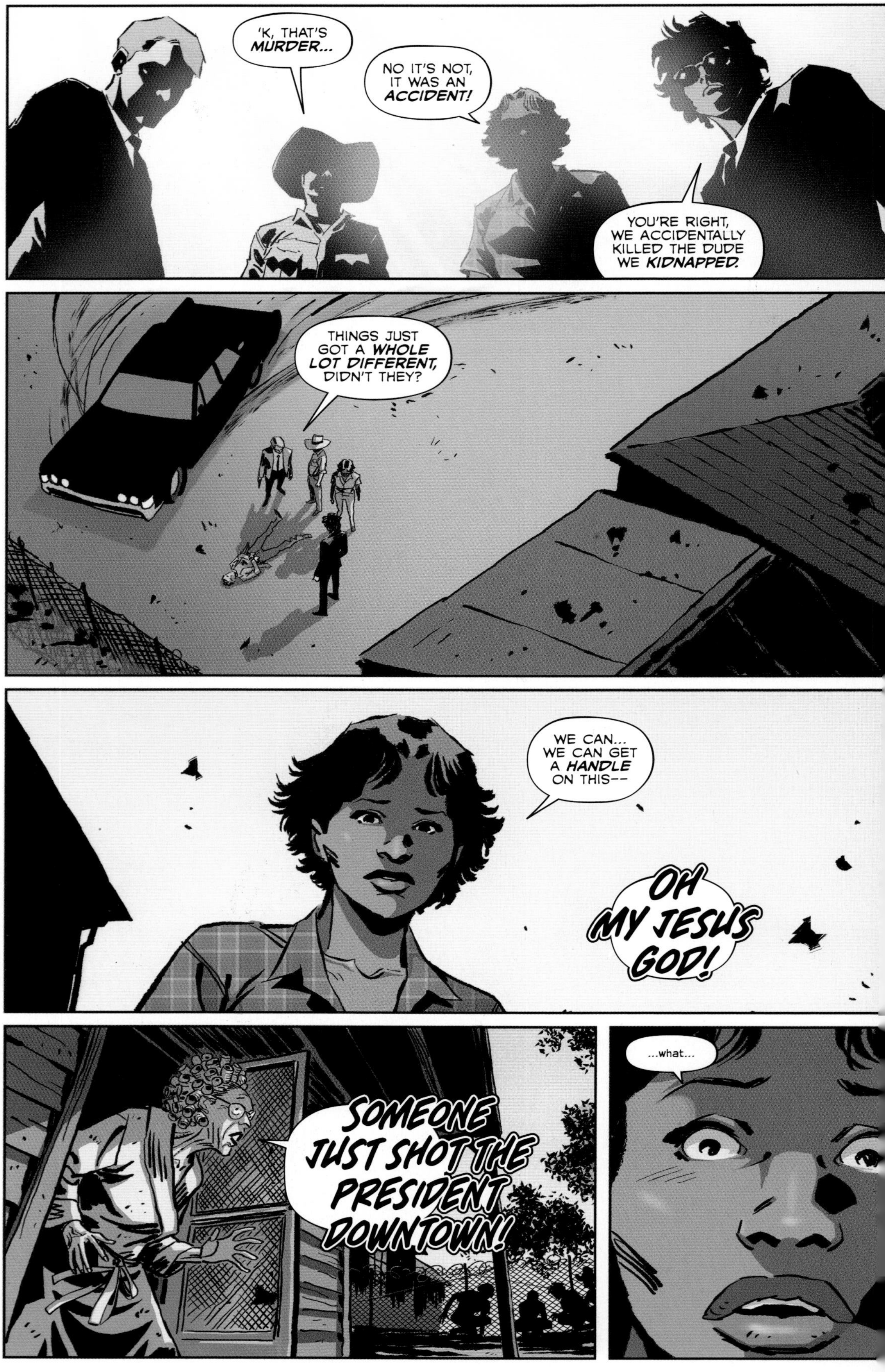
'K, THAT'S MURDER...
NO IT'S NOT, IT WAS AN ACCIDENT!
YOU'RE RIGHT, WE ACCIDENTALLY KILLED THE DUDE WE KIDNAPPED.
THINGS JUST GOT A WHOLE LOT DIFFERENT, DIDN'T THEY?
WE CAN... WE CAN GET A HANDLE ON THIS--
OH MY JESUS GOD!
SOMEONE JUST SHOT THE PRESIDENT DOWNTOWN!
...what...

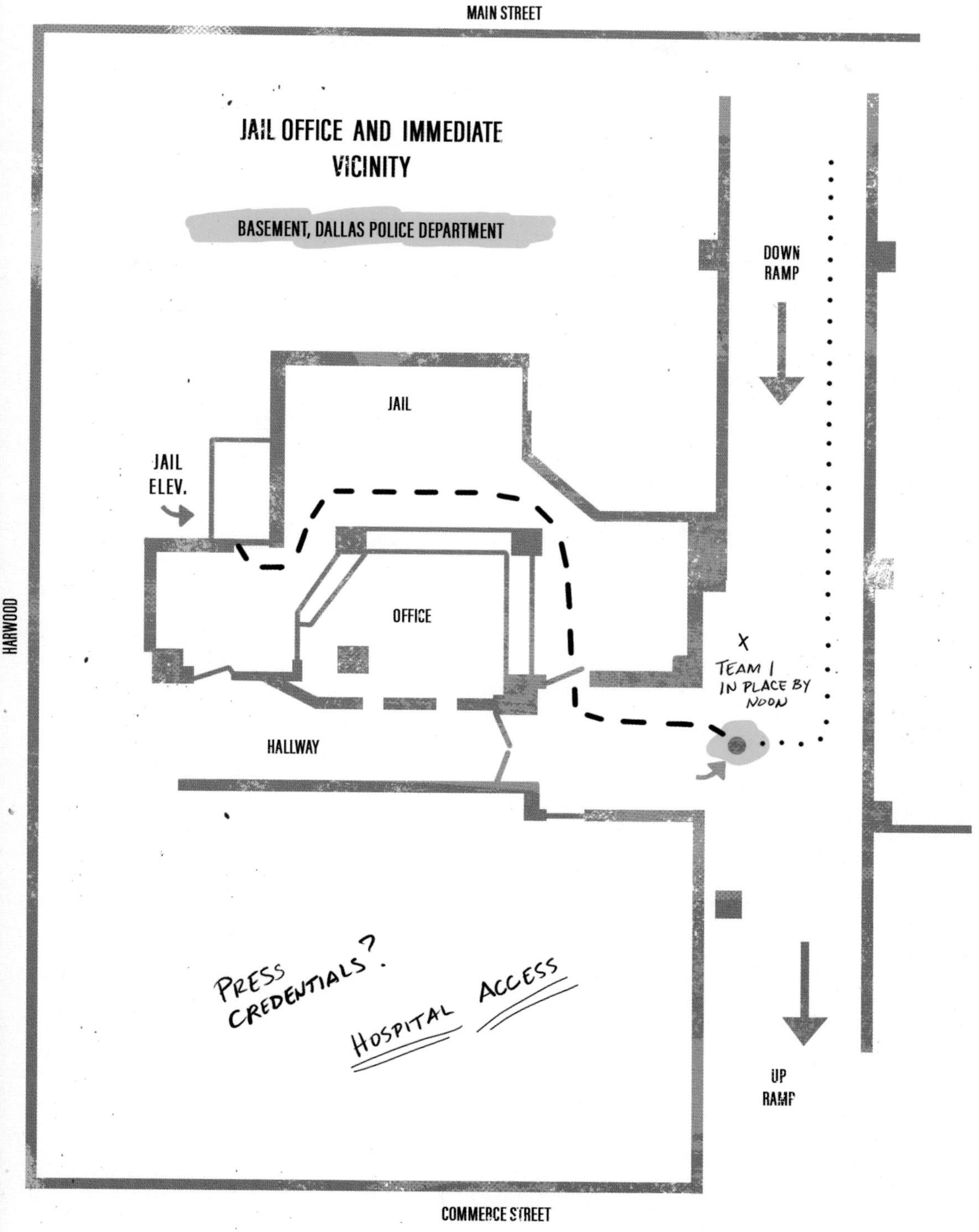
MAIN STREET
JAIL OFFICE AND IMMEDIATE VICINITY
BASEMENT, DALLAS POLICE DEPARTMENT
DOWN RAMP
JAIL
JAIL ELEV.
OFFICE
X
TEAM 1 IN PLACE BY NOON
HALLWAY
HARWOOD
PRESS CREDENTIALS?
HOSPITAL ACCESS
UP RAMP
COMMERCE STREET

WHO THE FUCK
IS JD TIPPIT?

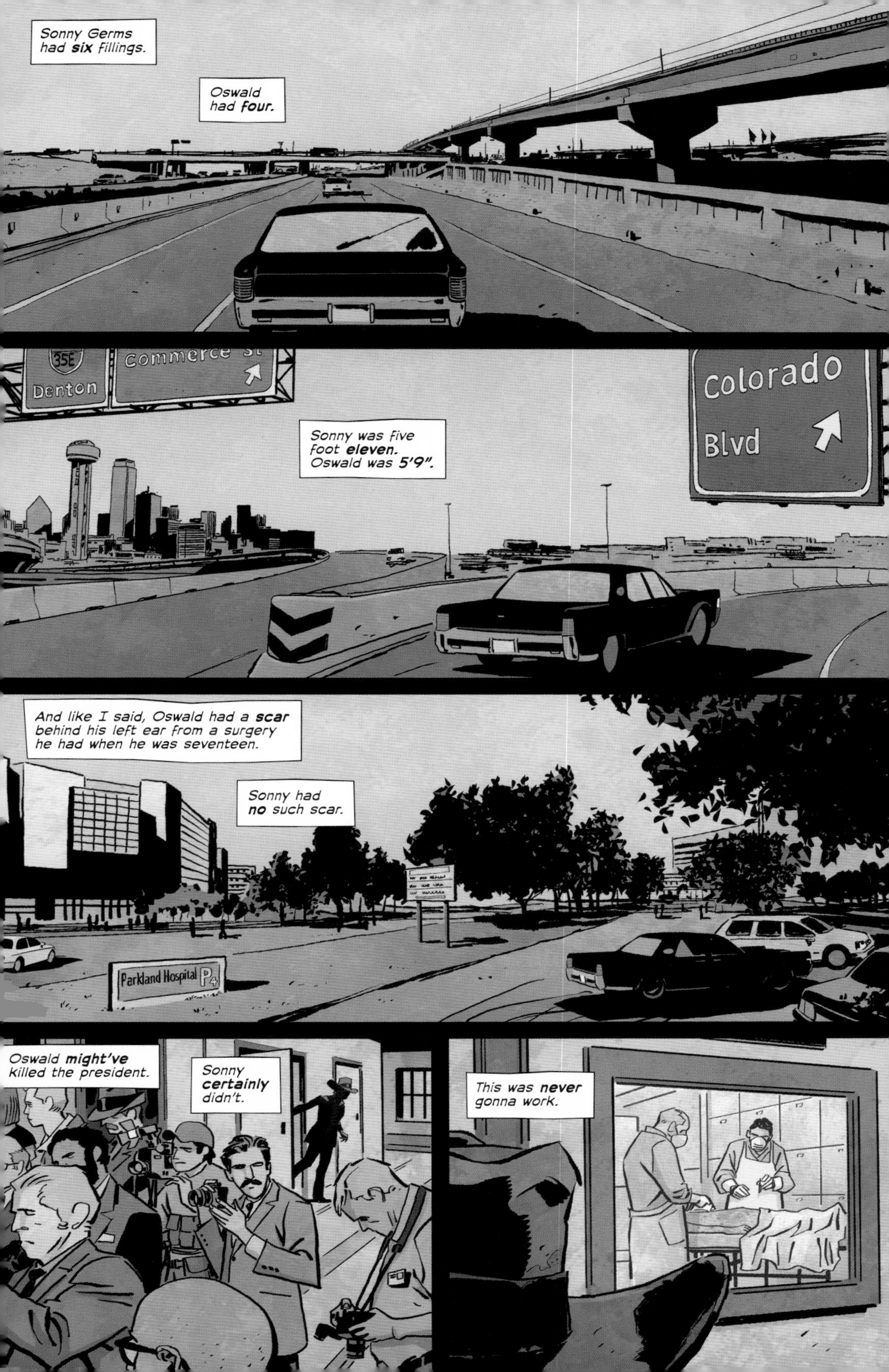
Sonny Germs had **six** fillings.
Oswald had **four.**
35E
Denton
Commerce St
Colorado Blvd
Sonny was five foot **eleven.** Oswald was **5'9".**
And like I said, Oswald had a **scar** behind his left ear from a surgery he had when he was seventeen.
Sonny had **no** such scar.
Parkland Hospital P4
Oswald **might've** killed the president.
Sonny **certainly** didn't.
This was **never** gonna work.

Dallas, somewhere near Fair Park. November 23rd, 1963.

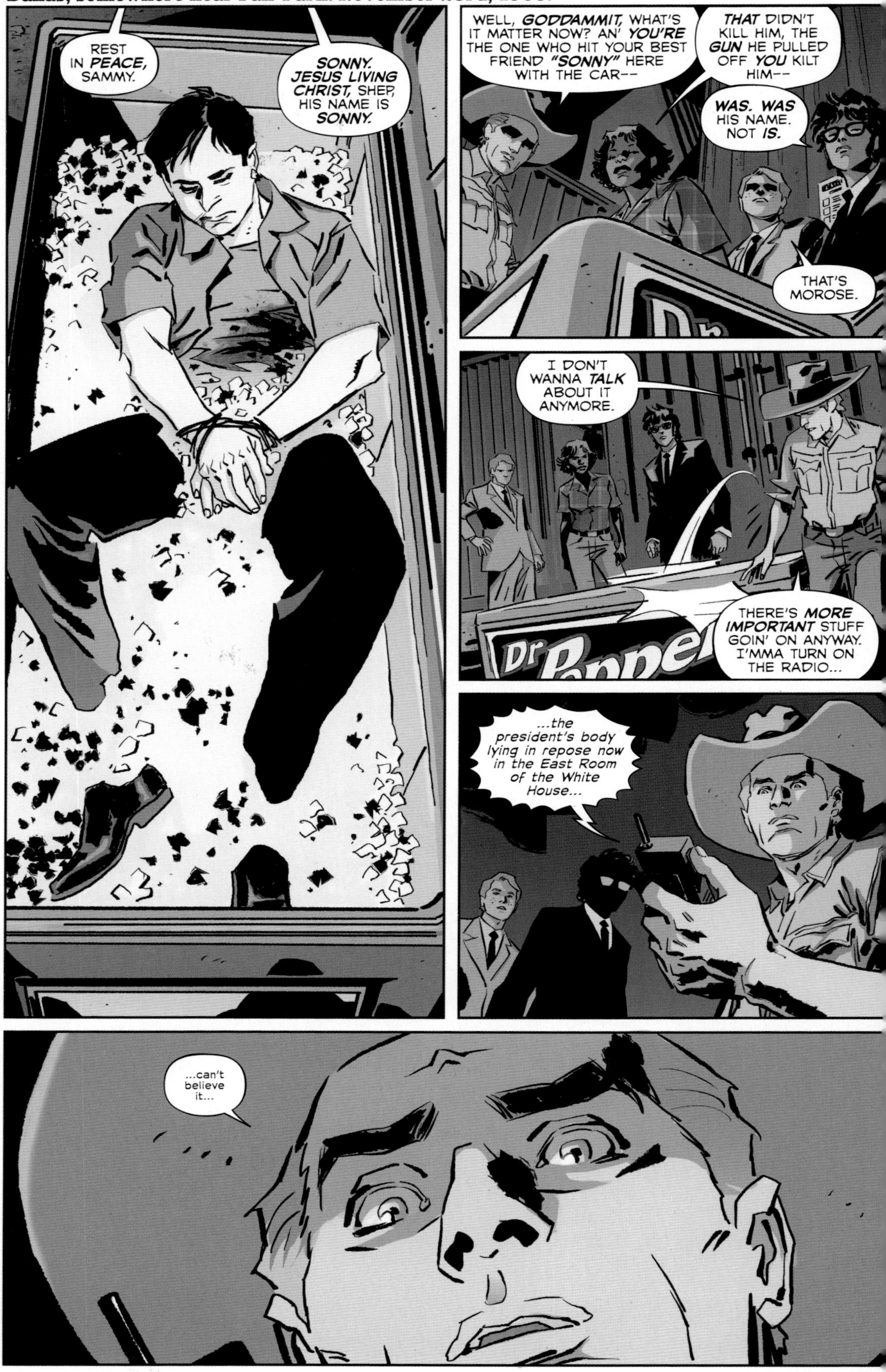
REST IN PEACE, SAMMY.
SONNY. JESUS LIVING CHRIST, SHEP, HIS NAME IS SONNY.
WELL, GODDAMMIT, WHAT'S IT MATTER NOW? AN' YOU'RE THE ONE WHO HIT YOUR BEST FRIEND "SONNY" HERE WITH THE CAR--
THAT DIDN'T KILL HIM, THE GUN HE PULLED OFF YOU KILT HIM--
WAS. WAS HIS NAME. NOT IS.
THAT'S MOROSE.
I DON'T WANNA TALK ABOUT IT ANYMORE.
THERE'S MORE IMPORTANT STUFF GOIN' ON ANYWAY. I'MMA TURN ON THE RADIO...
...the president's body lying in repose now in the East Room of the White House...
...can't believe it...

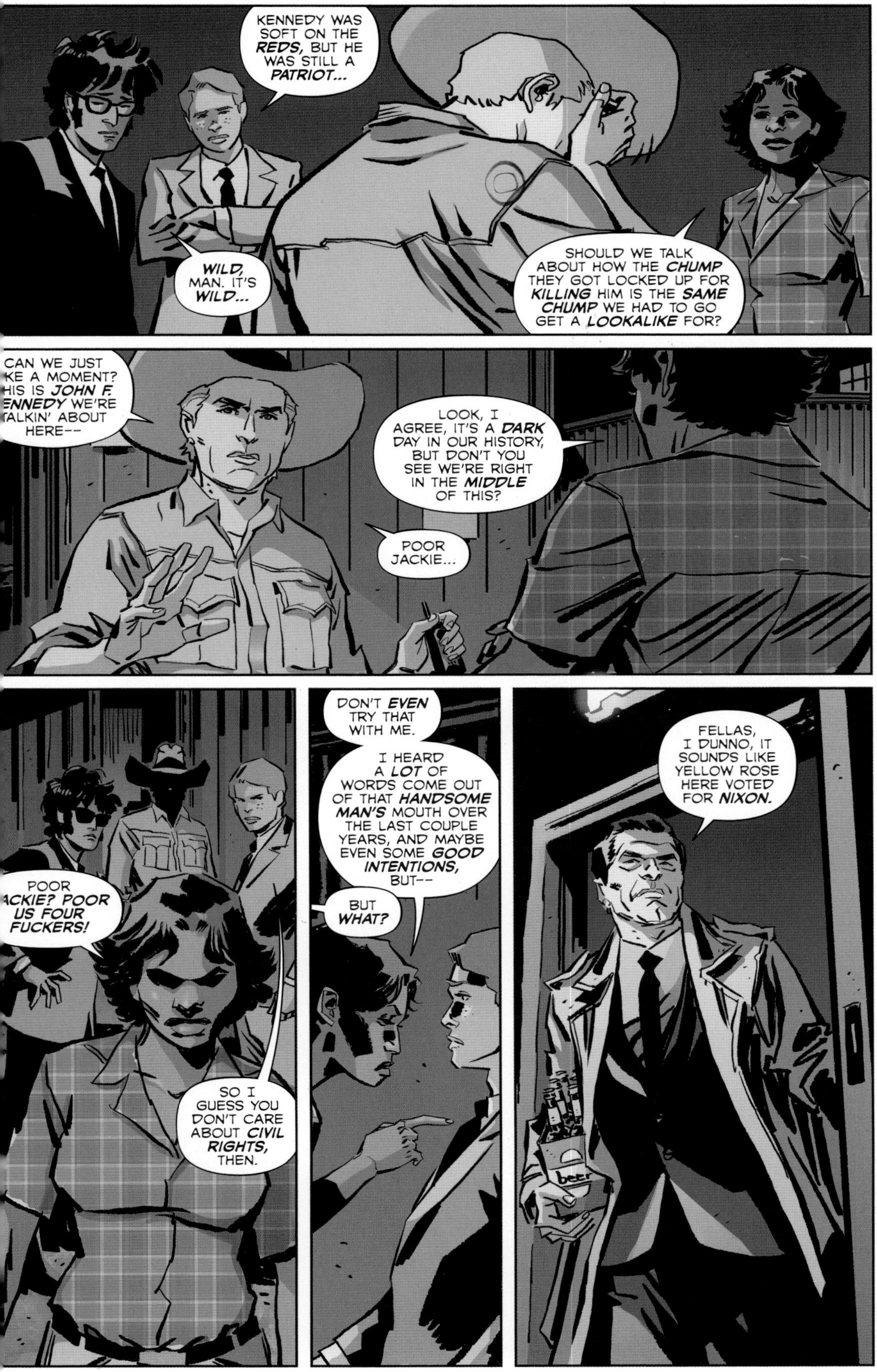
KENNEDY WAS SOFT ON THE REDS, BUT HE WAS STILL A PATRIOT...
WILD, MAN. IT'S WILD...
SHOULD WE TALK ABOUT HOW THE CHUMP THEY GOT LOCKED UP FOR KILLING HIM IS THE SAME CHUMP WE HAD TO GO GET A LOOKALIKE FOR?
CAN WE JUST KE A MOMENT? HIS IS JOHN F. ENNEDY WE'RE TALKIN' ABOUT HERE--
LOOK, I AGREE, IT'S A DARK DAY IN OUR HISTORY, BUT DON'T YOU SEE WE'RE RIGHT IN THE MIDDLE OF THIS?
POOR JACKIE...
POOR ACKIE? POOR US FOUR FUCKERS!
SO I GUESS YOU DON'T CARE ABOUT CIVIL RIGHTS, THEN.
DON'T EVEN TRY THAT WITH ME.
I HEARD A LOT OF WORDS COME OUT OF THAT HANDSOME MAN'S MOUTH OVER THE LAST COUPLE YEARS, AND MAYBE EVEN SOME GOOD INTENTIONS, BUT--
BUT WHAT?
FELLAS, I DUNNO, IT SOUNDS LIKE YELLOW ROSE HERE VOTED FOR NIXON.
beer

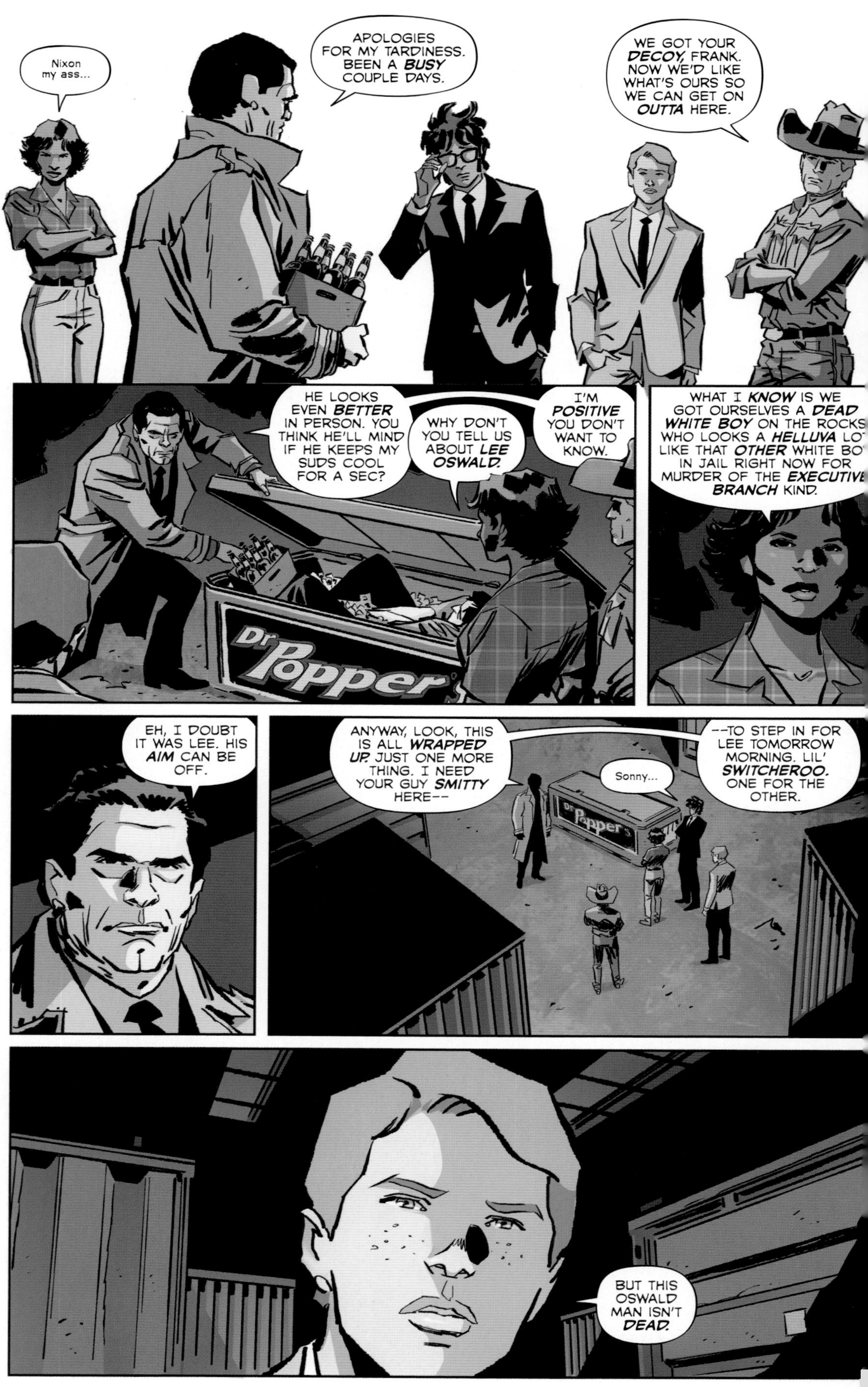
Nixon my ass...
APOLOGIES FOR MY TARDINESS. BEEN A BUSY COUPLE DAYS.
WE GOT YOUR DECOY, FRANK. NOW WE'D LIKE WHAT'S OURS SO WE CAN GET ON OUTTA HERE.
HE LOOKS EVEN BETTER IN PERSON. YOU THINK HE'LL MIND IF HE KEEPS MY SUDS COOL FOR A SEC?
WHY DON'T YOU TELL US ABOUT LEE OSWALD.
I'M POSITIVE YOU DON'T WANT TO KNOW.
Dr Popper
WHAT I KNOW IS WE GOT OURSELVES A DEAD WHITE BOY ON THE ROCKS WHO LOOKS A HELLUVA LOT LIKE THAT OTHER WHITE BOY IN JAIL RIGHT NOW FOR MURDER OF THE EXECUTIVE BRANCH KIND.
EH, I DOUBT IT WAS LEE. HIS AIM CAN BE OFF.
ANYWAY, LOOK, THIS IS ALL WRAPPED UP. JUST ONE MORE THING. I NEED YOUR GUY SMITTY HERE--
Sonny...
--TO STEP IN FOR LEE TOMORROW MORNING. LIL' SWITCHEROO. ONE FOR THE OTHER.
BUT THIS OSWALD MAN ISN'T DEAD.

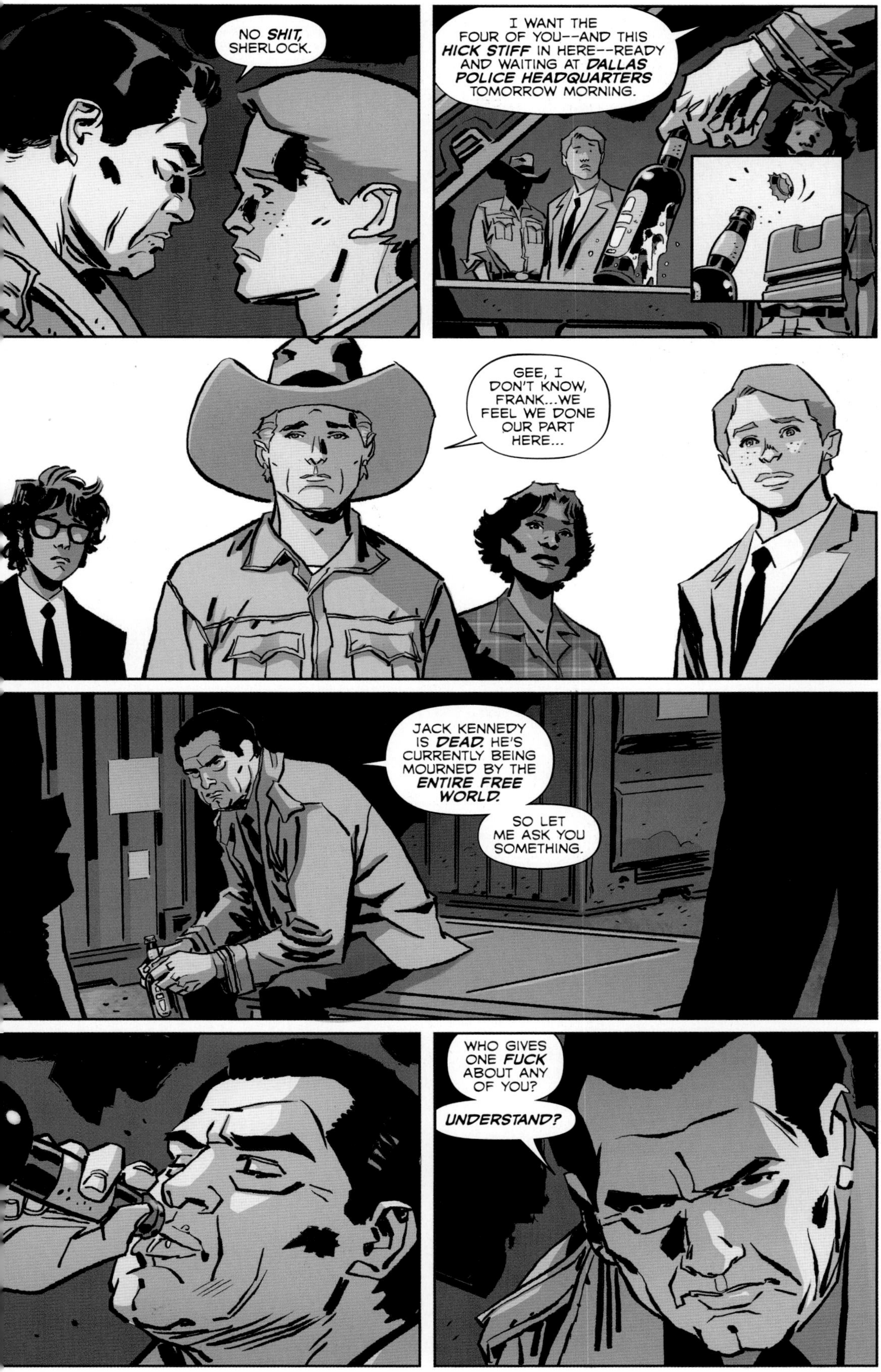
NO SHIT, SHERLOCK.
I WANT THE FOUR OF YOU--AND THIS HICK STIFF IN HERE--READY AND WAITING AT DALLAS POLICE HEADQUARTERS TOMORROW MORNING.
GEE, I DON'T KNOW, FRANK...WE FEEL WE DONE OUR PART HERE...
JACK KENNEDY IS DEAD. HE'S CURRENTLY BEING MOURNED BY THE ENTIRE FREE WORLD.
SO LET ME ASK YOU SOMETHING.
WHO GIVES ONE FUCK ABOUT ANY OF YOU?
UNDERSTAND?

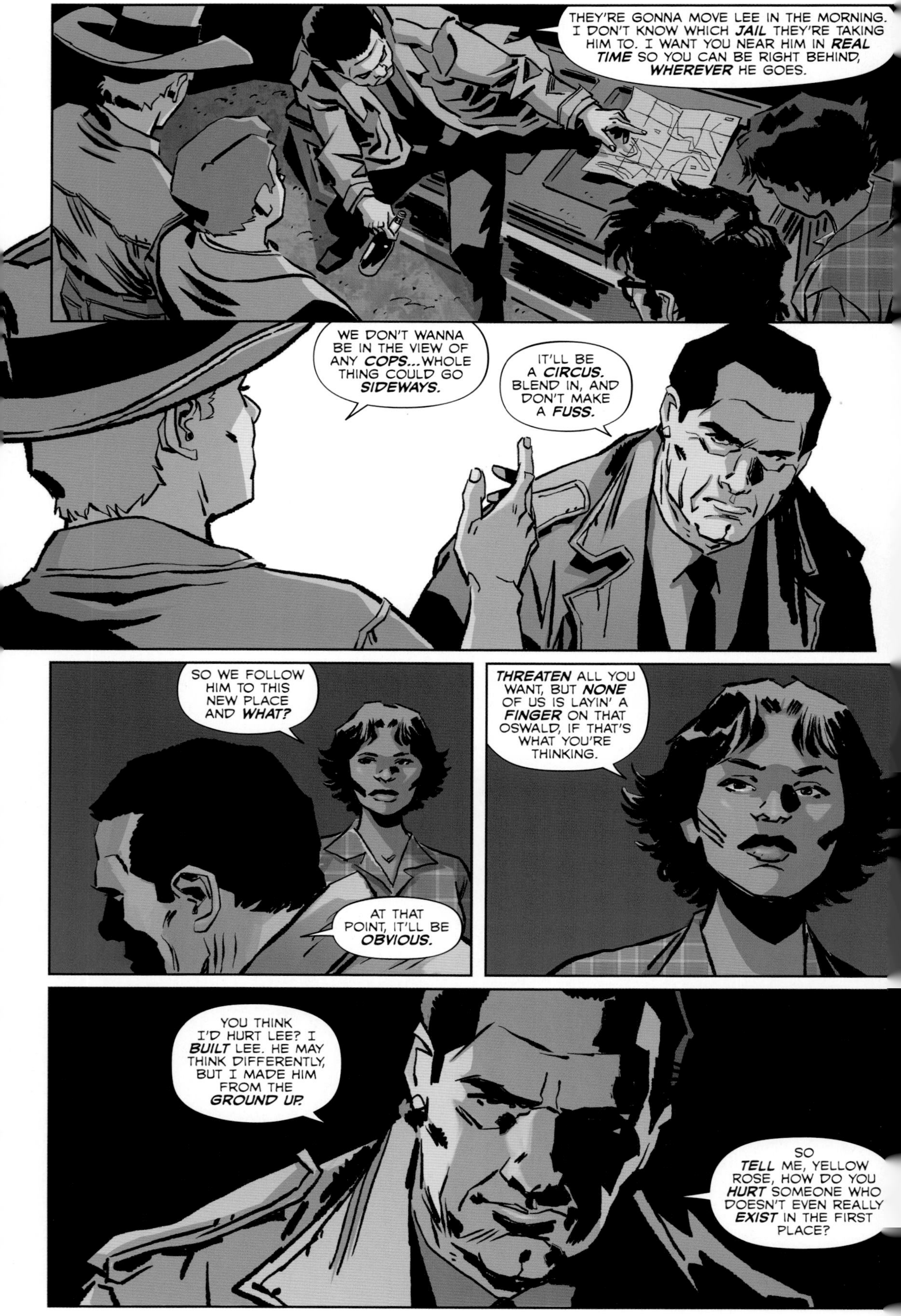
THEY'RE GONNA MOVE LEE IN THE MORNING. I DON'T KNOW WHICH JAIL THEY'RE TAKING HIM TO. I WANT YOU NEAR HIM IN REAL TIME SO YOU CAN BE RIGHT BEHIND, WHEREVER HE GOES.
WE DON'T WANNA BE IN THE VIEW OF ANY COPS...WHOLE THING COULD GO SIDEWAYS.
IT'LL BE A CIRCUS. BLEND IN, AND DON'T MAKE A FUSS.
SO WE FOLLOW HIM TO THIS NEW PLACE AND WHAT?
AT THAT POINT, IT'LL BE OBVIOUS.
THREATEN ALL YOU WANT, BUT NONE OF US IS LAYIN' A FINGER ON THAT OSWALD, IF THAT'S WHAT YOU'RE THINKING.
YOU THINK I'D HURT LEE? I BUILT LEE. HE MAY THINK DIFFERENTLY, BUT I MADE HIM FROM THE GROUND UP.
SO TELL ME, YELLOW ROSE, HOW DO YOU HURT SOMEONE WHO DOESN'T EVEN REALLY EXIST IN THE FIRST PLACE?

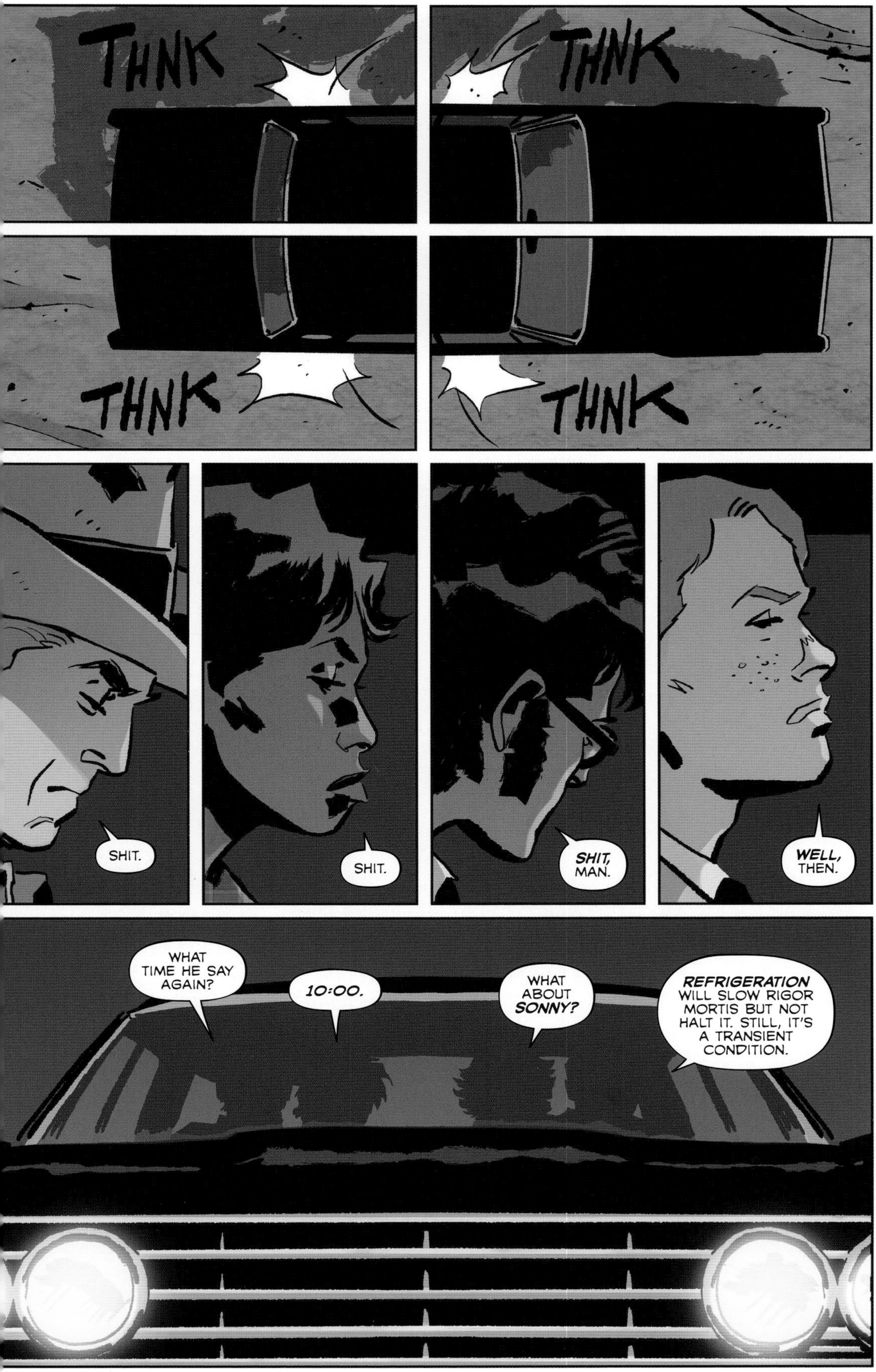
THNK
THNK
THNK
THNK
SHIT.
SHIT.
SHIT, MAN.
WELL, THEN.
WHAT TIME HE SAY AGAIN?
10:00.
WHAT ABOUT SONNY?
REFRIGERATION WILL SLOW RIGOR MORTIS BUT NOT HALT IT. STILL, IT'S A TRANSIENT CONDITION.

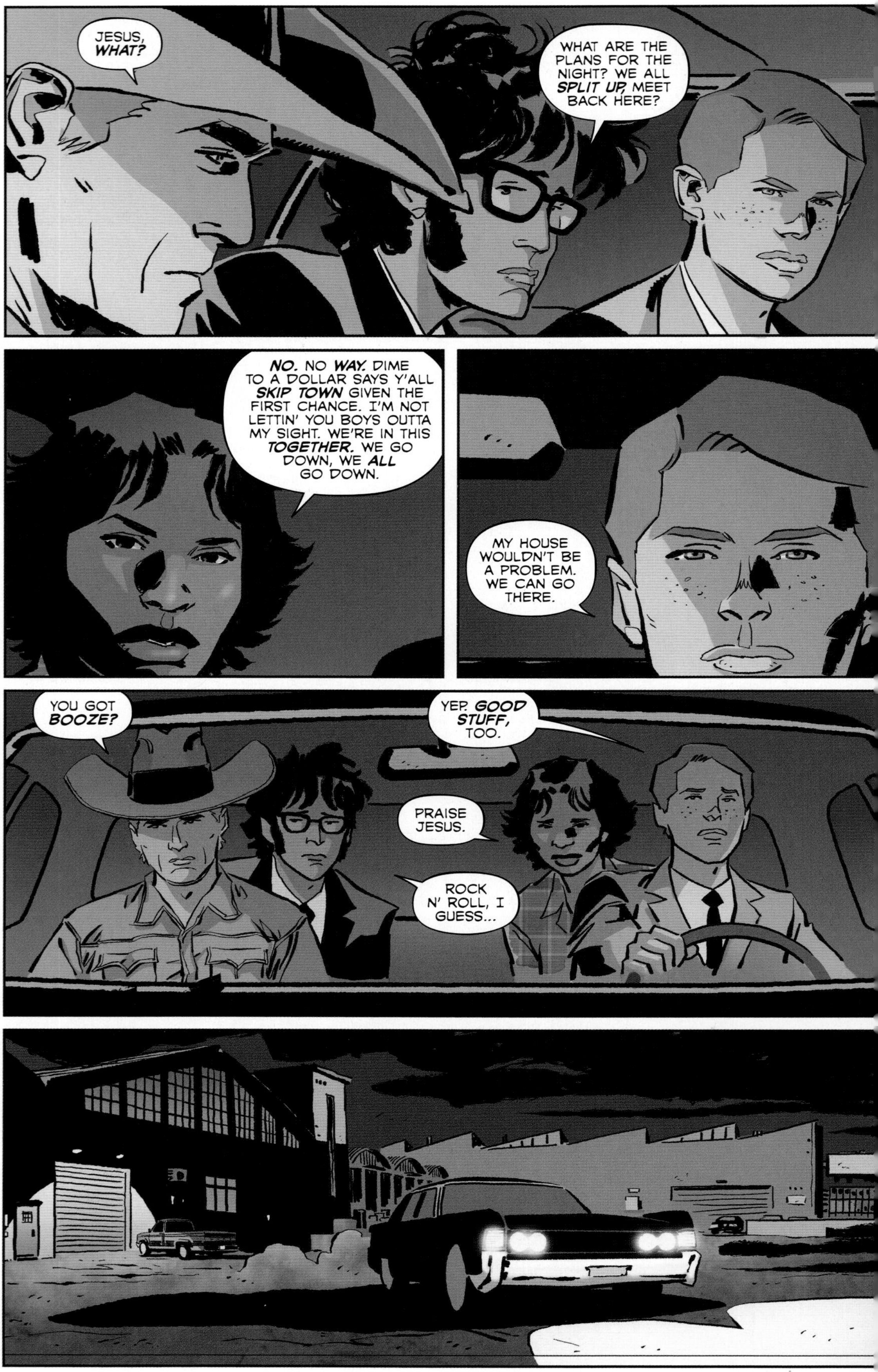
JESUS, WHAT?
WHAT ARE THE PLANS FOR THE NIGHT? WE ALL SPLIT UP, MEET BACK HERE?
NO. NO WAY. DIME TO A DOLLAR SAYS Y'ALL SKIP TOWN GIVEN THE FIRST CHANCE. I'M NOT LETTIN' YOU BOYS OUTTA MY SIGHT. WE'RE IN THIS TOGETHER. WE GO DOWN, WE ALL GO DOWN.
MY HOUSE WOULDN'T BE A PROBLEM. WE CAN GO THERE.
YOU GOT BOOZE?
YEP. GOOD STUFF, TOO.
PRAISE JESUS.
ROCK N' ROLL, I GUESS...

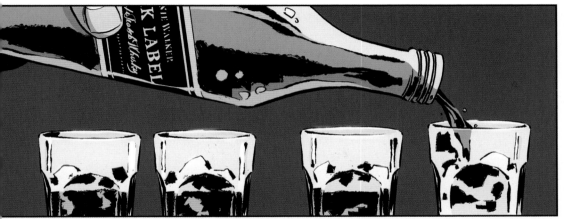

TO **SONNY GERMS**... REST IN PEACE...

THIS HAS **ALL** THE MAKIN'S OF A **RIGHT CRISIS**.

WHO YOU THINK **GRANDDADDY FRANK** WORKS FOR?

HIMSELF. AT LEAST THAT'S WHAT HE THINKS.

MOB, MAYBE? THOSE **ITALIAN** GUYS FROM **NEW YORK** AN' SUCH.

WHAT IF IT'S, LIKE...THE **RUSSIANS?**

THAT'D BE **ODD**, CONSIDERING HE TOLD ME I CAN GET A JOB WITH THE **CIA** IN MEXICO CITY.

JEEPERS, OUR OWN *GOVERNMENT* THEN...?

MAKES THE MOST SENSE TO ME.

REALLY?

WHO *ELSE* GETS THE MOST OUTTA THE PRESIDENT BEIN' GONE? *DOZENS* OF GUYS IN D.C. GOT A LOT OF *MONEY AMBITIONS,* AND KENNEDY MIGHTA BEEN IN THE *WAY.*

OR IT REALLY WAS THAT CREEPY CRAWLY *OSWALD,* AND FRANK IS JUST LOOKIN' FOR A WAY TO *CASH IN* ON HIM.

DANG, MAN... DANG.

I THINK... OUR BEST BET... IS TO TAKE CARE OF *EACH OTHER* RIGHT NOW. 'CAUSE NO ONE *ELSE* IN THE WORLD IS.

YEAH. THAT SOUNDS GOOD TO ME, ROSE.

ALRIGHT THEN, SHEP, OL' BOY...

CLNK

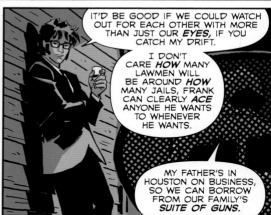

IT'D BE GOOD IF WE COULD WATCH OUT FOR EACH OTHER WITH MORE THAN JUST OUR *EYES,* IF YOU CATCH MY DRIFT.

I DON'T CARE *HOW* MANY LAWMEN WILL BE AROUND *HOW* MANY JAILS, FRANK CAN CLEARLY *ACE* ANYONE HE WANTS TO WHENEVER HE WANTS.

MY FATHER'S IN HOUSTON ON BUSINESS, SO WE CAN BORROW FROM OUR FAMILY'S *SUITE OF GUNS.*

SMARTEST THING YOU SAID SINCE WE MET, WAINRIGHT.

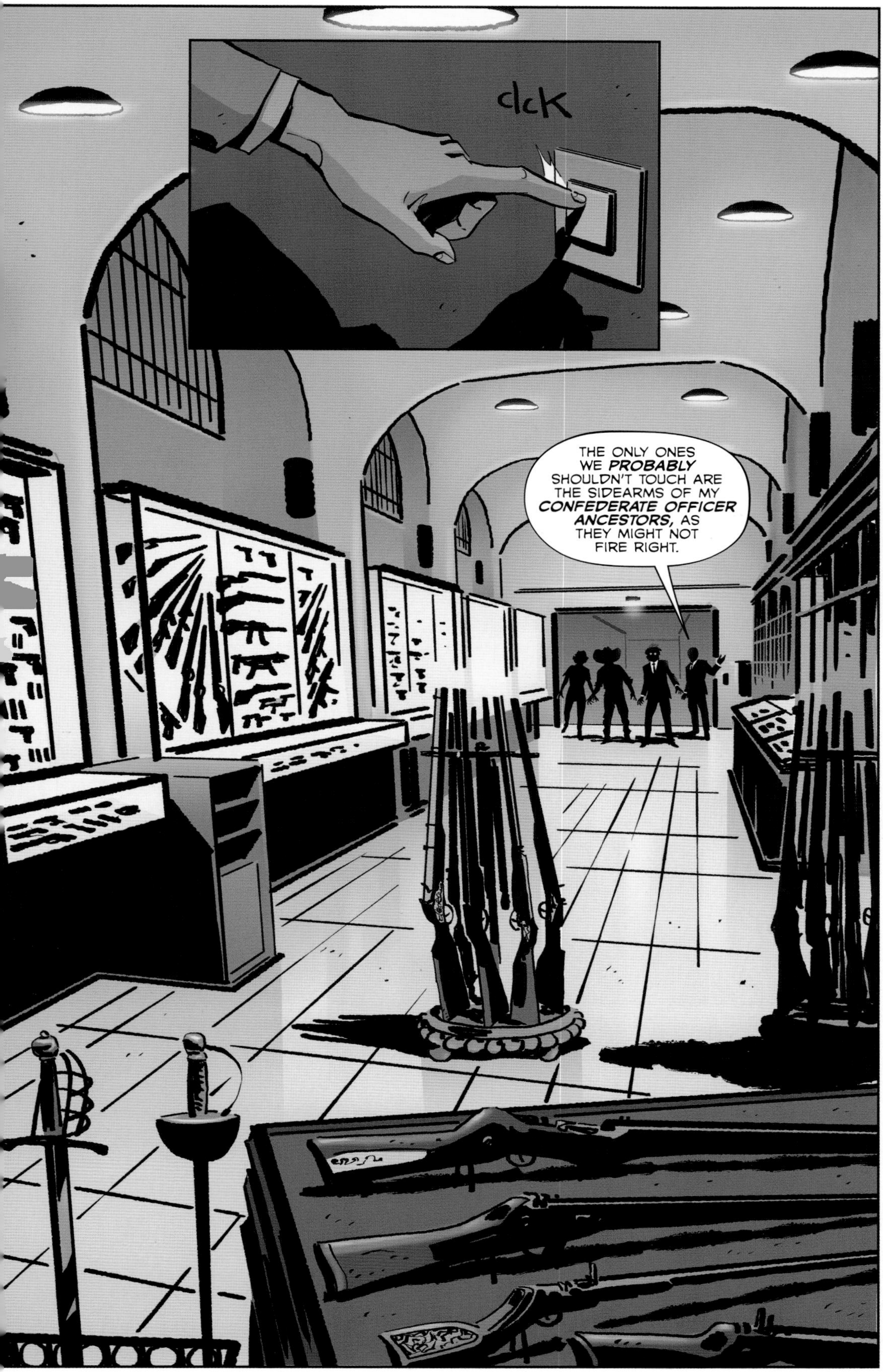
clcK
THE ONLY ONES WE *PROBABLY* SHOULDN'T TOUCH ARE THE SIDEARMS OF MY ***CONFEDERATE OFFICER ANCESTORS,*** AS THEY MIGHT NOT FIRE RIGHT.

Dallas Police Headquarters, 11:10 A.M.
November 24th, 1963.

"*HELL* WE EVEN *DOIN'* HERE? IT'S BEEN AN *HOUR.* THERE'S MORE *COPS* THAN I CAN SHAKE A STICK AT AN' WE GOT SONNY PARKED IN THE GODDAMN *SUN* OUTSIDE."

FRANK SAID *WE* GO WHERE *OSWALD* GOES, AND WE GOTTA WAIT *HERE* TO FIND OUT WHERE THAT *IS.*

I TALKED TO A MORNING NEWS GUY OVER THERE WHO SAID HE'S HEADED TO *CITY JAIL.* BINGO, LET'S *HIT THE ROAD.*

CAN'T BE THAT SIMPLE...

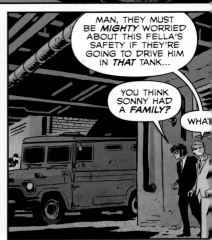

MAN, THEY MUST BE *MIGHTY* WORRIED ABOUT THIS FELLA'S SAFETY IF THEY'RE GOING TO DRIVE HIM IN *THAT* TANK...

YOU THINK SONNY HAD A *FAMILY?*

WHAT

A *FAMILY.* PEOPLE WHO CARED ABOUT HIM, MAN.

BUCK, HE WAS A *DRUNK LONER.* WE PROPERLY STAKED HIM OUT.

EVERYBODY'S GOT A *DADDY* AN' A *MOMMY.*

I CAN BARELY *MOVE*...WISH WE HAD A *POINT OF CONTACT*... SOME *COVER,* SOMETHIN'...

HEY, WE'RE JUST DOIN OUR MORNING DELIVERY OF DR. *POPPER'S* TO *POLICE HQ*...

RIGHT, KEEP POLISHIN' *THAT* TURD...

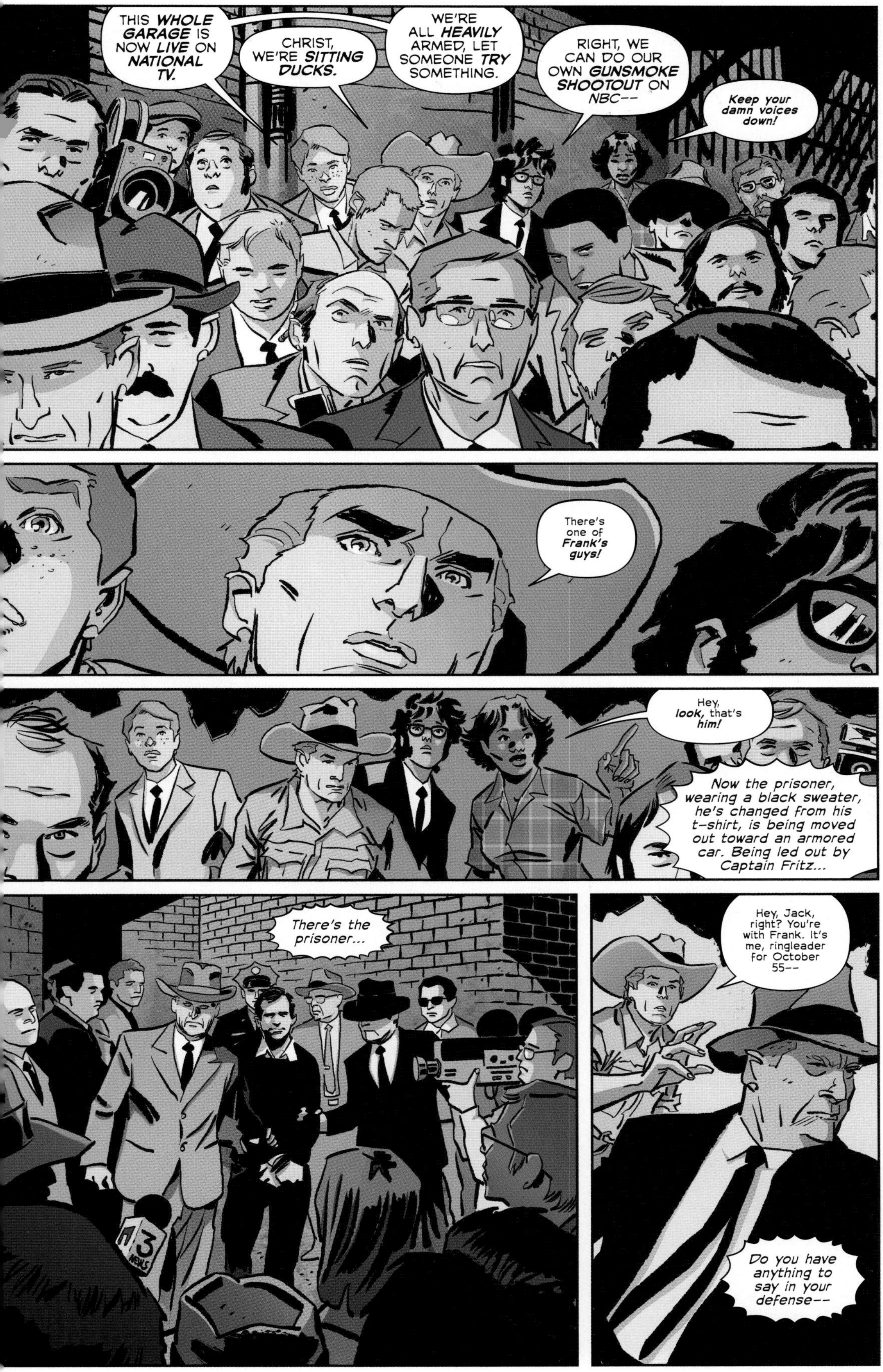
THIS WHOLE GARAGE IS NOW LIVE ON NATIONAL TV.
CHRIST, WE'RE SITTING DUCKS.
WE'RE ALL HEAVILY ARMED, LET SOMEONE TRY SOMETHING.
RIGHT, WE CAN DO OUR OWN GUNSMOKE SHOOTOUT ON NBC--
Keep your damn voices down!
There's one of Frank's guys!
Hey, look, that's him!
Now the prisoner, wearing a black sweater, he's changed from his t-shirt, is being moved out toward an armored car. Being led out by Captain Fritz...
There's the prisoner...
3 NEWS
Hey, Jack, right? You're with Frank. It's me, ringleader for October 55--
Do you have anything to say in your defense--

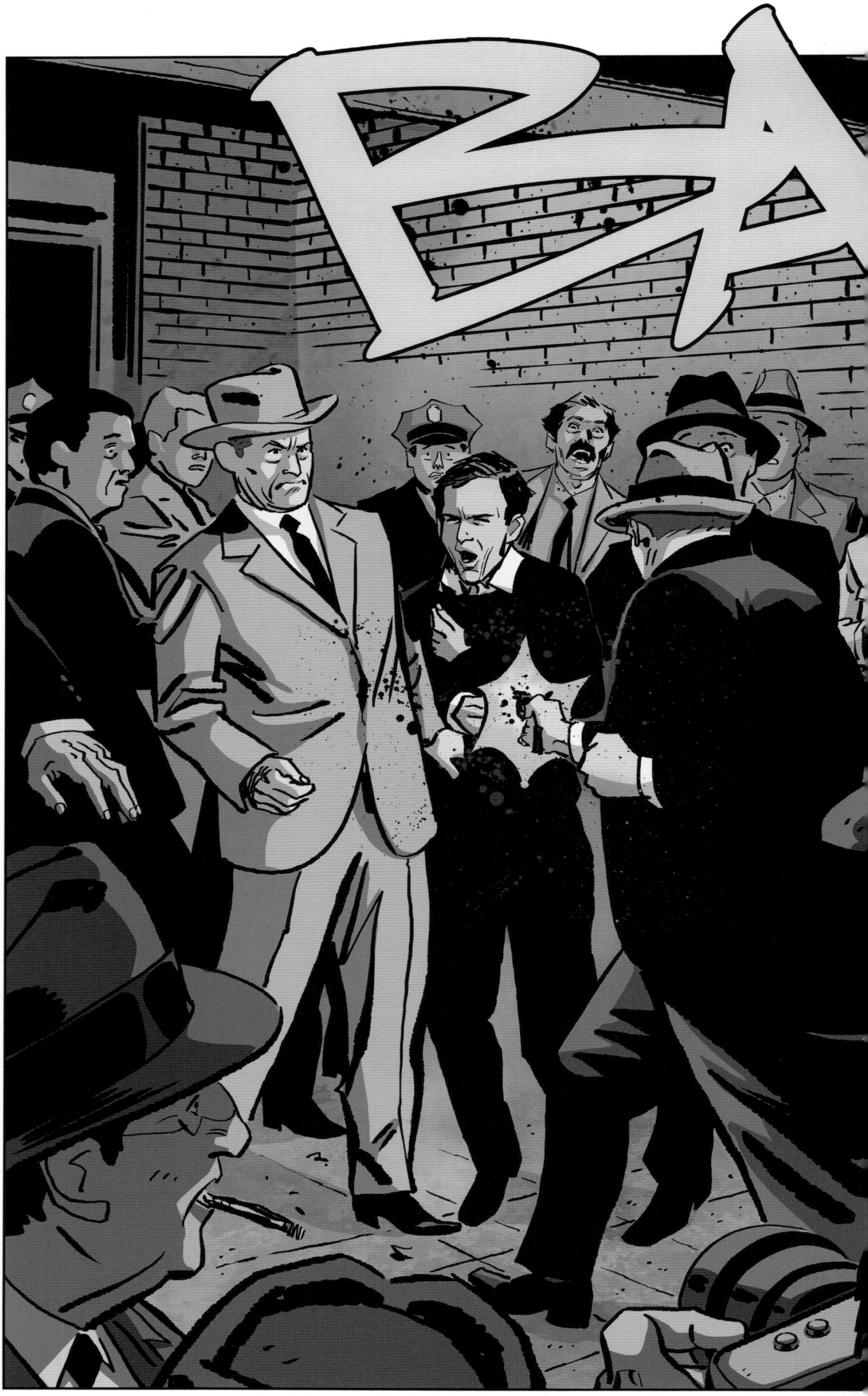
BA

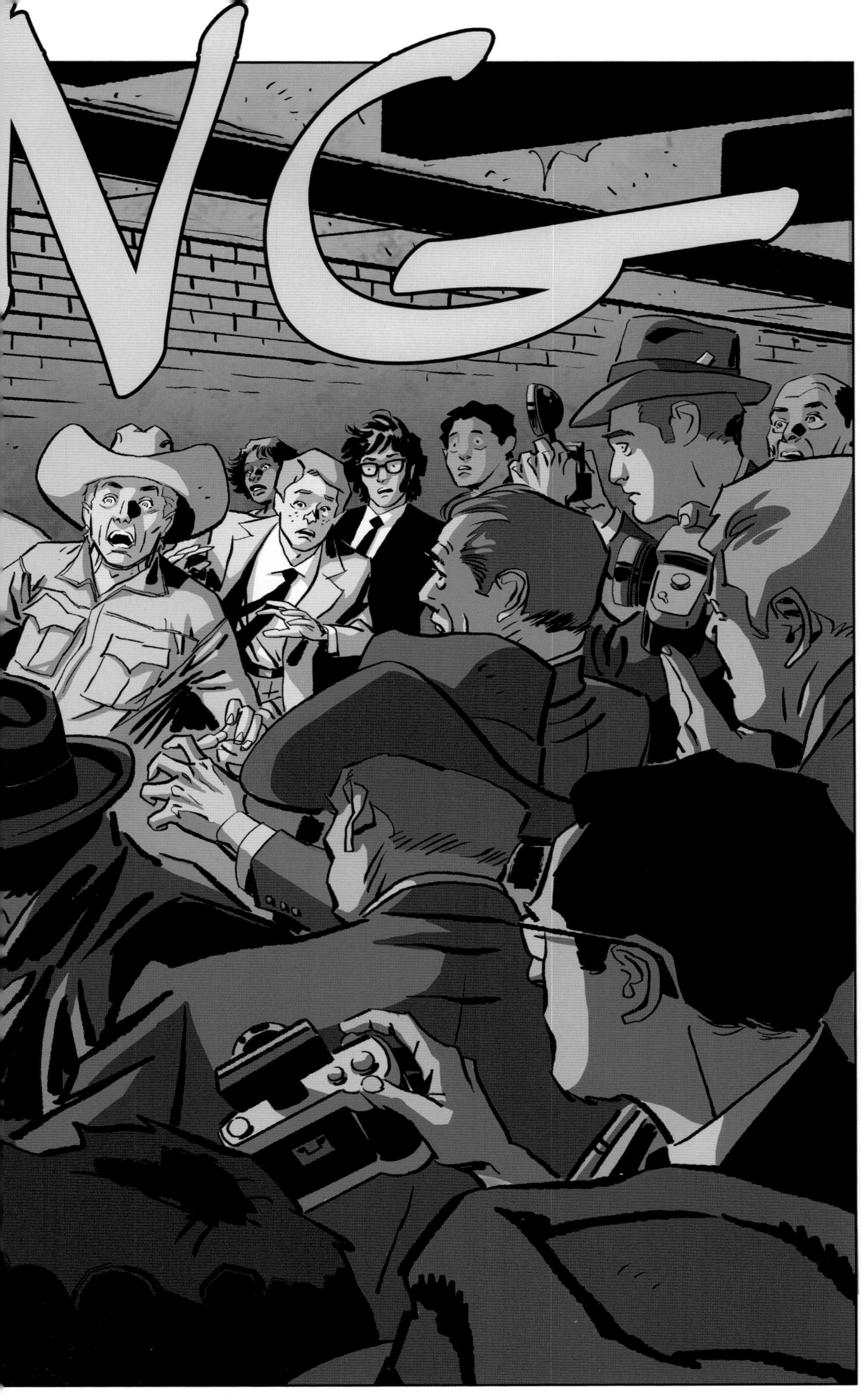
NG

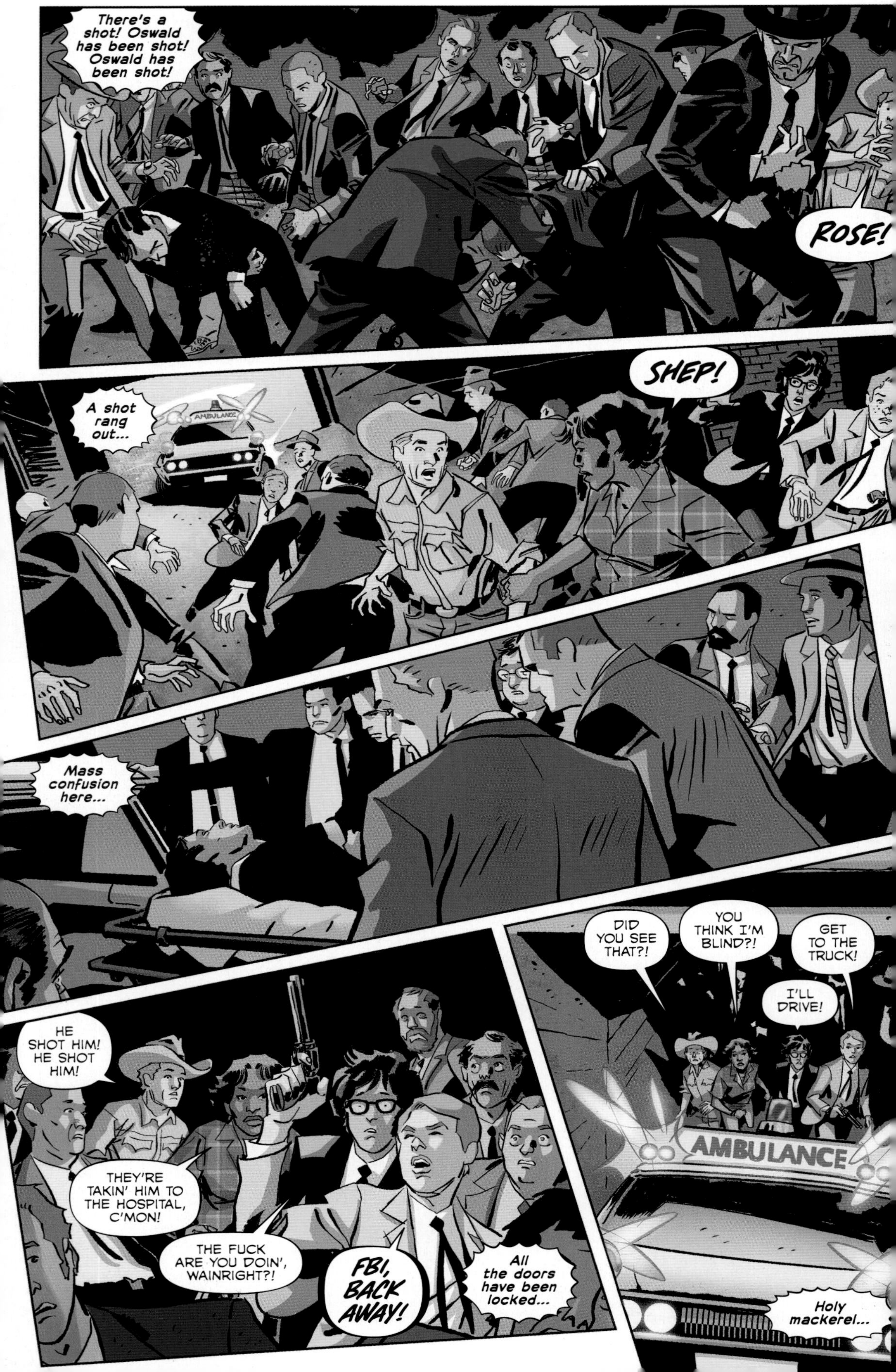
There's a shot! Oswald has been shot! Oswald has been shot!
ROSE!
A shot rang out...
SHEP!
Mass confusion here...
HE SHOT HIM! HE SHOT HIM!
THEY'RE TAKIN' HIM TO THE HOSPITAL, C'MON!
THE FUCK ARE YOU DOIN', WAINRIGHT?!
FBI, BACK AWAY!
All the doors have been locked...
DID YOU SEE THAT?!
YOU THINK I'M BLIND?!
GET TO THE TRUCK!
I'LL DRIVE!
AMBULANCE
Holy mackerel...

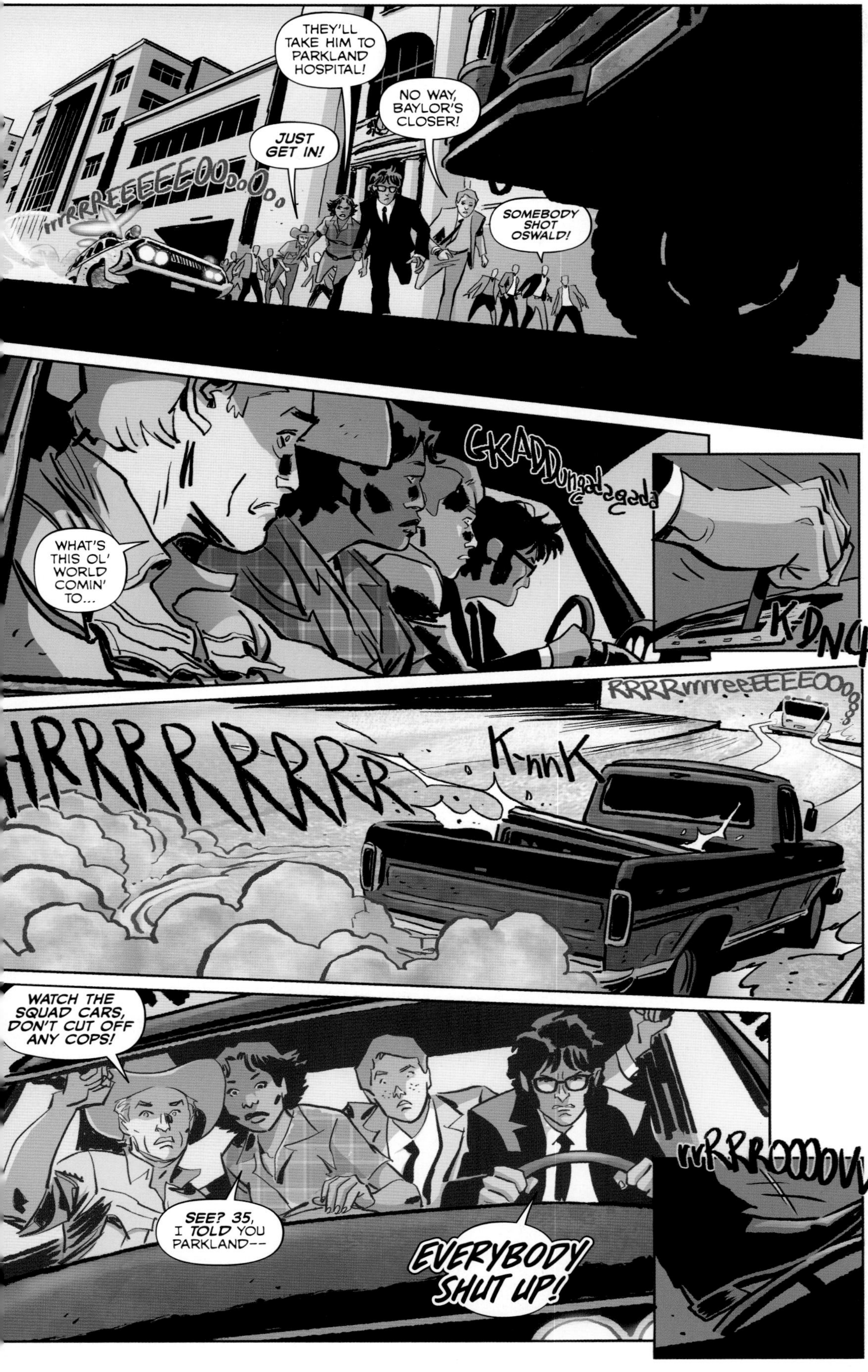
THEY'LL TAKE HIM TO PARKLAND HOSPITAL!
NO WAY, BAYLOR'S CLOSER!
JUST GET IN!
rrrRRREEEEEEOOoooOoo
SOMEBODY SHOT OSWALD!
CKADDungadagada
WHAT'S THIS OL' WORLD COMIN' TO...
KDNCH
RRRRrrrreeEEEEOooooo
HRRRRRRRRR
K-nnK
WATCH THE SQUAD CARS, DON'T CUT OFF ANY COPS!
SEE? 35, I TOLD YOU PARKLAND--
EVERYBODY SHUT UP!
rrRRROOOOW

DAMN, BUCK! JUST PARK US INSIDE THE *MORGUE,* 'CAUSE THAT'S WHERE WE'RE ALL HEADED ANYWAY WITH THE WAY *YOU'RE* DRIVIN'!

EEEEEEEEEEEEEEEEEEE

WHAT *NOW?*

SHOT LIKE THAT, GUY'S GOT *MASSIVE* HEART AND LIVER DAMAGE. HE'S PROBABLY ALREADY *DEAD.*

THEN WE NEED TO GET THE *HELL* INSIDE WITH SONNY BOY OR IT'S *OUR* ASS.

EEEEEE

OFFICER-- MY...*HUSBAND,* HE'S IN THE *ER--*

AUTHORIZED ONLY

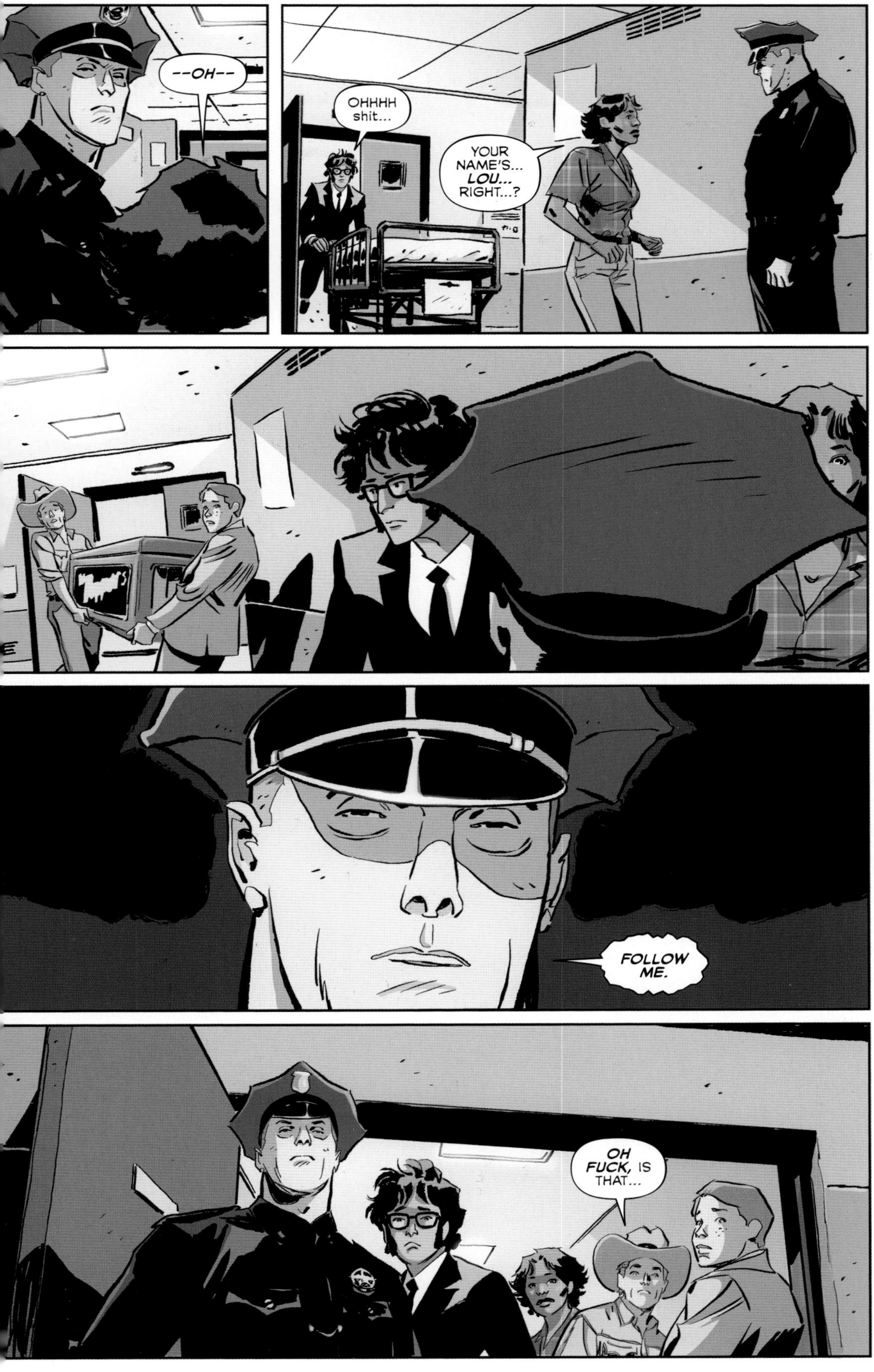
--OH--
OHHHH shit...
YOUR NAME'S... LOU... RIGHT...?
FOLLOW ME.
OH FUCK, IS THAT...

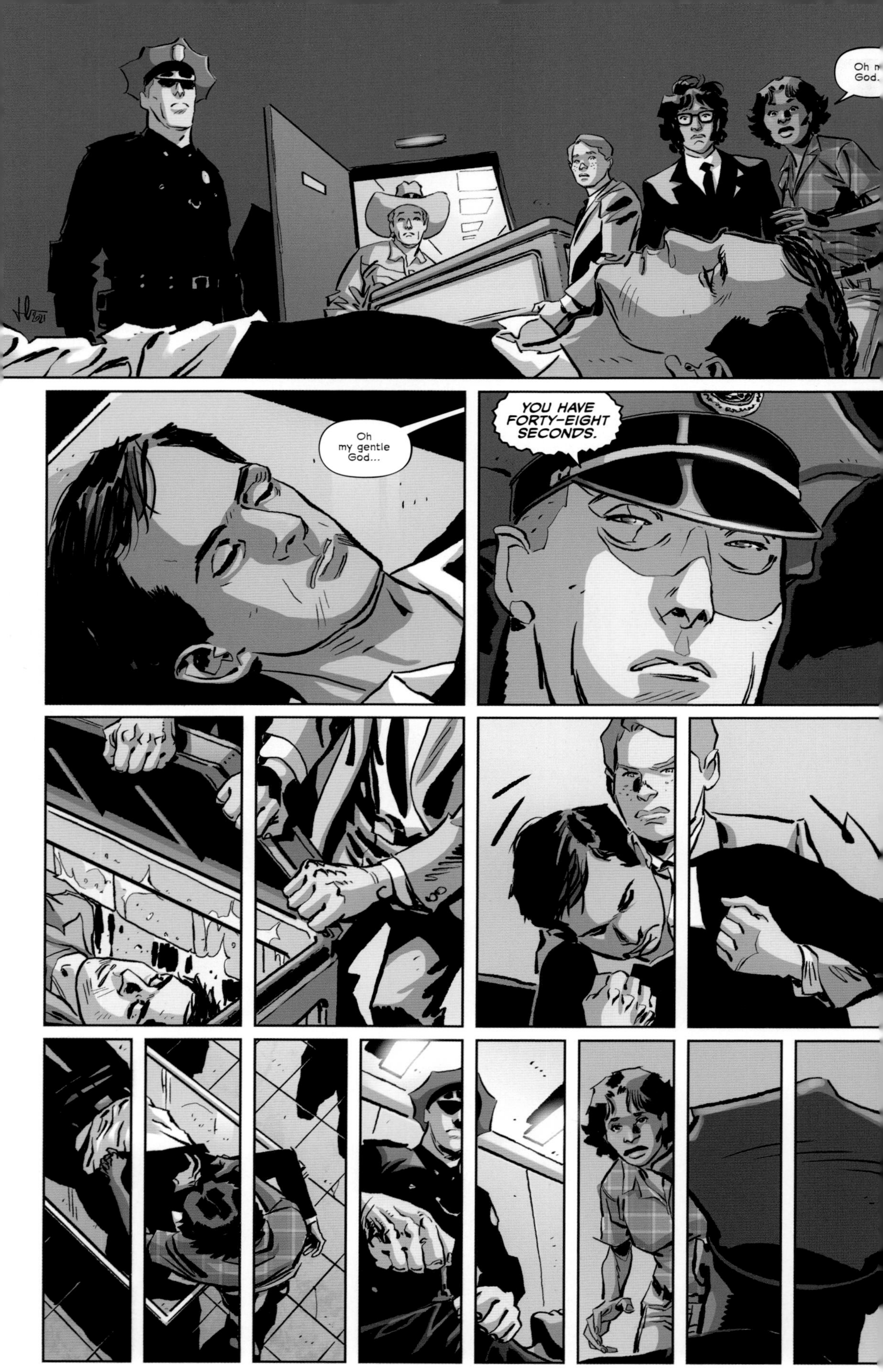
Oh m
God.
Oh
my gentle
God...
YOU HAVE
FORTY-EIGHT
SECONDS.

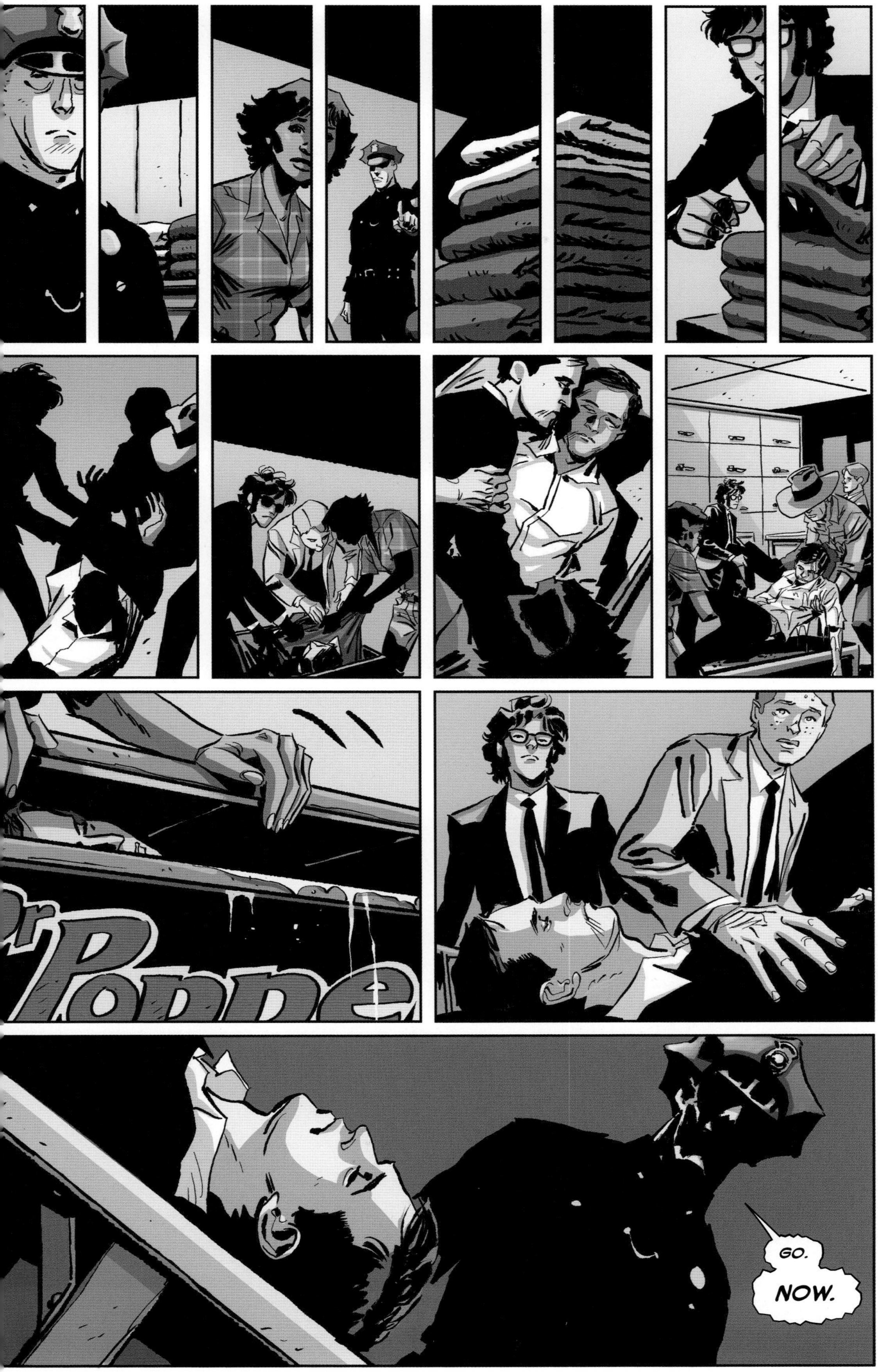
Dr Peppe
GO.
NOW.

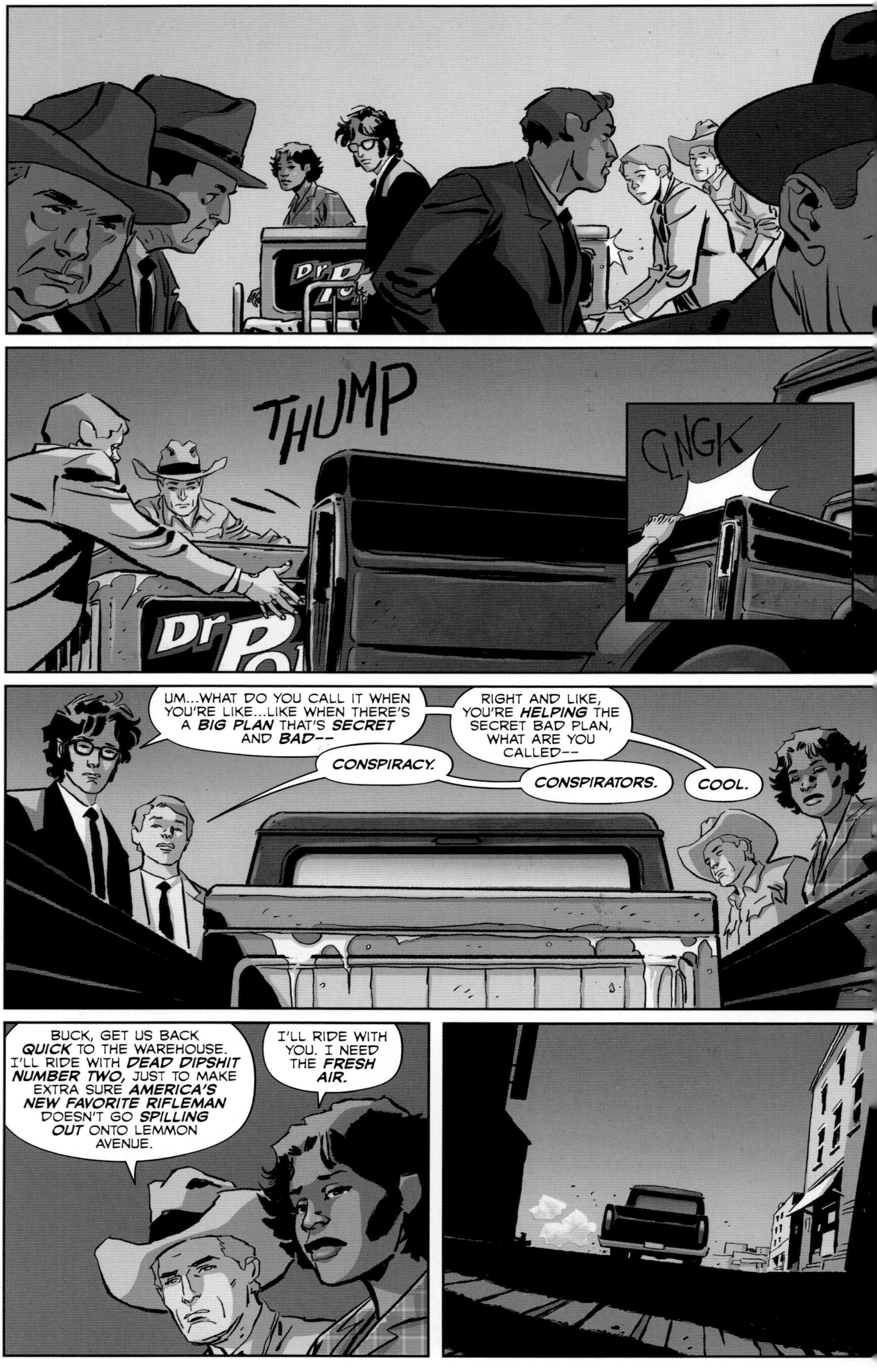
THUMP
CLNGK
UM...WHAT DO YOU CALL IT WHEN YOU'RE LIKE...LIKE WHEN THERE'S A BIG PLAN THAT'S SECRET AND BAD--
CONSPIRACY.
RIGHT AND LIKE, YOU'RE HELPING THE SECRET BAD PLAN, WHAT ARE YOU CALLED--
CONSPIRATORS.
COOL.
BUCK, GET US BACK QUICK TO THE WAREHOUSE. I'LL RIDE WITH DEAD DIPSHIT NUMBER TWO, JUST TO MAKE EXTRA SURE AMERICA'S NEW FAVORITE RIFLEMAN DOESN'T GO SPILLING OUT ONTO LEMMON AVENUE.
I'LL RIDE WITH YOU. I NEED THE FRESH AIR.

TEXAS.

HUH?

ONLY IN *TEXAS* DOES SOMETHING THIS CRAZY O DOWN LIKE *THIS*...AND *KEEP* GOING. ONE *DEAD BODY* FOR ANOTHER *DEAD BODY*...I MEAN...WHO CARES WHO'S BURIED WHERE...MAKES NO *SENSE.* YOU GET WHAT I'M SAYIN', *COWBOY.*

I'M...FROM *WISCONSIN.*

NO *SHIT?*

NO *SHIT.* I WORKED IN A *GROCERY STORE.*

CAME DOWN HERE WITH...I DUNNO. HOPES OF...BEING...SOMETHING *WORTH A SHIT.* THINK I MIGHTA *MISSED THE MARK.*

WELL...YOUR *HAT'S* TOO DAMN BIG...BUT I'LL ADMIT. YOU HAD *ME* FOOLED.

YEAH?

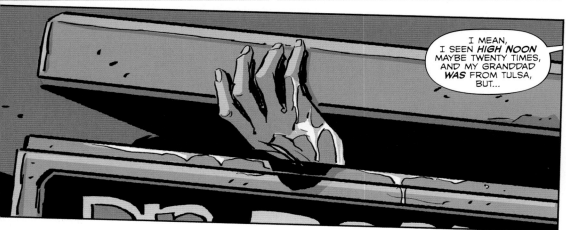

I MEAN, I SEEN *HIGH NOON* MAYBE TWENTY TIMES, AND MY GRANDDAD *WAS* FROM TULSA, BUT...

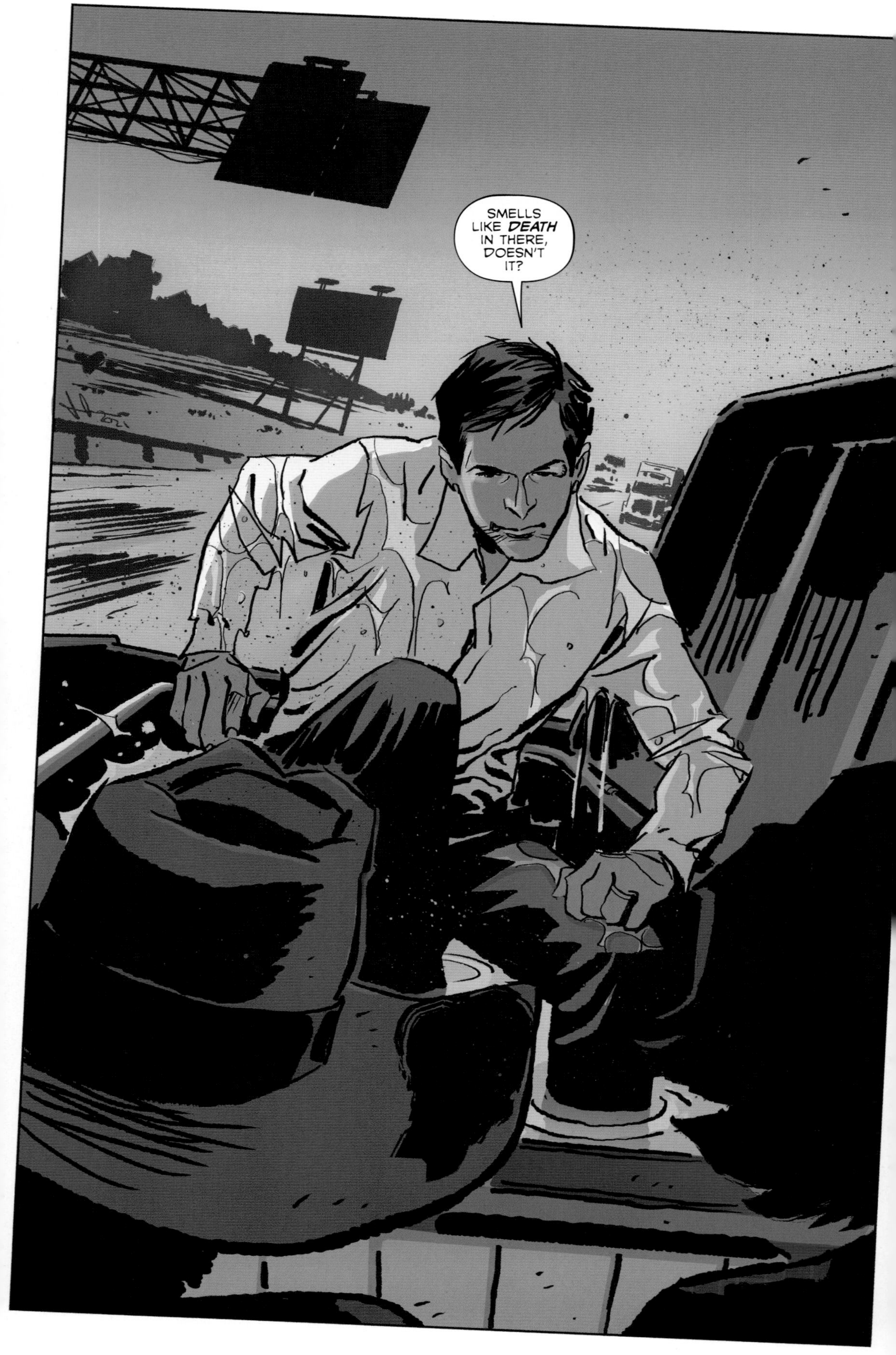
SMELLS LIKE DEATH IN THERE, DOESN'T IT?

ICE DEPARTMENT
Y OF DALLAS
—J5-000

ARREST REPORT
ON
INVESTIGATIVE PRISONER

RT. THUMB PRINT

ST NAME	MIDDLE NAME	LAST NAME	DATE	TIME
LEE	HARVEY	OSWALD	11-22-63	140 pm

L.D. NUMBER   ARREST NUMBER   63-98155

PLACE   E ☒ COLORED ☐   SEX MALE ☒ FEMALE ☐   AGE 24   DATE OF BIRTH OCT 18-39   HOME ADDRESS 1026 N. BECKLEY

RESS WHERE ARREST WAS MADE 231 W. JEFFERSON   TYPE PREMISES (IF BUSINESS, GIVE TRADE NAME ALSO) THEATRE

RGE INV. MURDER

BUSINESS WHERE ARREST MADE HAS: BEER LICENSE ☐   LIQUOR LICENSE ☐   STATE LIC. NO.

V ARREST WAS MADE   VIEW ☐   CALL ☐   WARRANT ☐

LOCATION OF OFFENSE (IF OTHER THAN PLACE OF ARREST)

PLAINANT (NAME-RACE-SEX-AGE)   HOME ADDRESS-PHONE NO.   BUSINESS ADDRESS-PHONE NO.

NESS   HOME ADDRESS-PHONE NO.   BUSINESS ADDRESS-PHONE NO.

NESS   HOME ADDRESS-PHONE NO.   BUSINESS ADDRESS-PHONE NO.

PERTY PLACED IN POUND (MAKE, MODEL, LICENSE NO. OF AUTO)   PROPERTY PLACED IN PROPERTY ROOM

ES OF OTHERS ARRESTED AT THE SAME TIME IN CONNECTION TO THE SAME OR SIMILAR OFFENSE

E OF AND/OR INFORMATION CONCERING OTHER SUSPECTS NOT APPREHENDED

OTHER DETAILS ON THE ARREST

This man shot and killed President John F. Kennedy and Police Officer J. D. Tippit. He also shot and wounded Governor John Connally.

DECEASED
11-24-63
Parkland Story

RK ALL ITEMS WHICH APPLY   NK ☐ DRINKING ☐ CURSED ☐ RESISTED ☐ FOUGHT ☐   INJURED BEFORE ARREST ☐   INJURED DURING OR AFTER ARREST ☐   OFFICER INJURED ☐   SPECIAL REPORT ☐

ESTING OFFICER	I.D. NO.	ARRESTING OFFICER	I.D. NO.
M.N. MCDONALD	1178	K.E. LYONS	1276

ER OFFICER   I.D. NO.   OTHER OFFICER   I.D. NO.
LT. EJ. CUNNINGHAM   PJ. BENTLEY   526

INVESTIGATION ASSIGNED TO   CHARGE FILED   FILED BY   DATE   DATE - TIME TO CO JAIL

VESTIGATION ASSIGNED TO   DATE-TIME   H.C. BOND BY   DATE-TIME   COURT   DATE   TIME

TRIBUTION (REMOVE CARSON- CHCECK ORIGINAL FOR RECORDS BU-- CHECK COPY FOR EACH BUREAU CONCERNED)
RDS ☐   SPEC. PER BUREAU ☐   HOMICIDE ROBBERY ☐   AUTO THEFT ☐   BURGLARY THEFT ☐   FORGERY ☐   JUVENILE ☐   TRAFFIC ☐   ☐

USE REVERSE SIDE IF MORE SPACE IS NEEDED

LOOSE ENDS

—Kodak film facing N, red head scarf

—Nix?

—Craig Mauser story

—14k gold, size 15+, hammer & sickle stamp
—> NEEDS TO GET TO PAINE HOUSE ASAP,
Marina must find before burial

Dallas, Parkland Memorial Hospital. October 5th, 1981.

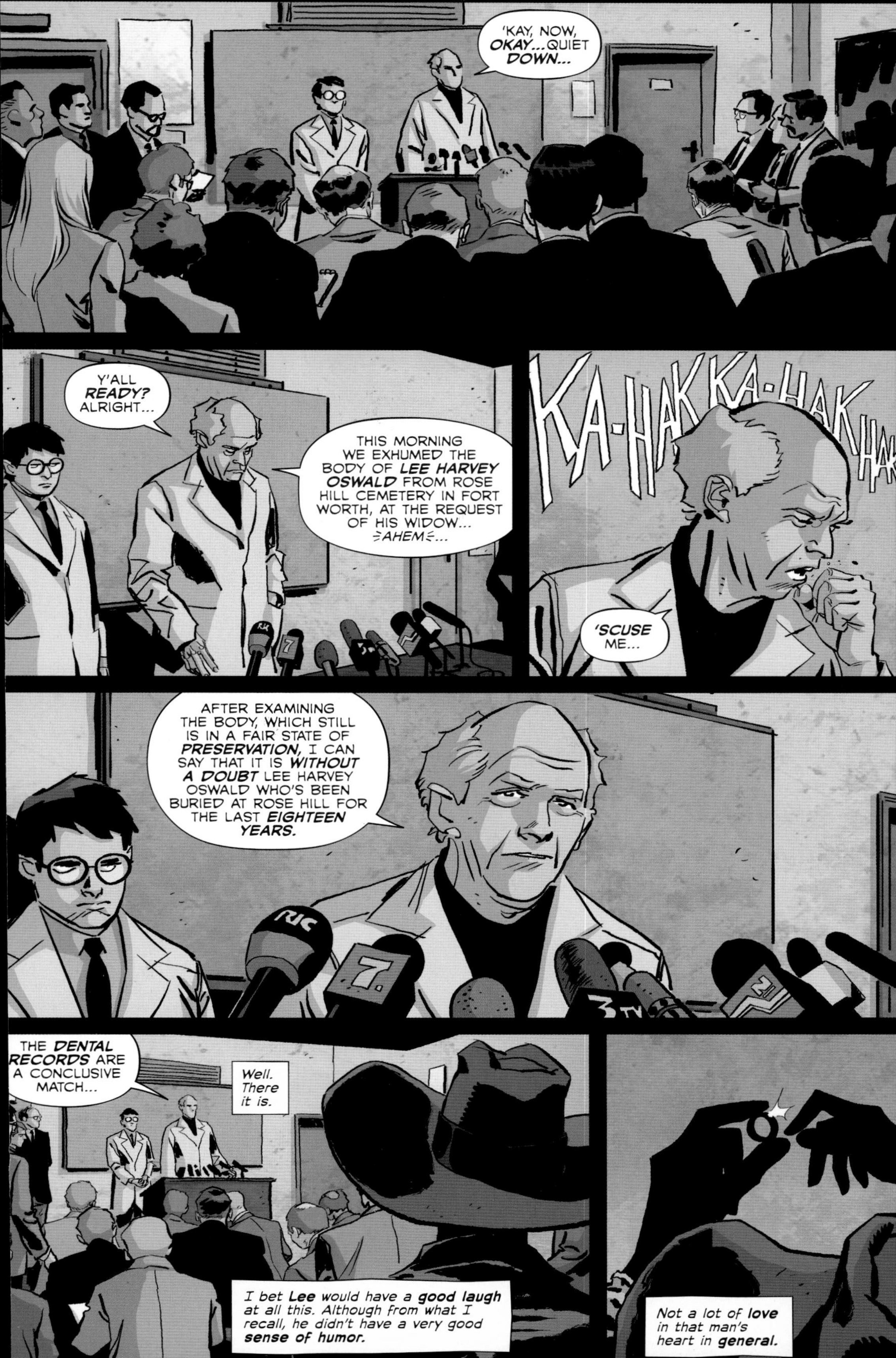
'KAY, NOW, OKAY... QUIET DOWN...
Y'ALL READY? ALRIGHT...
THIS MORNING WE EXHUMED THE BODY OF LEE HARVEY OSWALD FROM ROSE HILL CEMETERY IN FORT WORTH, AT THE REQUEST OF HIS WIDOW... AHEM...
KA-HAK KA-HAK HAK
'SCUSE ME...
AFTER EXAMINING THE BODY, WHICH STILL IS IN A FAIR STATE OF PRESERVATION, I CAN SAY THAT IT IS WITHOUT A DOUBT LEE HARVEY OSWALD WHO'S BEEN BURIED AT ROSE HILL FOR THE LAST EIGHTEEN YEARS.
THE DENTAL RECORDS ARE A CONCLUSIVE MATCH...
Well. There it is.
I bet Lee would have a good laugh at all this. Although from what I recall, he didn't have a very good sense of humor.
Not a lot of love in that man's heart in general.

Just outside Vidor, Texas, near the Louisiana border. November 24th, 1963.

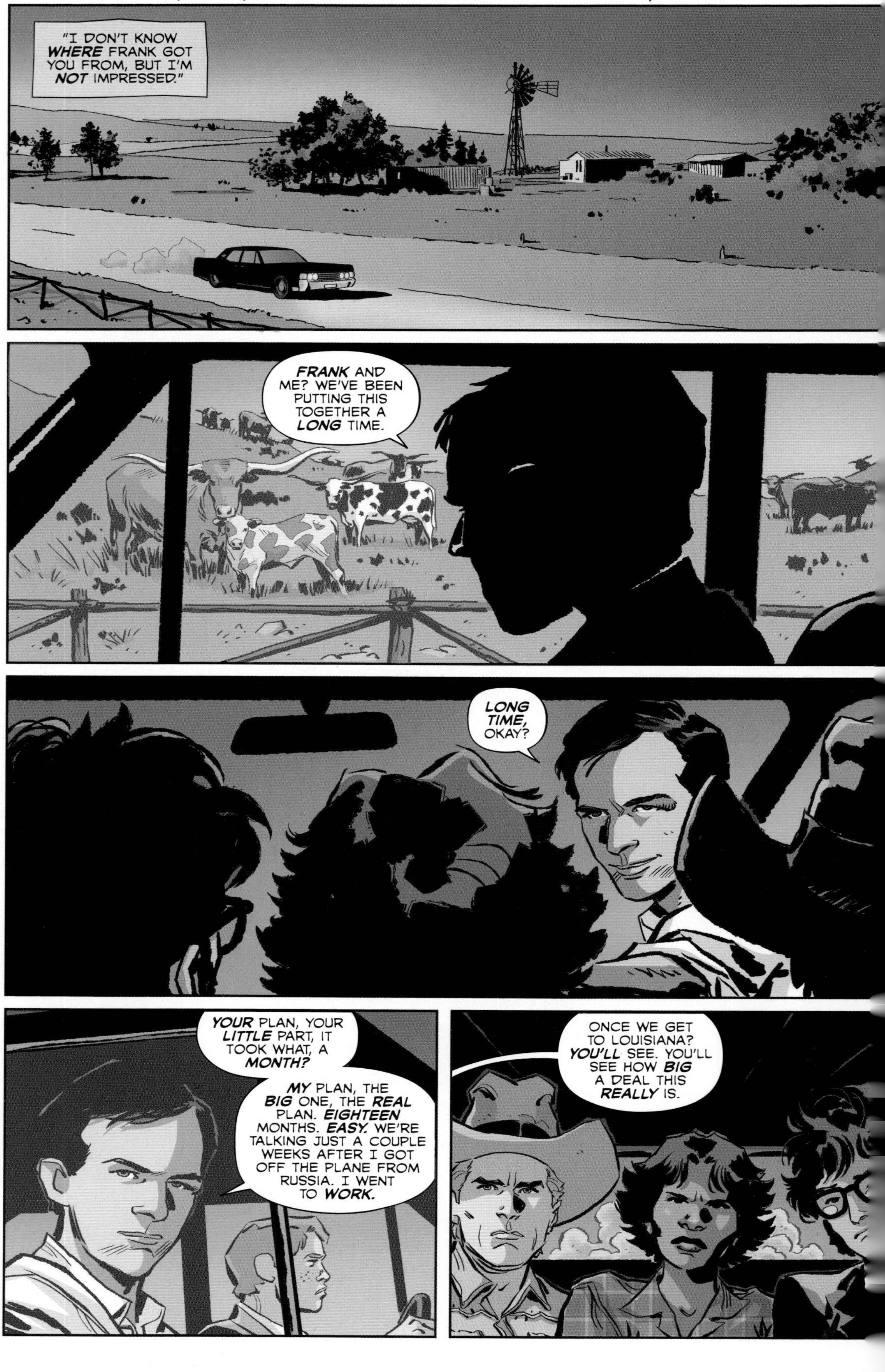
"I DON'T KNOW WHERE FRANK GOT YOU FROM, BUT I'M NOT IMPRESSED."
FRANK AND ME? WE'VE BEEN PUTTING THIS TOGETHER A LONG TIME.
LONG TIME, OKAY?
YOUR PLAN, YOUR LITTLE PART, IT TOOK WHAT, A MONTH?
MY PLAN, THE BIG ONE, THE REAL PLAN. EIGHTEEN MONTHS. EASY. WE'RE TALKING JUST A COUPLE WEEKS AFTER I GOT OFF THE PLANE FROM RUSSIA. I WENT TO WORK.
ONCE WE GET TO LOUISIANA? YOU'LL SEE. YOU'LL SEE HOW BIG A DEAL THIS REALLY IS.

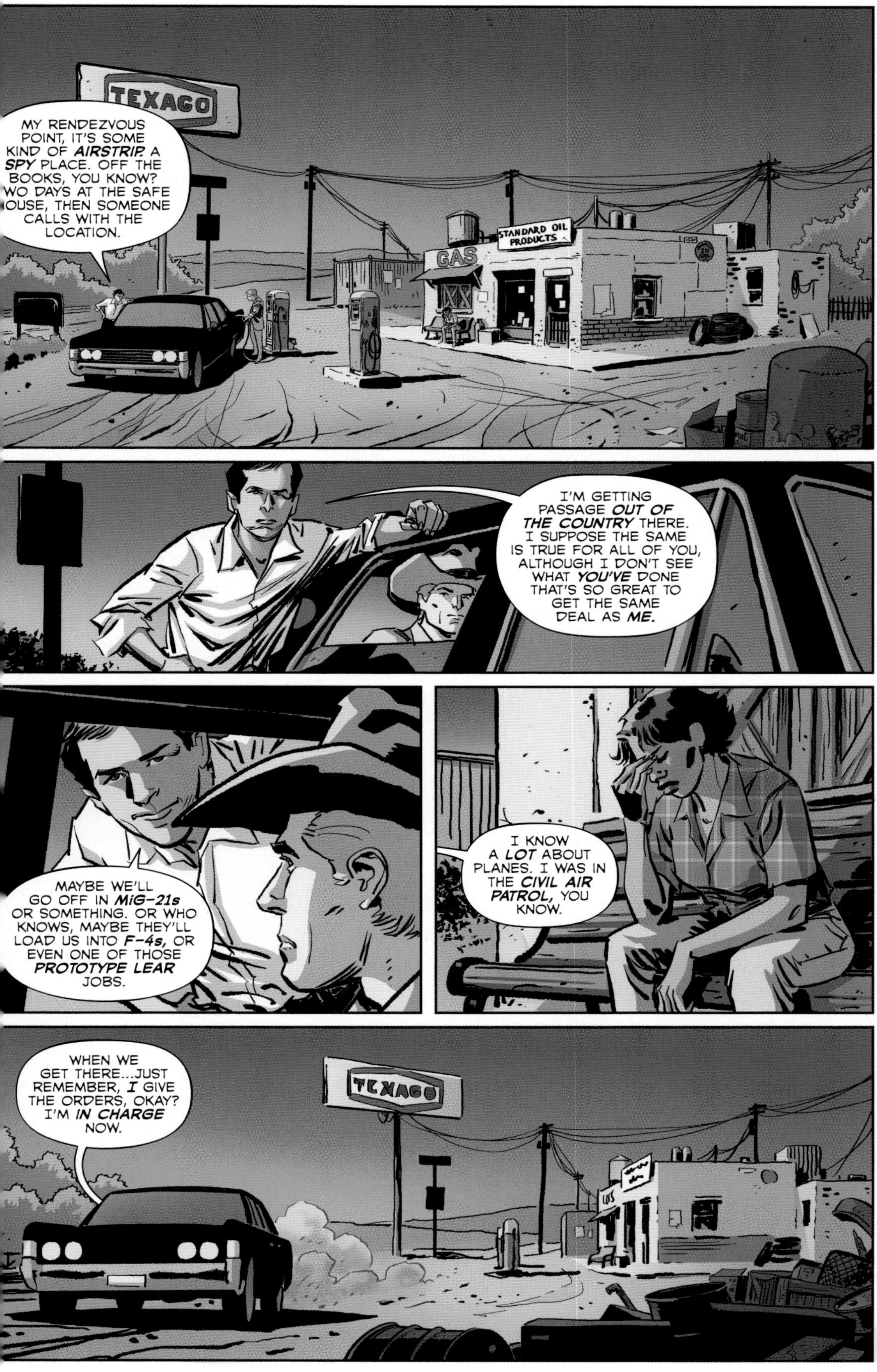
TEXAGO
MY RENDEZVOUS POINT, IT'S SOME KIND OF AIRSTRIP. A SPY PLACE. OFF THE BOOKS, YOU KNOW? WO DAYS AT THE SAFE OUSE, THEN SOMEONE CALLS WITH THE LOCATION.
STANDARD OIL PRODUCTS
GAS
I'M GETTING PASSAGE OUT OF THE COUNTRY THERE. I SUPPOSE THE SAME IS TRUE FOR ALL OF YOU, ALTHOUGH I DON'T SEE WHAT YOU'VE DONE THAT'S SO GREAT TO GET THE SAME DEAL AS ME.
MAYBE WE'LL GO OFF IN MiG-21s OR SOMETHING. OR WHO KNOWS, MAYBE THEY'LL LOAD US INTO F-4s, OR EVEN ONE OF THOSE PROTOTYPE LEAR JOBS.
I KNOW A LOT ABOUT PLANES. I WAS IN THE CIVIL AIR PATROL, YOU KNOW.
WHEN WE GET THERE...JUST REMEMBER, I GIVE THE ORDERS, OKAY? I'M IN CHARGE NOW.

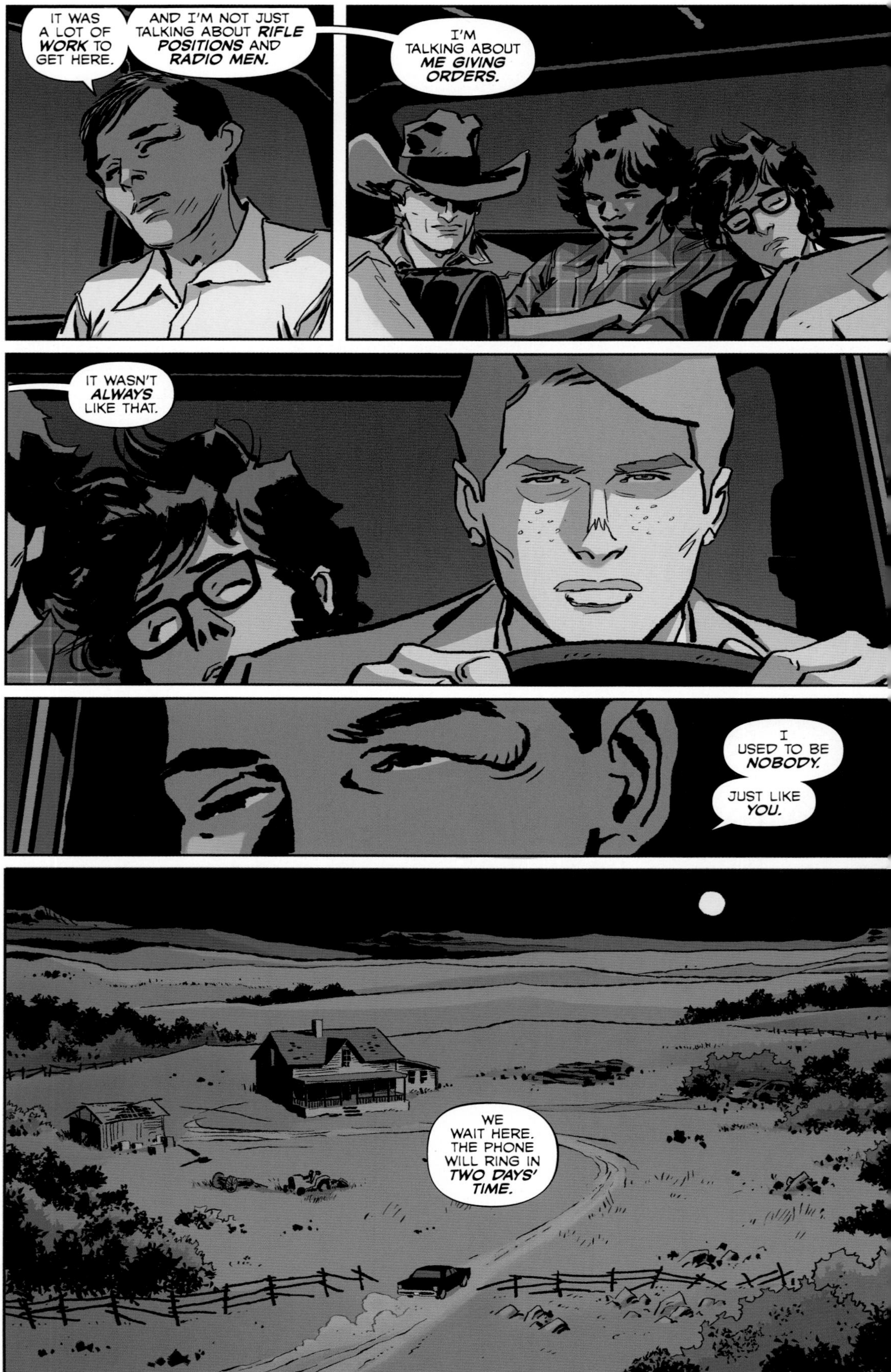
IT WAS A LOT OF WORK TO GET HERE.
AND I'M NOT JUST TALKING ABOUT RIFLE POSITIONS AND RADIO MEN.
I'M TALKING ABOUT ME GIVING ORDERS.
IT WASN'T ALWAYS LIKE THAT.
I USED TO BE NOBODY.
JUST LIKE YOU.
WE WAIT HERE. THE PHONE WILL RING IN TWO DAYS' TIME.

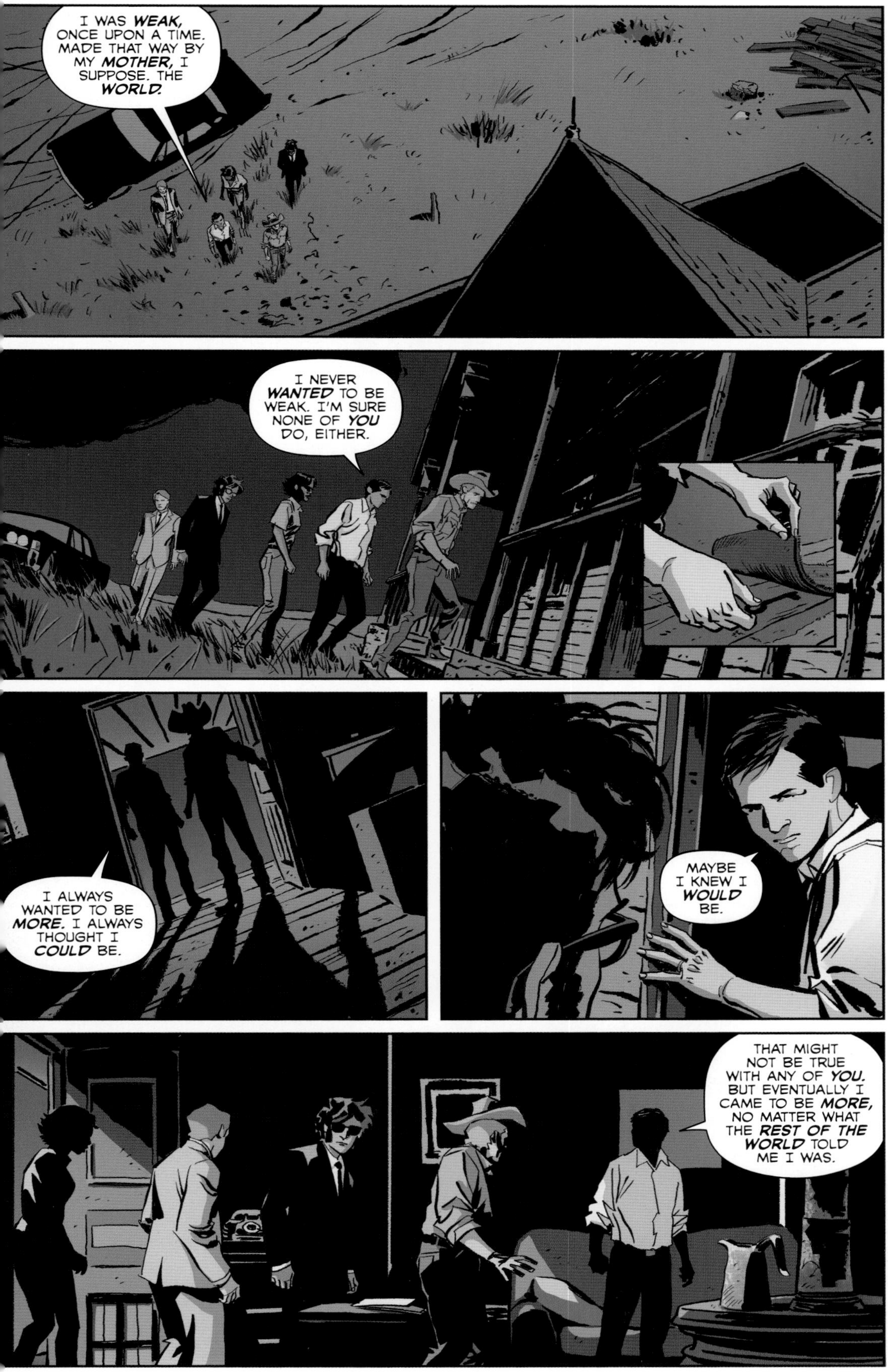
I WAS WEAK, ONCE UPON A TIME. MADE THAT WAY BY MY MOTHER, I SUPPOSE. THE WORLD.
I NEVER WANTED TO BE WEAK. I'M SURE NONE OF YOU DO, EITHER.
I ALWAYS WANTED TO BE MORE. I ALWAYS THOUGHT I COULD BE.
MAYBE I KNEW I WOULD BE.
THAT MIGHT NOT BE TRUE WITH ANY OF YOU. BUT EVENTUALLY I CAME TO BE MORE, NO MATTER WHAT THE REST OF THE WORLD TOLD ME I WAS.

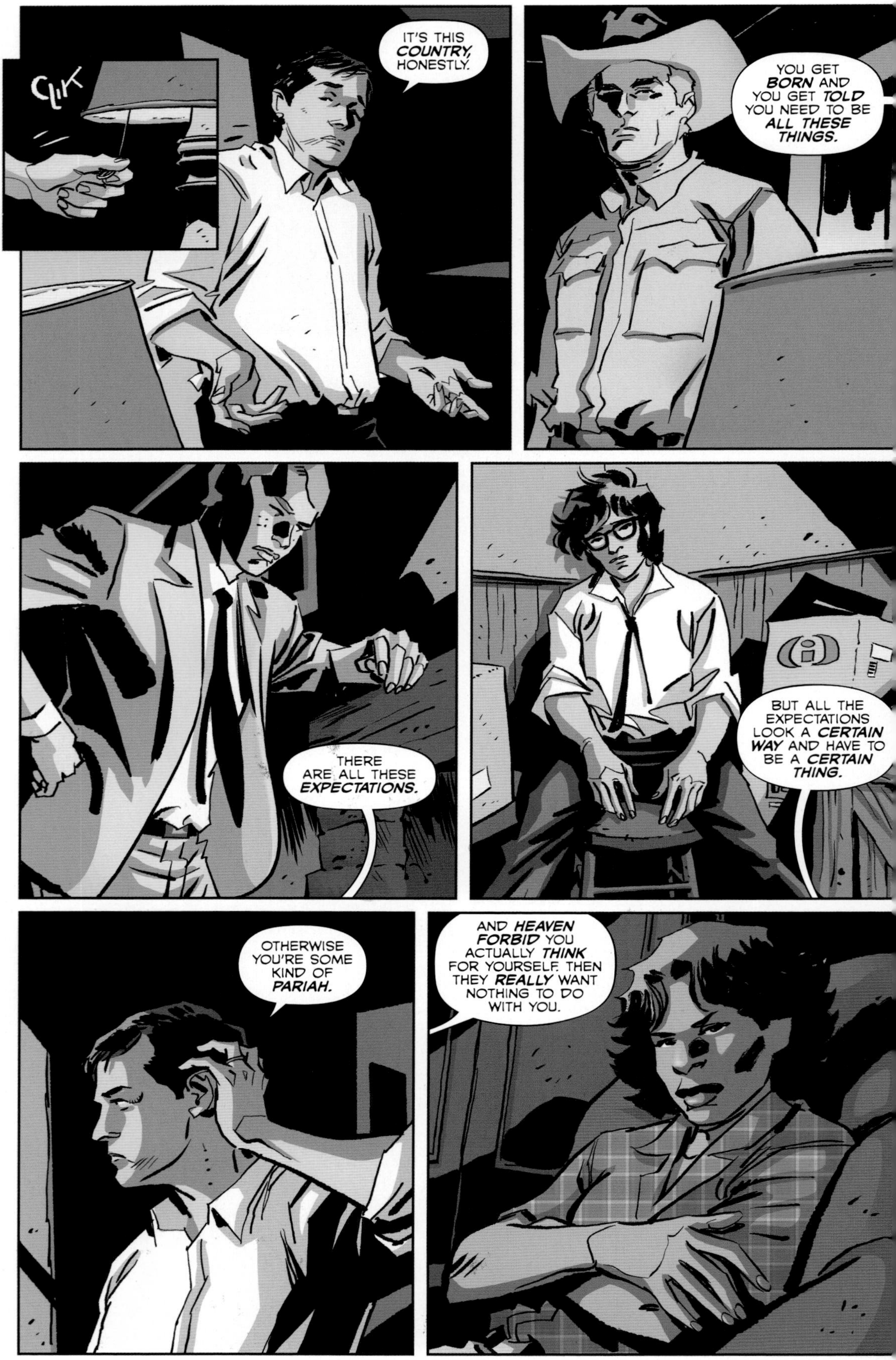
CLIK
IT'S THIS COUNTRY, HONESTLY.
YOU GET BORN AND YOU GET TOLD YOU NEED TO BE ALL THESE THINGS.
THERE ARE ALL THESE EXPECTATIONS.
BUT ALL THE EXPECTATIONS LOOK A CERTAIN WAY AND HAVE TO BE A CERTAIN THING.
OTHERWISE YOU'RE SOME KIND OF PARIAH.
AND HEAVEN FORBID YOU ACTUALLY THINK FOR YOURSELF. THEN THEY REALLY WANT NOTHING TO DO WITH YOU.

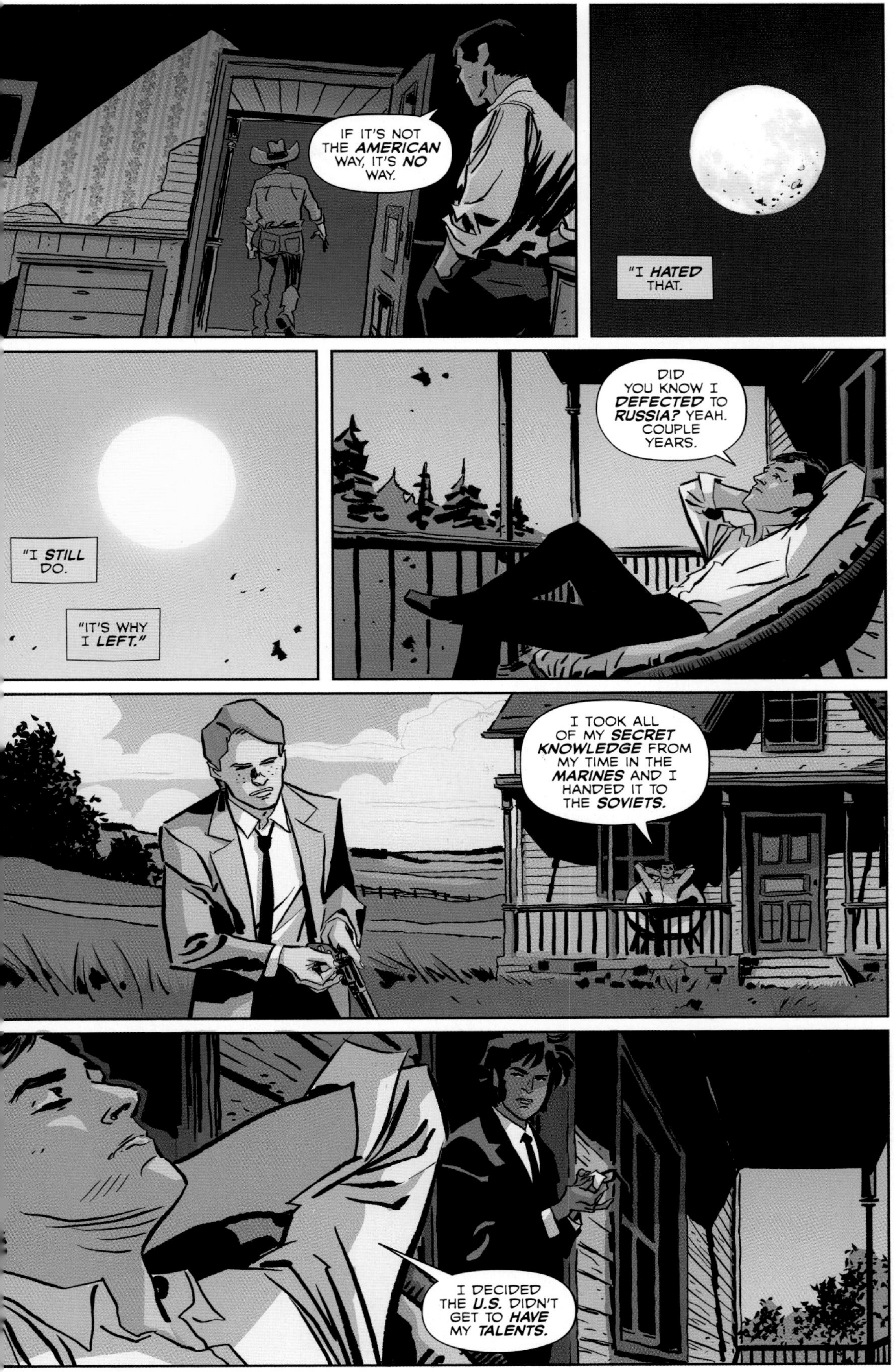
IF IT'S NOT THE AMERICAN WAY, IT'S NO WAY.
"I HATED THAT.
"I STILL DO.
"IT'S WHY I LEFT."
DID YOU KNOW I DEFECTED TO RUSSIA? YEAH. COUPLE YEARS.
I TOOK ALL OF MY SECRET KNOWLEDGE FROM MY TIME IN THE MARINES AND I HANDED IT TO THE SOVIETS.
I DECIDED THE U.S. DIDN'T GET TO HAVE MY TALENTS.

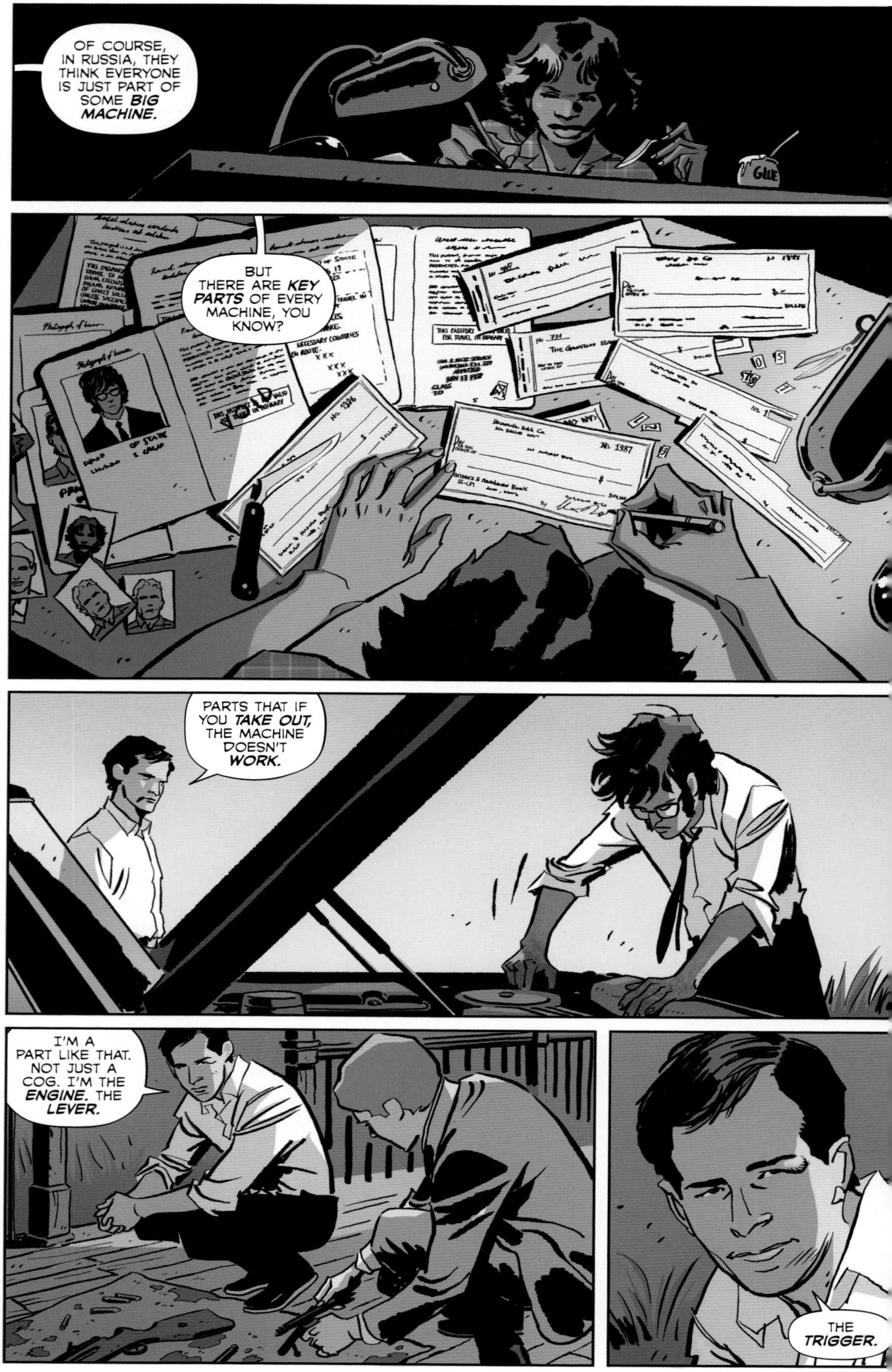
OF COURSE, IN RUSSIA, THEY THINK EVERYONE IS JUST PART OF SOME BIG MACHINE.
BUT THERE ARE KEY PARTS OF EVERY MACHINE, YOU KNOW?
PARTS THAT IF YOU TAKE OUT, THE MACHINE DOESN'T WORK.
I'M A PART LIKE THAT. NOT JUST A COG. I'M THE ENGINE. THE LEVER.
THE TRIGGER.

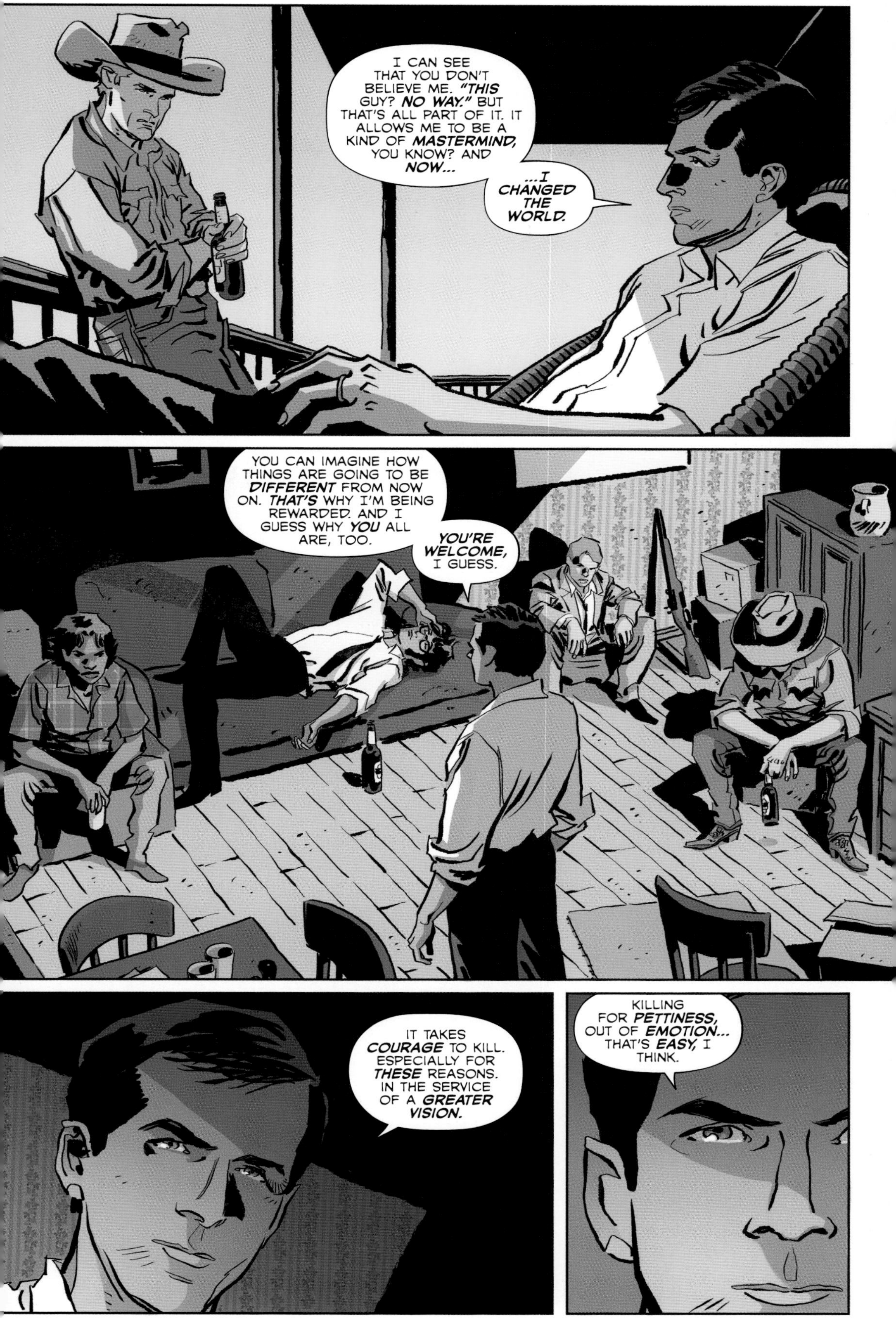
I CAN SEE THAT YOU DON'T BELIEVE ME. "THIS GUY? NO WAY." BUT THAT'S ALL PART OF IT. IT ALLOWS ME TO BE A KIND OF MASTERMIND, YOU KNOW? AND NOW...
...I CHANGED THE WORLD.
YOU CAN IMAGINE HOW THINGS ARE GOING TO BE DIFFERENT FROM NOW ON. THAT'S WHY I'M BEING REWARDED. AND I GUESS WHY YOU ALL ARE, TOO.
YOU'RE WELCOME, I GUESS.
IT TAKES COURAGE TO KILL. ESPECIALLY FOR THESE REASONS. IN THE SERVICE OF A GREATER VISION.
KILLING FOR PETTINESS, OUT OF EMOTION... THAT'S EASY, I THINK.

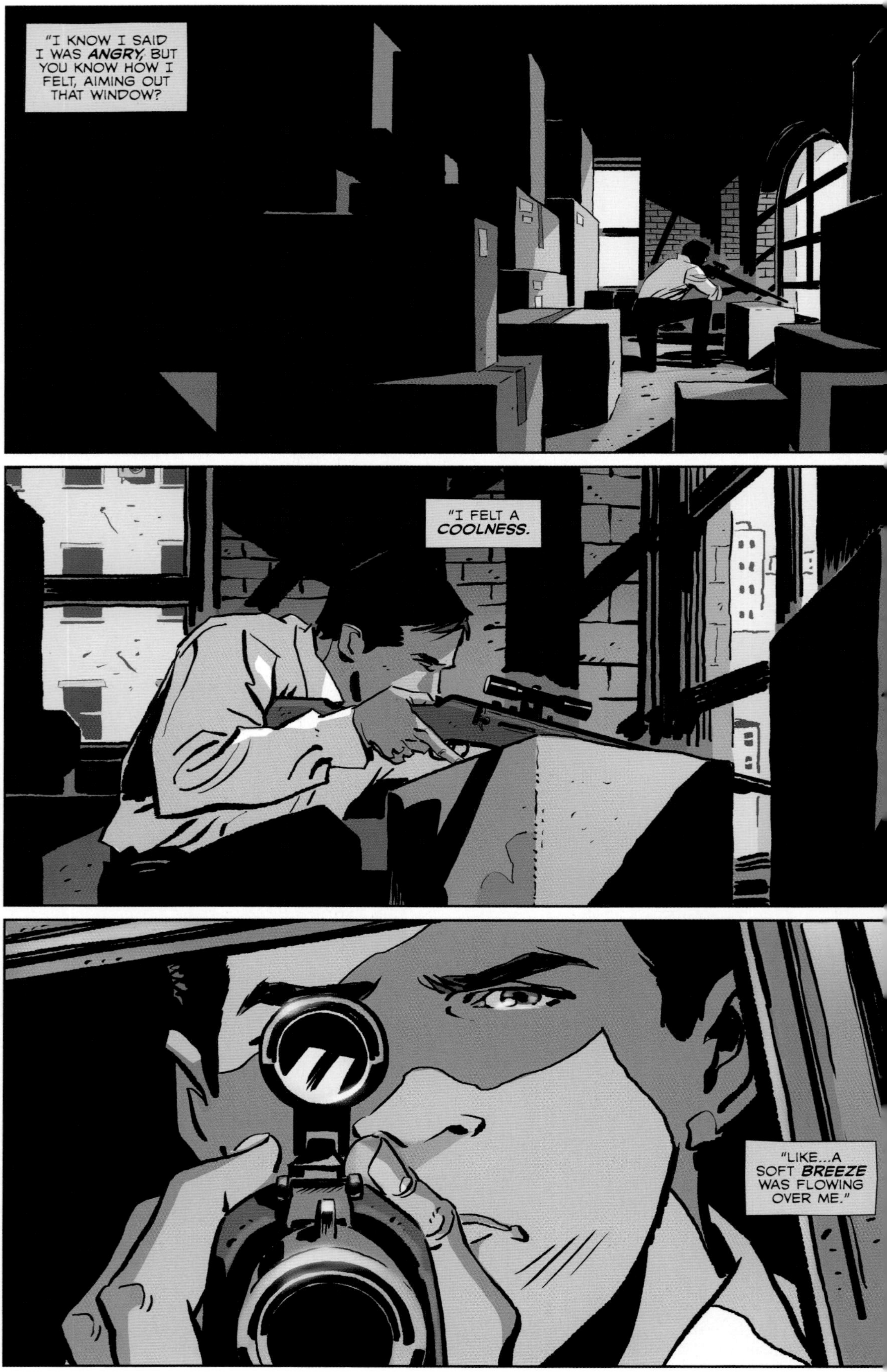
"I KNOW I SAID I WAS ANGRY, BUT YOU KNOW HOW I FELT, AIMING OUT THAT WINDOW?
"I FELT A COOLNESS.
"LIKE...A SOFT BREEZE WAS FLOWING OVER ME."

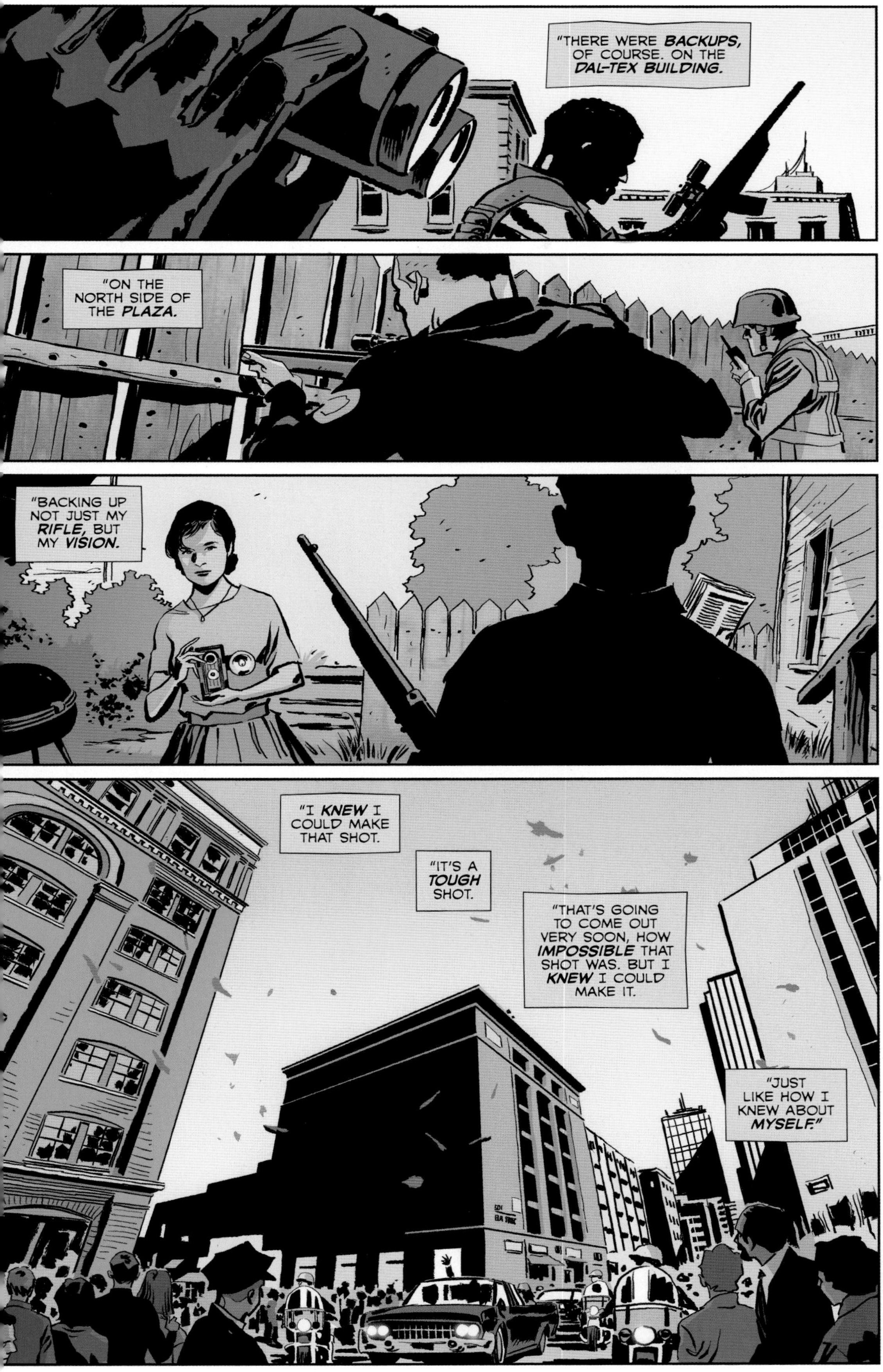
"THERE WERE BACKUPS, OF COURSE. ON THE DAL-TEX BUILDING.
"ON THE NORTH SIDE OF THE PLAZA.
"BACKING UP NOT JUST MY RIFLE, BUT MY VISION.
"I KNEW I COULD MAKE THAT SHOT.
"IT'S A TOUGH SHOT.
"THAT'S GOING TO COME OUT VERY SOON, HOW IMPOSSIBLE THAT SHOT WAS. BUT I KNEW I COULD MAKE IT.
"JUST LIKE HOW I KNEW ABOUT MYSELF."

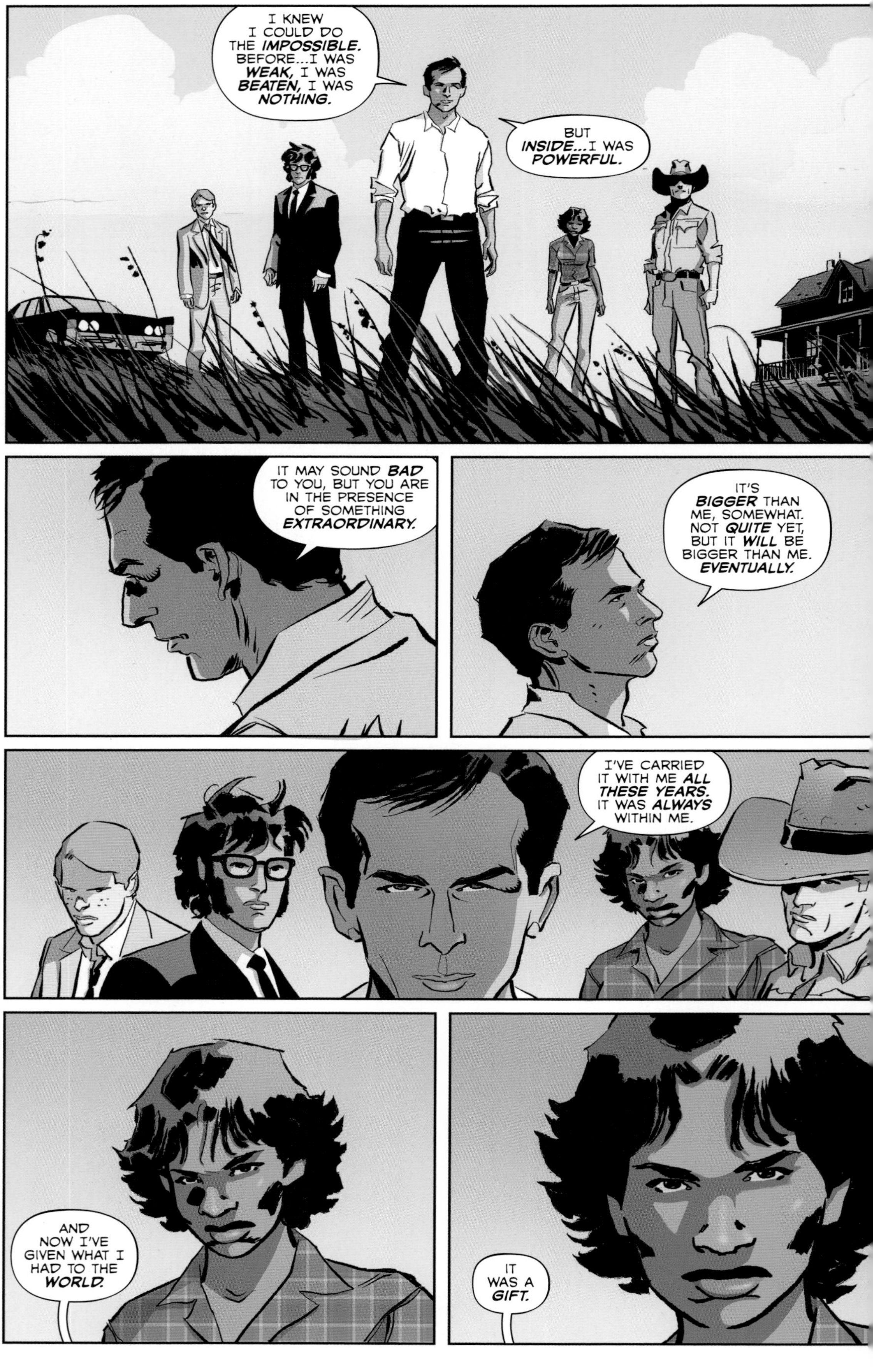
I KNEW I COULD DO THE IMPOSSIBLE. BEFORE...I WAS WEAK, I WAS BEATEN, I WAS NOTHING.
BUT INSIDE...I WAS POWERFUL.
IT MAY SOUND BAD TO YOU, BUT YOU ARE IN THE PRESENCE OF SOMETHING EXTRAORDINARY.
IT'S BIGGER THAN ME, SOMEWHAT. NOT QUITE YET, BUT IT WILL BE BIGGER THAN ME. EVENTUALLY.
I'VE CARRIED IT WITH ME ALL THESE YEARS. IT WAS ALWAYS WITHIN ME.
AND NOW I'VE GIVEN WHAT I HAD TO THE WORLD.
IT WAS A GIFT.

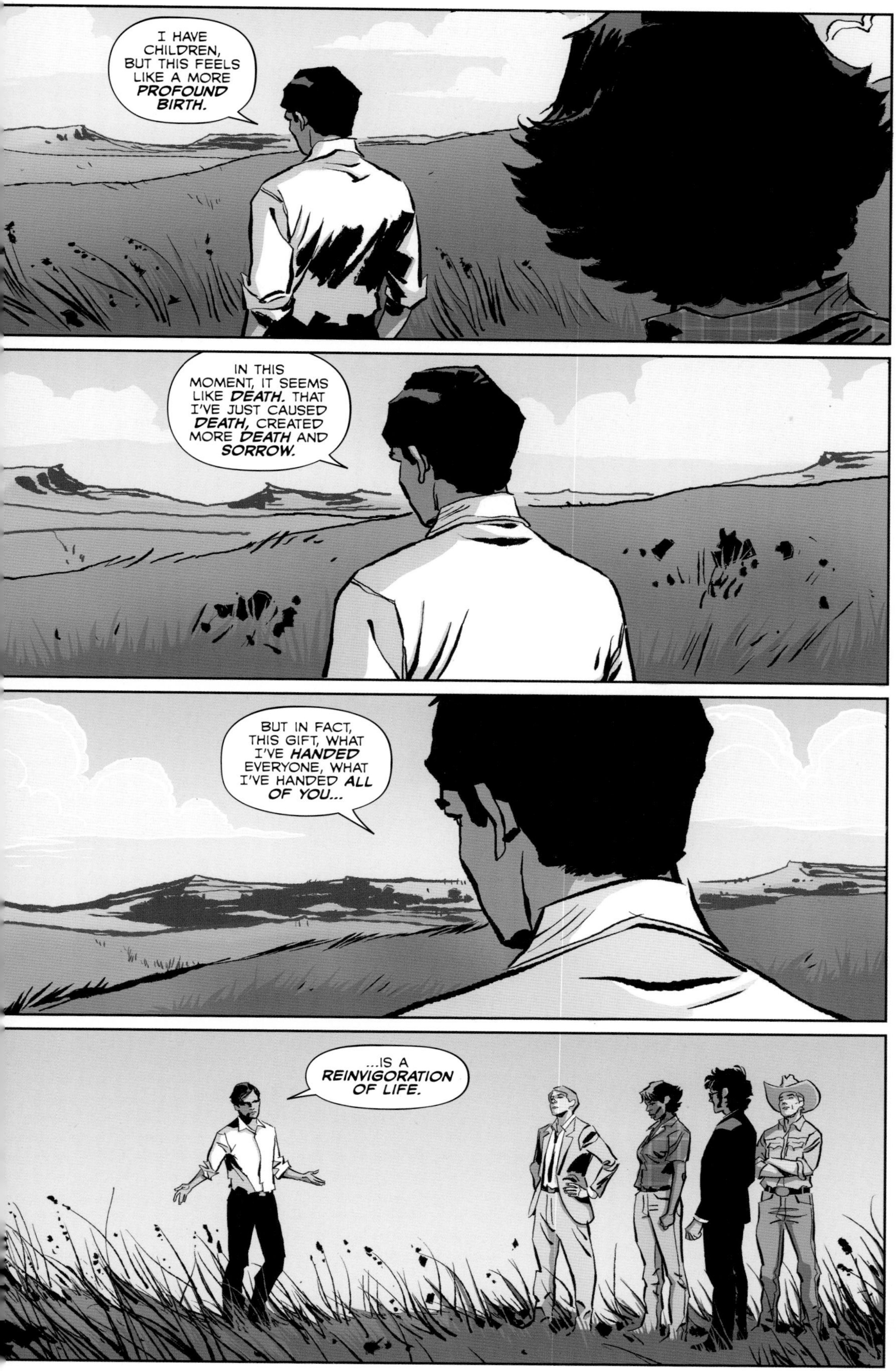
I HAVE CHILDREN, BUT THIS FEELS LIKE A MORE *PROFOUND BIRTH.*
IN THIS MOMENT, IT SEEMS LIKE *DEATH.* THAT I'VE JUST CAUSED *DEATH,* CREATED MORE *DEATH* AND *SORROW.*
BUT IN FACT, THIS GIFT, WHAT I'VE *HANDED* EVERYONE, WHAT I'VE HANDED *ALL OF YOU...*
...IS A *REINVIGORATION OF LIFE.*

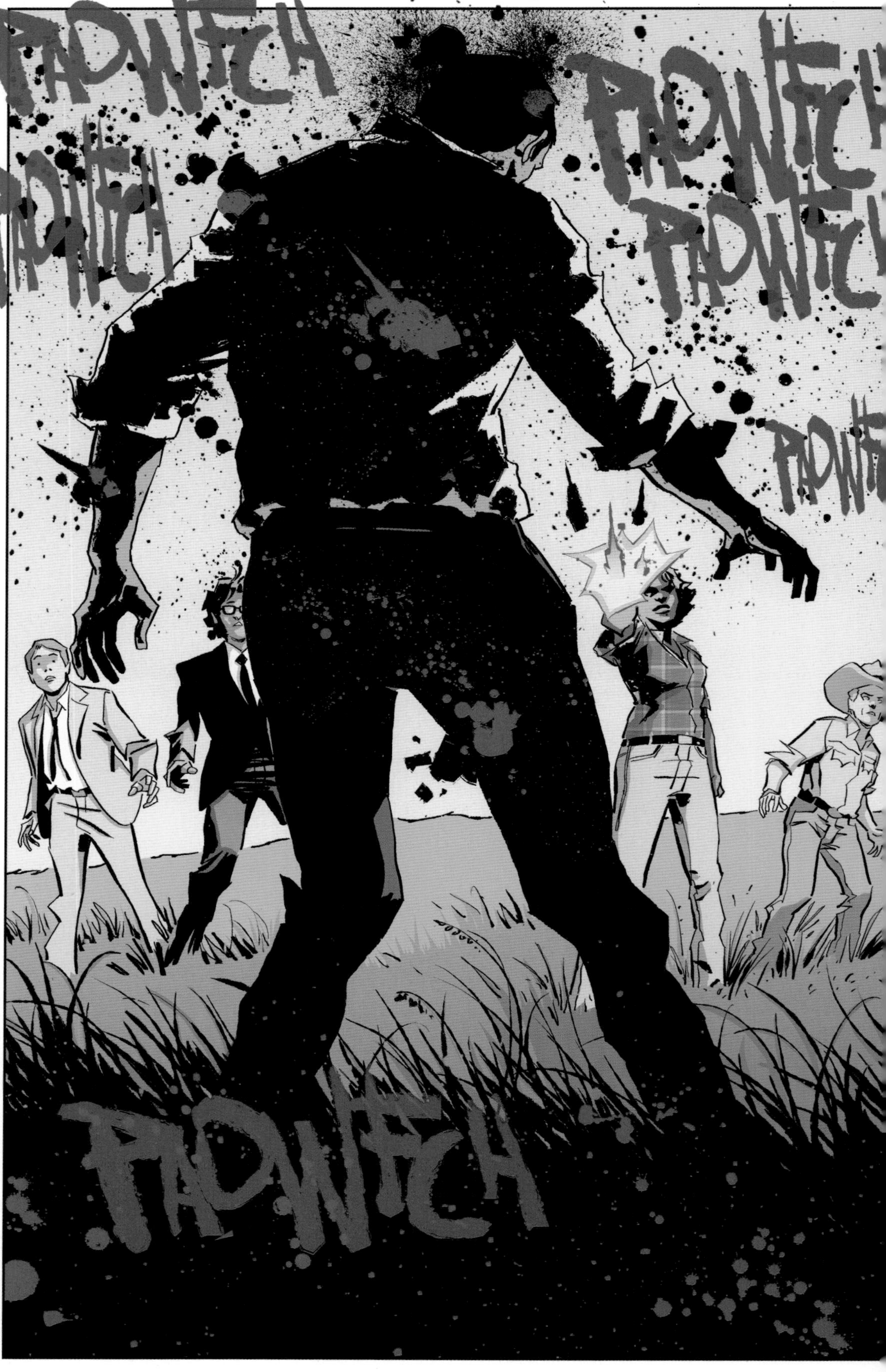
PAOWTCH
PAOWTCH
PAOWTCH

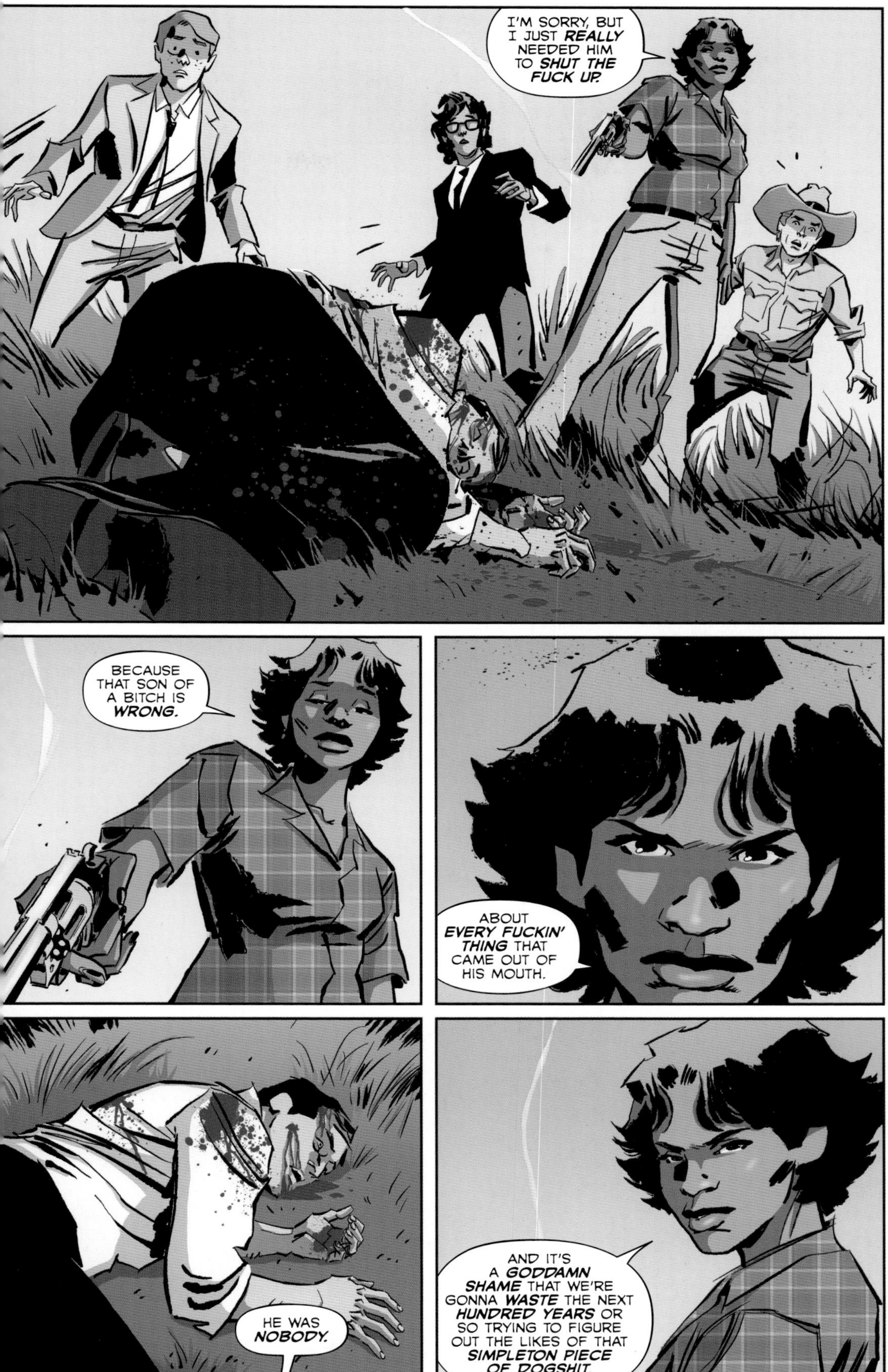
I'M SORRY, BUT I JUST **REALLY** NEEDED HIM TO **SHUT THE FUCK UP.**
BECAUSE THAT SON OF A BITCH IS **WRONG.**
ABOUT **EVERY FUCKIN' THING** THAT CAME OUT OF HIS MOUTH.
HE WAS **NOBODY.**
AND IT'S A **GODDAMN SHAME** THAT WE'RE GONNA **WASTE** THE NEXT **HUNDRED YEARS** OR SO TRYING TO FIGURE OUT THE LIKES OF THAT **SIMPLETON PIECE OF DOGSHIT.**

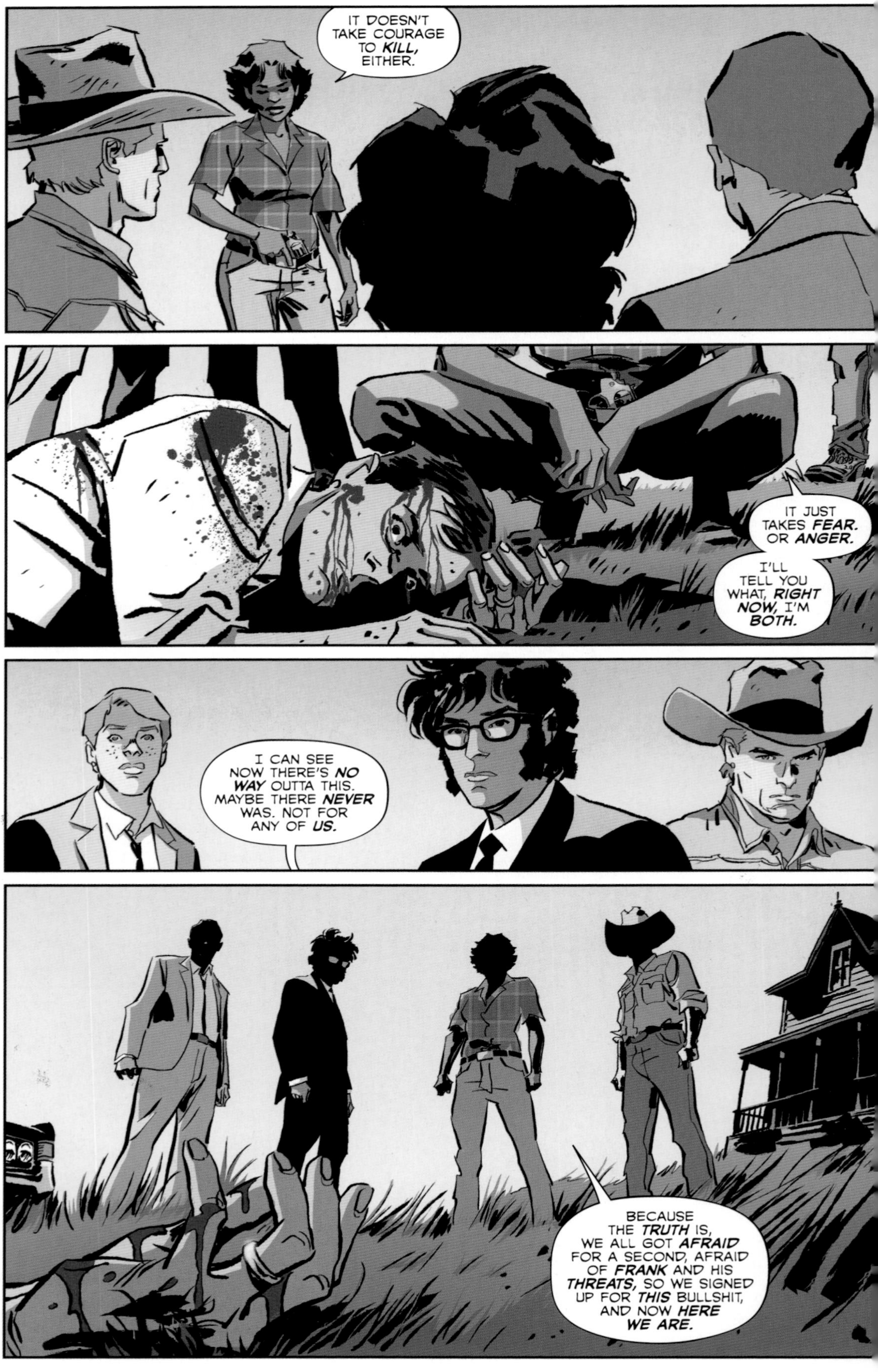
IT DOESN'T TAKE COURAGE TO KILL, EITHER.
IT JUST TAKES FEAR. OR ANGER.
I'LL TELL YOU WHAT, RIGHT NOW, I'M BOTH.
I CAN SEE NOW THERE'S NO WAY OUTTA THIS. MAYBE THERE NEVER WAS. NOT FOR ANY OF US.
BECAUSE THE TRUTH IS, WE ALL GOT AFRAID FOR A SECOND, AFRAID OF FRANK AND HIS THREATS, SO WE SIGNED UP FOR THIS BULLSHIT, AND NOW HERE WE ARE.

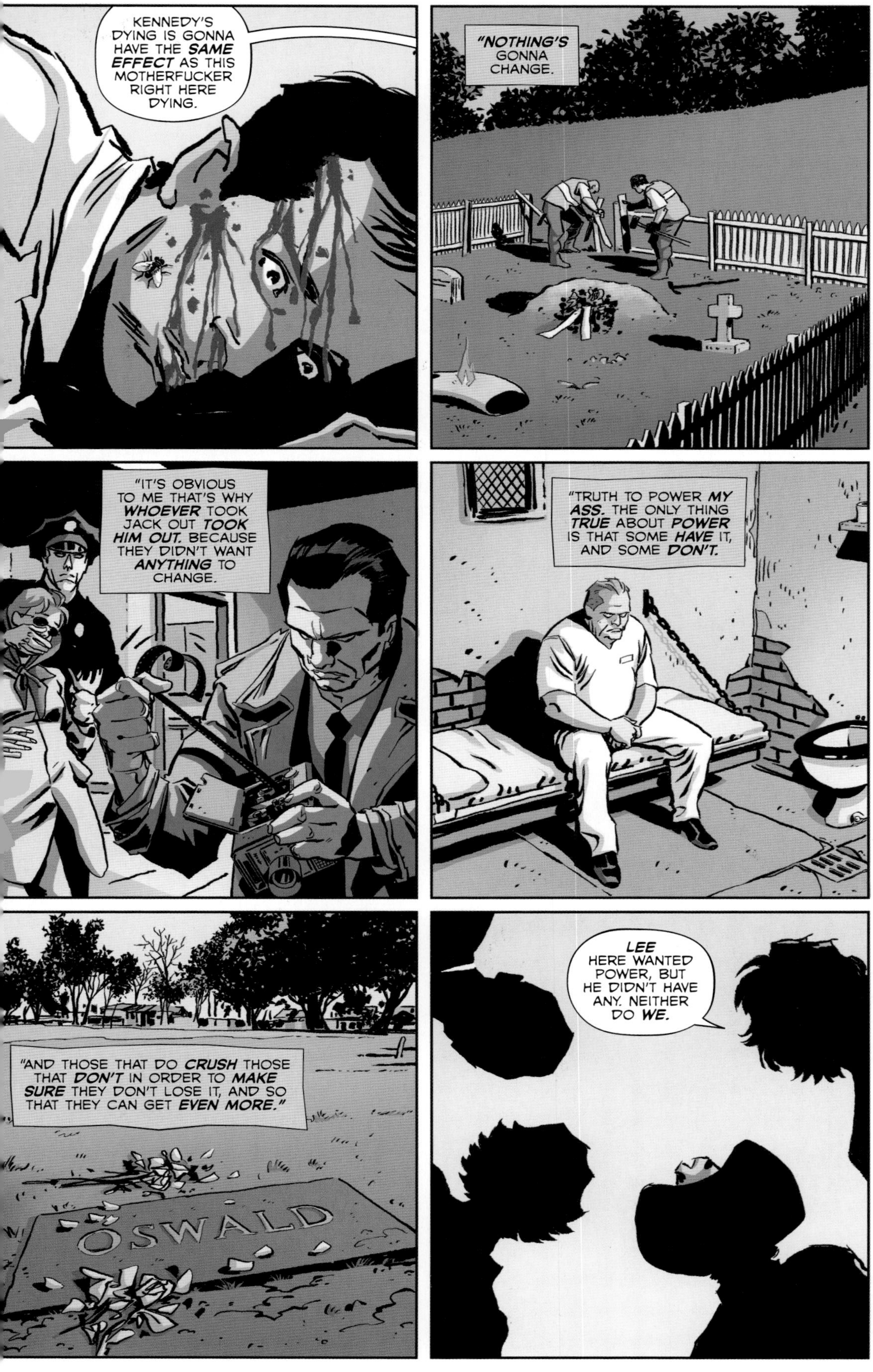
KENNEDY'S DYING IS GONNA HAVE THE SAME EFFECT AS THIS MOTHERFUCKER RIGHT HERE DYING.
"NOTHING'S GONNA CHANGE.
"IT'S OBVIOUS TO ME THAT'S WHY WHOEVER TOOK JACK OUT TOOK HIM OUT. BECAUSE THEY DIDN'T WANT ANYTHING TO CHANGE.
"TRUTH TO POWER MY ASS. THE ONLY THING TRUE ABOUT POWER IS THAT SOME HAVE IT, AND SOME DON'T.
"AND THOSE THAT DO CRUSH THOSE THAT DON'T IN ORDER TO MAKE SURE THEY DON'T LOSE IT, AND SO THAT THEY CAN GET EVEN MORE."
OSWALD
LEE HERE WANTED POWER, BUT HE DIDN'T HAVE ANY. NEITHER DO WE.

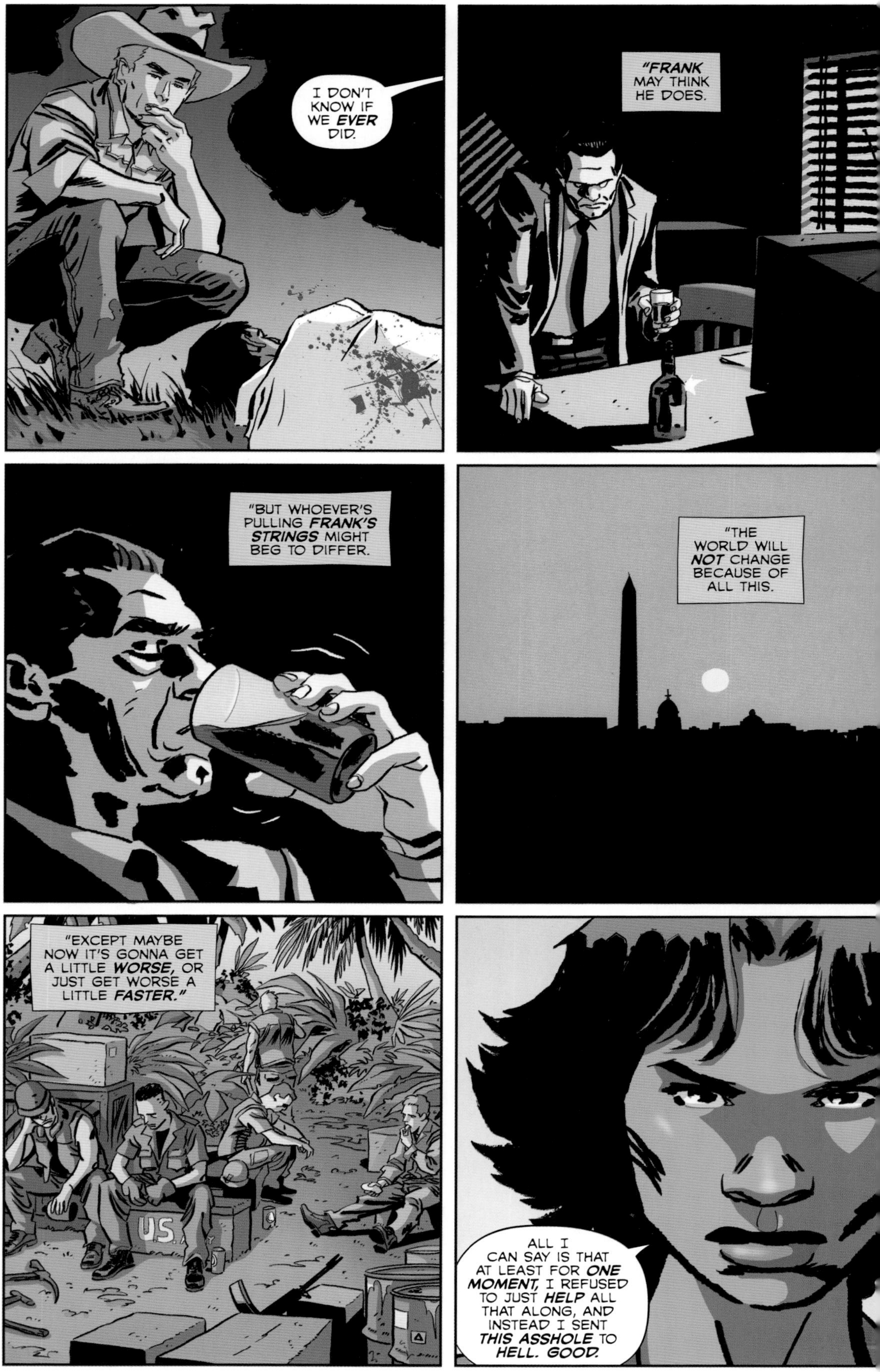
I DON'T KNOW IF WE EVER DID.
"FRANK MAY THINK HE DOES.
"BUT WHOEVER'S PULLING FRANK'S STRINGS MIGHT BEG TO DIFFER.
"THE WORLD WILL NOT CHANGE BECAUSE OF ALL THIS.
"EXCEPT MAYBE NOW IT'S GONNA GET A LITTLE WORSE, OR JUST GET WORSE A LITTLE FASTER."
U.S.
ALL I CAN SAY IS THAT AT LEAST FOR ONE MOMENT, I REFUSED TO JUST HELP ALL THAT ALONG, AND INSTEAD I SENT THIS ASSHOLE TO HELL. GOOD.

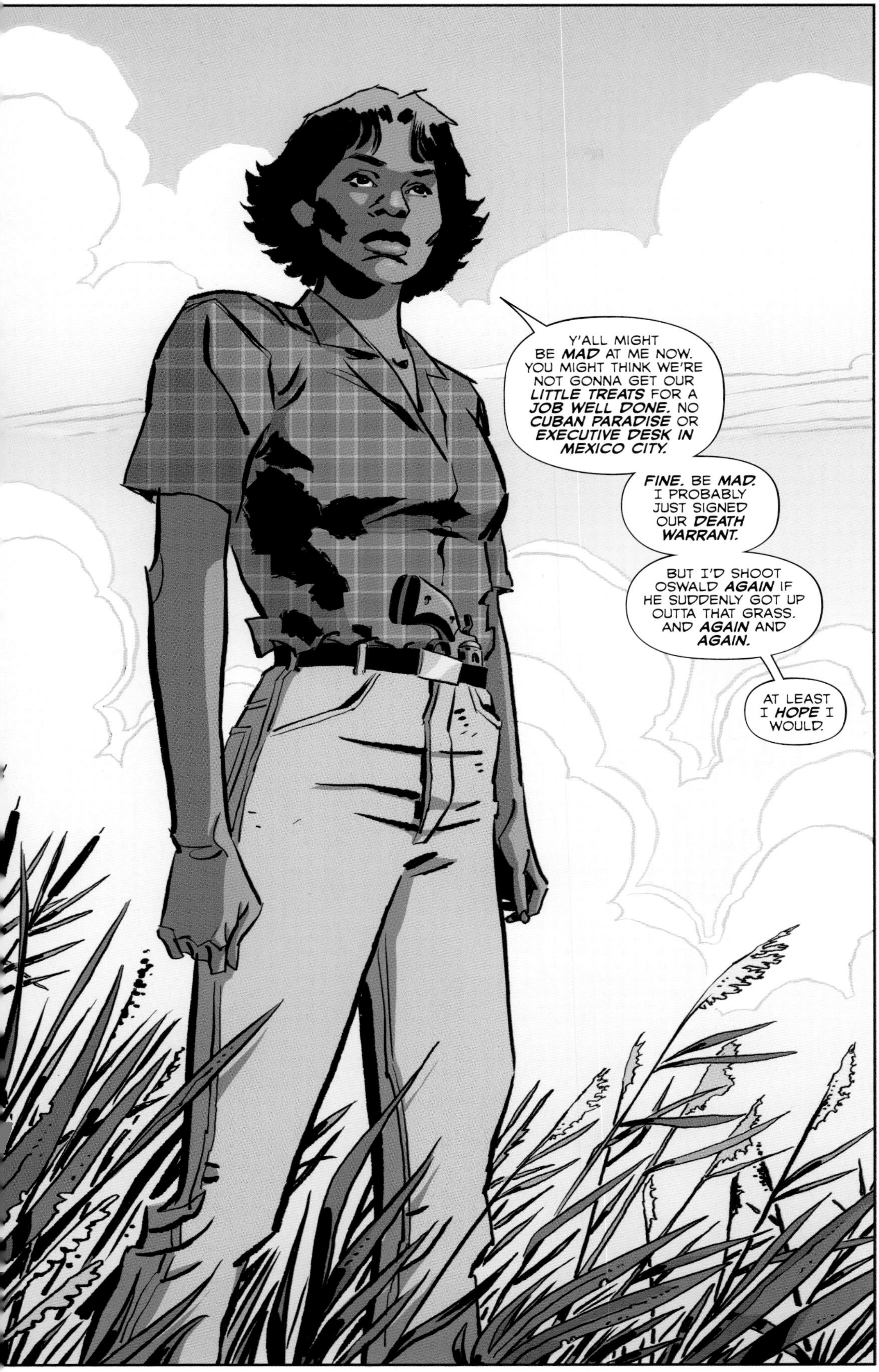
Y'ALL MIGHT BE MAD AT ME NOW. YOU MIGHT THINK WE'RE NOT GONNA GET OUR LITTLE TREATS FOR A JOB WELL DONE. NO CUBAN PARADISE OR EXECUTIVE DESK IN MEXICO CITY.
FINE. BE MAD. I PROBABLY JUST SIGNED OUR DEATH WARRANT.
BUT I'D SHOOT OSWALD AGAIN IF HE SUDDENLY GOT UP OUTTA THAT GRASS. AND AGAIN AND AGAIN.
AT LEAST I HOPE I WOULD.

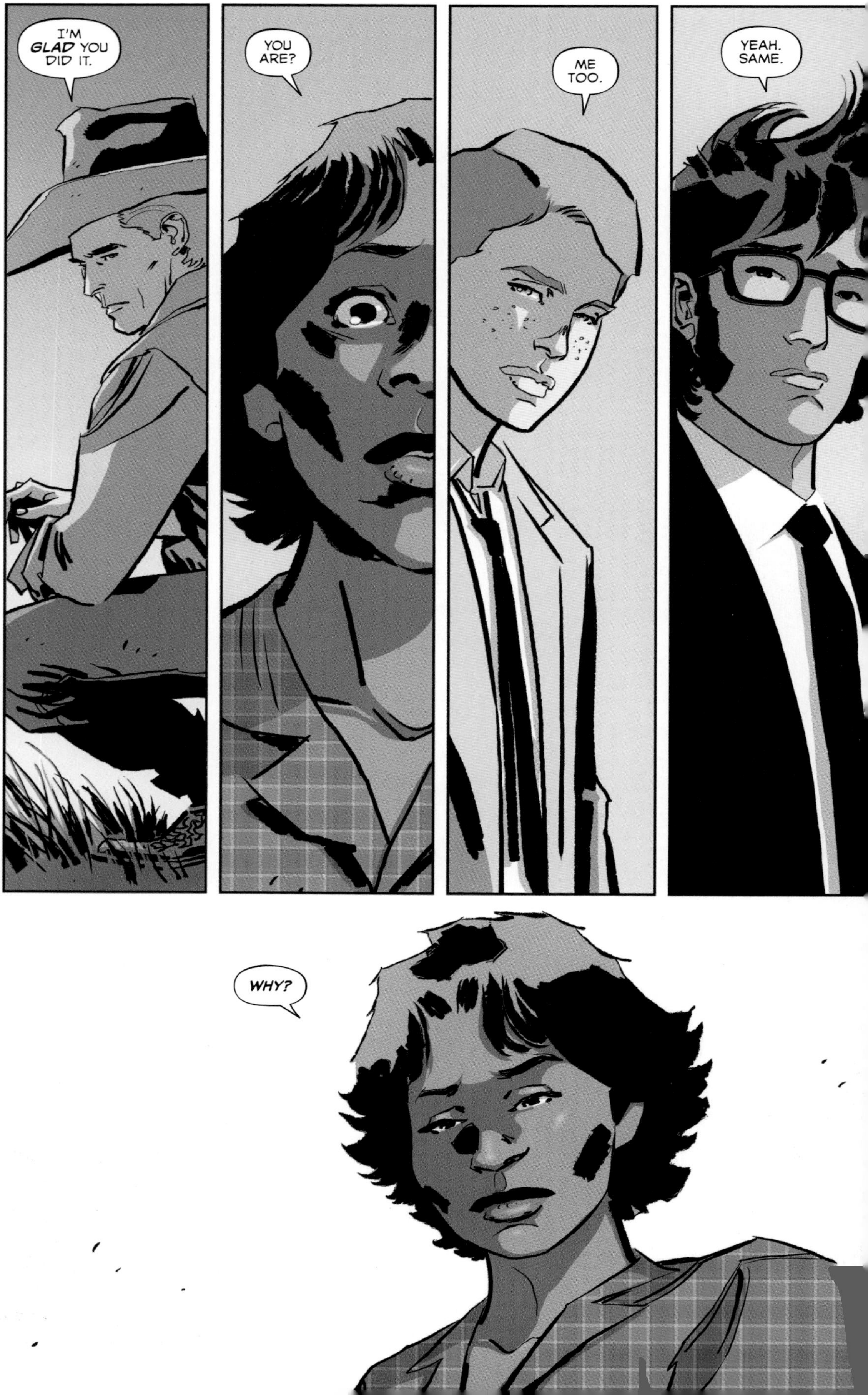
I'M **GLAD** YOU DID IT.
YOU ARE?
ME TOO.
YEAH. SAME.
WHY?

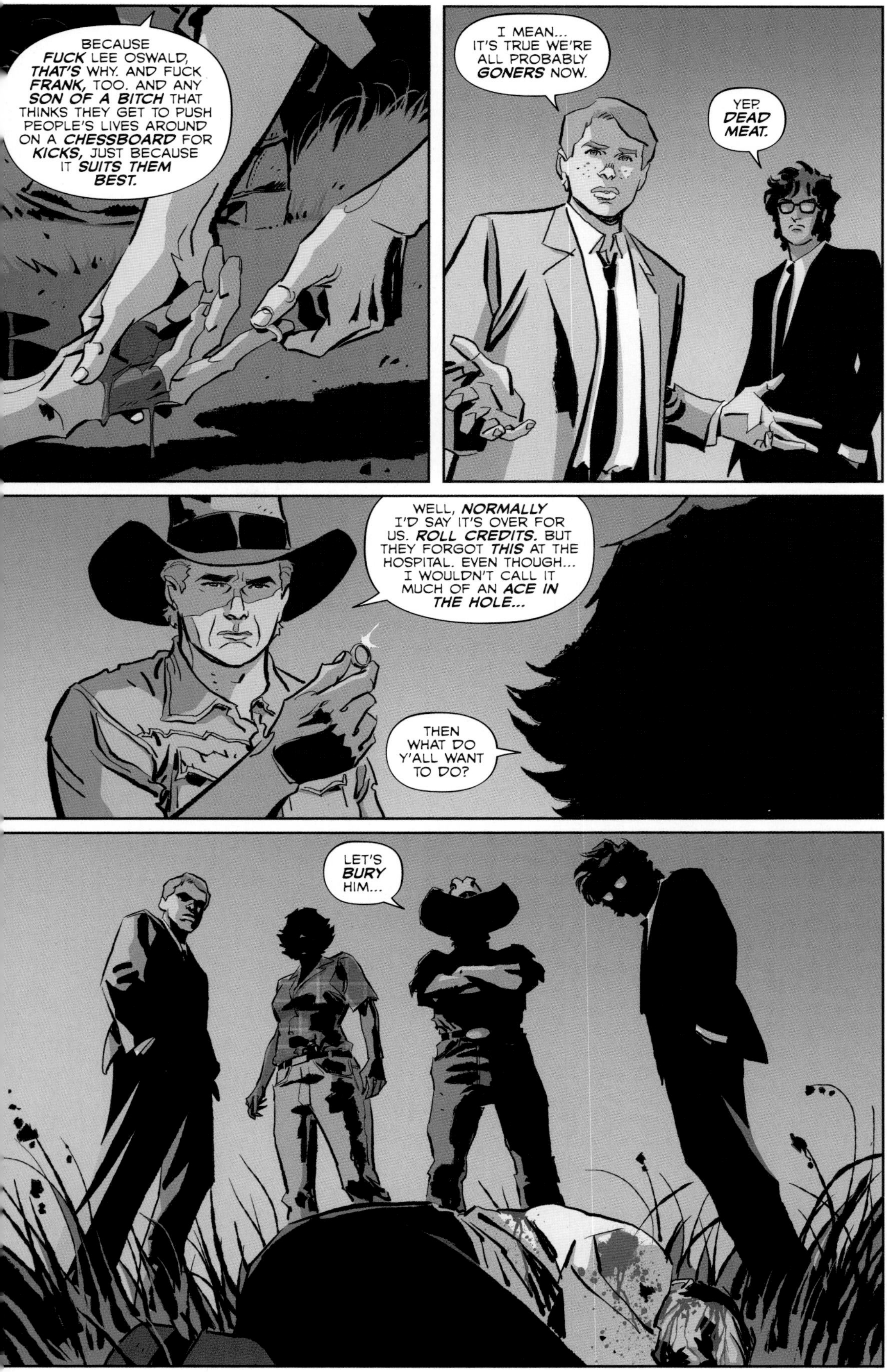
BECAUSE FUCK LEE OSWALD, THAT'S WHY. AND FUCK FRANK, TOO. AND ANY SON OF A BITCH THAT THINKS THEY GET TO PUSH PEOPLE'S LIVES AROUND ON A CHESSBOARD FOR KICKS, JUST BECAUSE IT SUITS THEM BEST.
I MEAN... IT'S TRUE WE'RE ALL PROBABLY GONERS NOW.
YEP. DEAD MEAT.
WELL, NORMALLY I'D SAY IT'S OVER FOR US. ROLL CREDITS. BUT THEY FORGOT THIS AT THE HOSPITAL. EVEN THOUGH... I WOULDN'T CALL IT MUCH OF AN ACE IN THE HOLE...
THEN WHAT DO Y'ALL WANT TO DO?
LET'S BURY HIM...

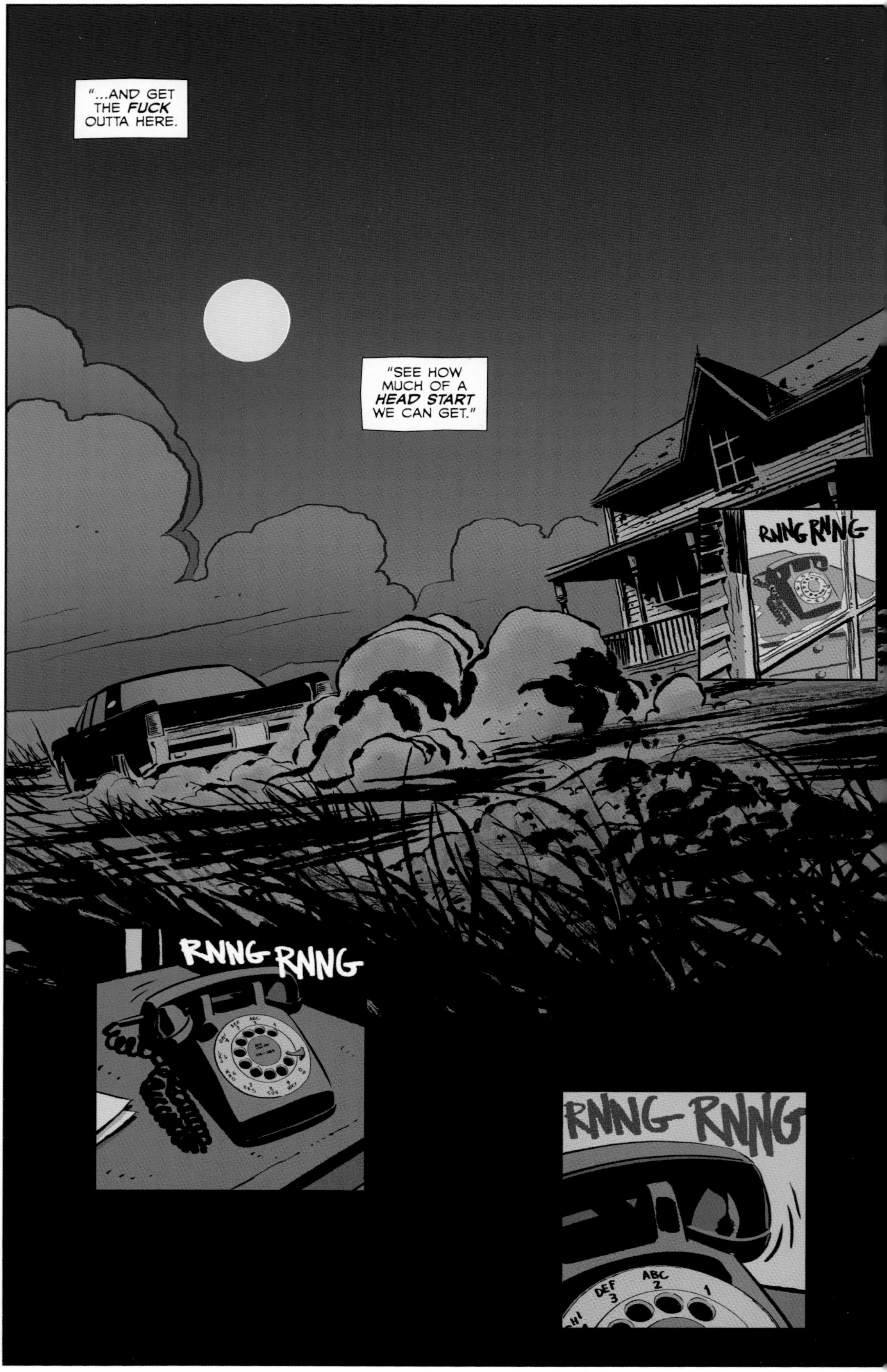
"...AND GET THE *FUCK* OUTTA HERE.
"SEE HOW MUCH OF A *HEAD START* WE CAN GET."
RNNG RNNG
RNNG RNNG
RNNG RNNG
ABC 2
DEF 3
1

Ring was found in cup on the nightstand.

Story goes he never took it off but did that morning and left it with some cash before going to work.

On body at time of burial.

No match second and third interior stamp inside the band but does have hammer and sickle.

Good here?

RCS

RALLO COLD STORAGE

Sonny,

After failure to show for your shift over the last three days, your loading position with RCS is hereby terminated. Last check will be mailed to address on file.

11/26/63

—Mgt

1008 COMMERCE, PHONE: EMERSON-723

Rose Hill Burial Park. Fort Worth, Texas. October 5th, 1981.

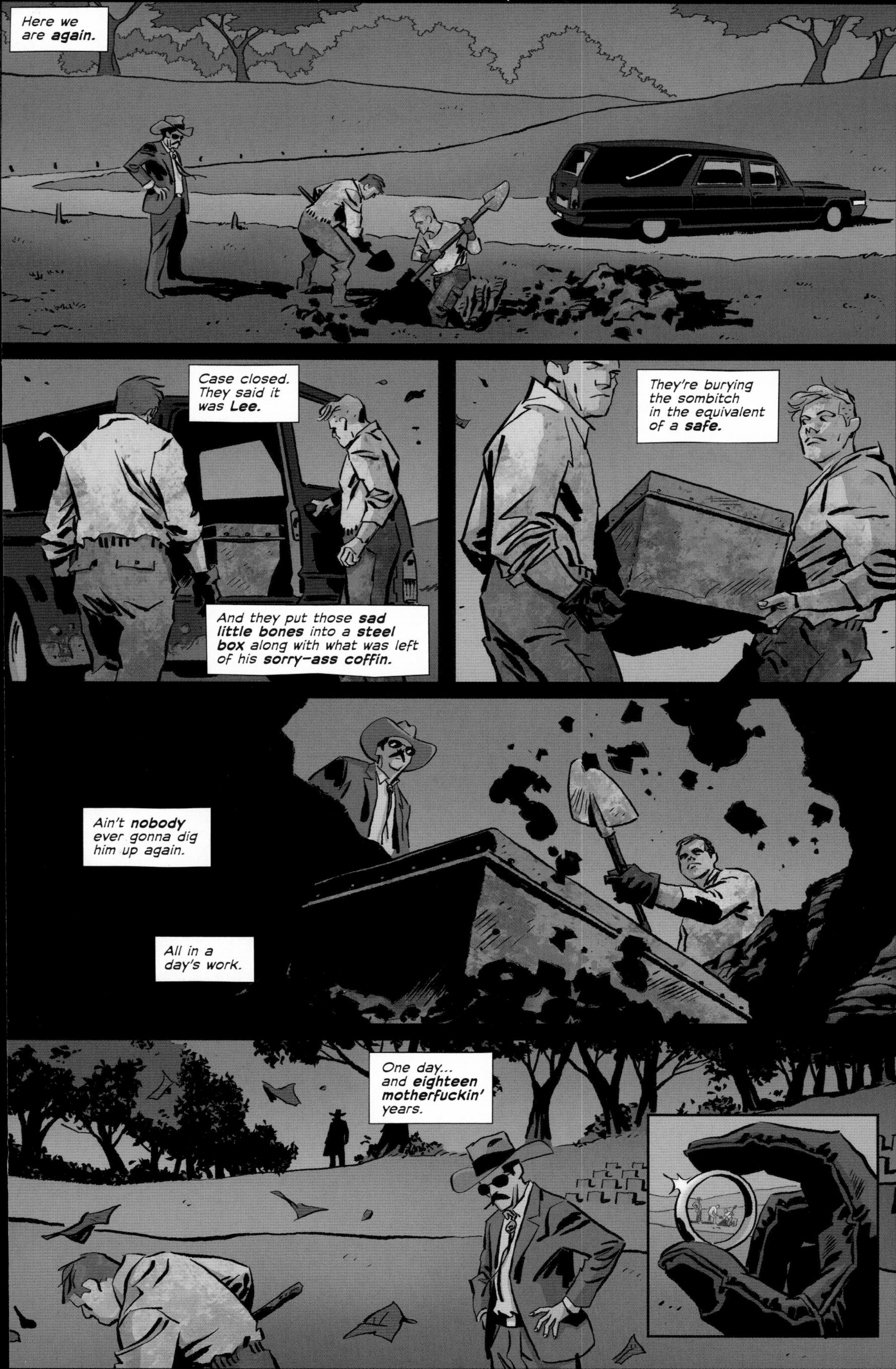

Here we are **again.**
Case closed. They said it was **Lee.**
And they put those **sad little bones** into a **steel box** along with what was left of his **sorry-ass coffin.**
They're burying the sombitch in the equivalent of a **safe.**
Ain't **nobody** ever gonna dig him up again.
All in a day's work.
One day... and **eighteen motherfuckin'** years.

Terlingua, Texas. November 26th, 1963.

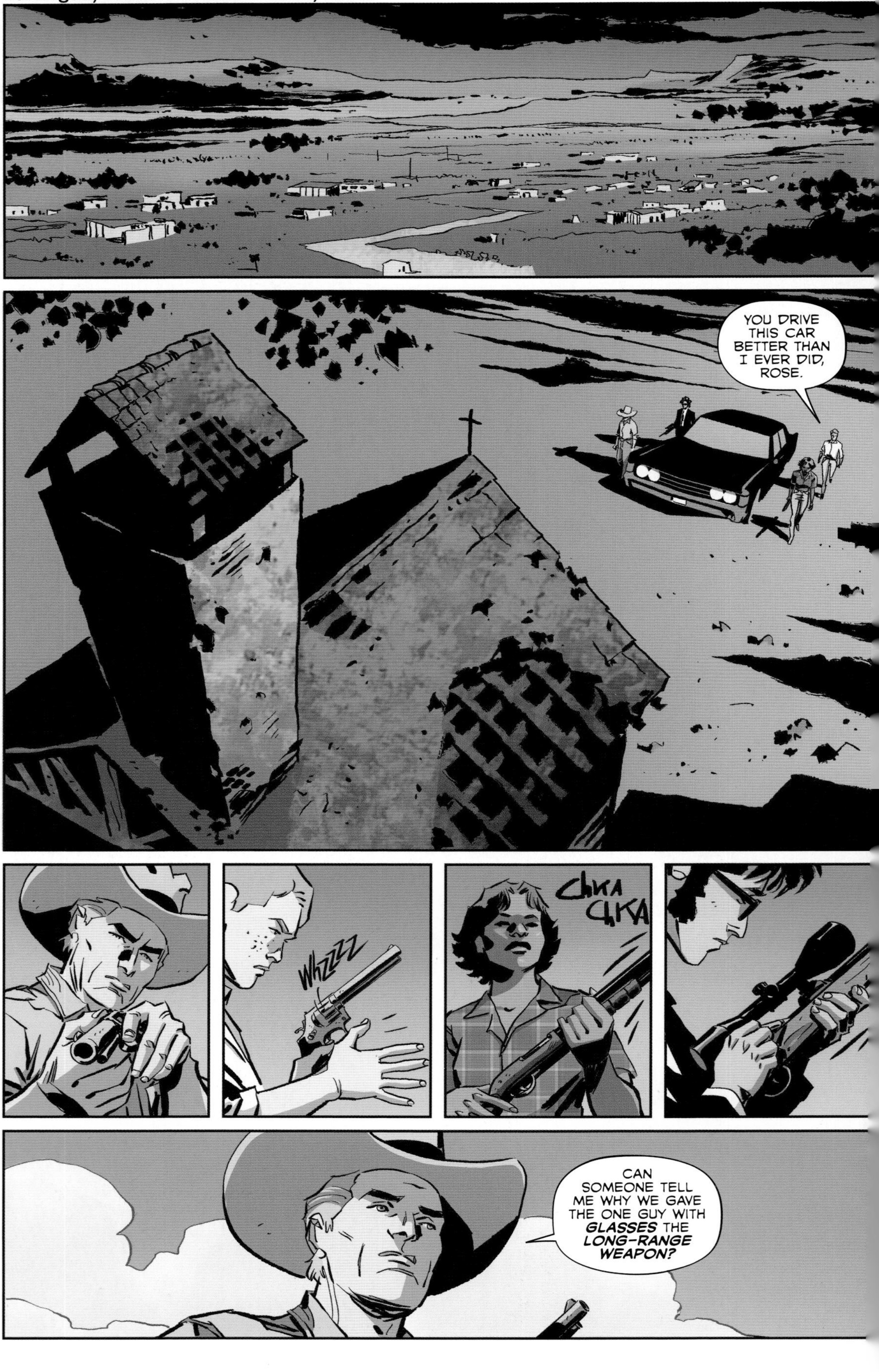
YOU DRIVE THIS CAR BETTER THAN I EVER DID, ROSE.
WhZZZZ
ChKA ChKA
CAN SOMEONE TELL ME WHY WE GAVE THE ONE GUY WITH **GLASSES** THE **LONG-RANGE WEAPON?**

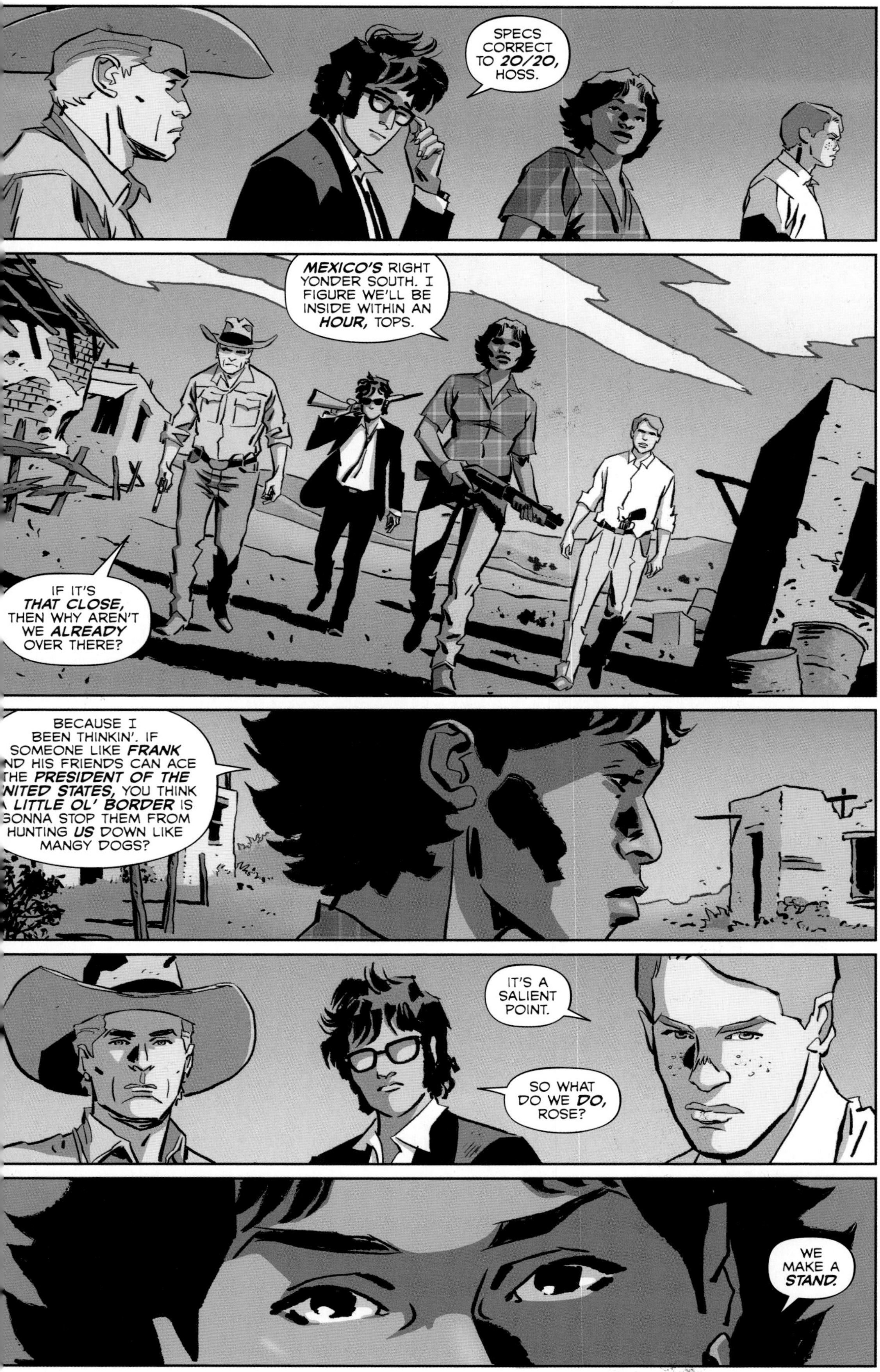

SPECS CORRECT TO 20/20, HOSS.
MEXICO'S RIGHT YONDER SOUTH. I FIGURE WE'LL BE INSIDE WITHIN AN HOUR, TOPS.
IF IT'S THAT CLOSE, THEN WHY AREN'T WE ALREADY OVER THERE?
BECAUSE I BEEN THINKIN'. IF SOMEONE LIKE FRANK ND HIS FRIENDS CAN ACE THE PRESIDENT OF THE NITED STATES, YOU THINK LITTLE OL' BORDER IS GONNA STOP THEM FROM HUNTING US DOWN LIKE MANGY DOGS?
IT'S A SALIENT POINT.
SO WHAT DO WE DO, ROSE?
WE MAKE A STAND.

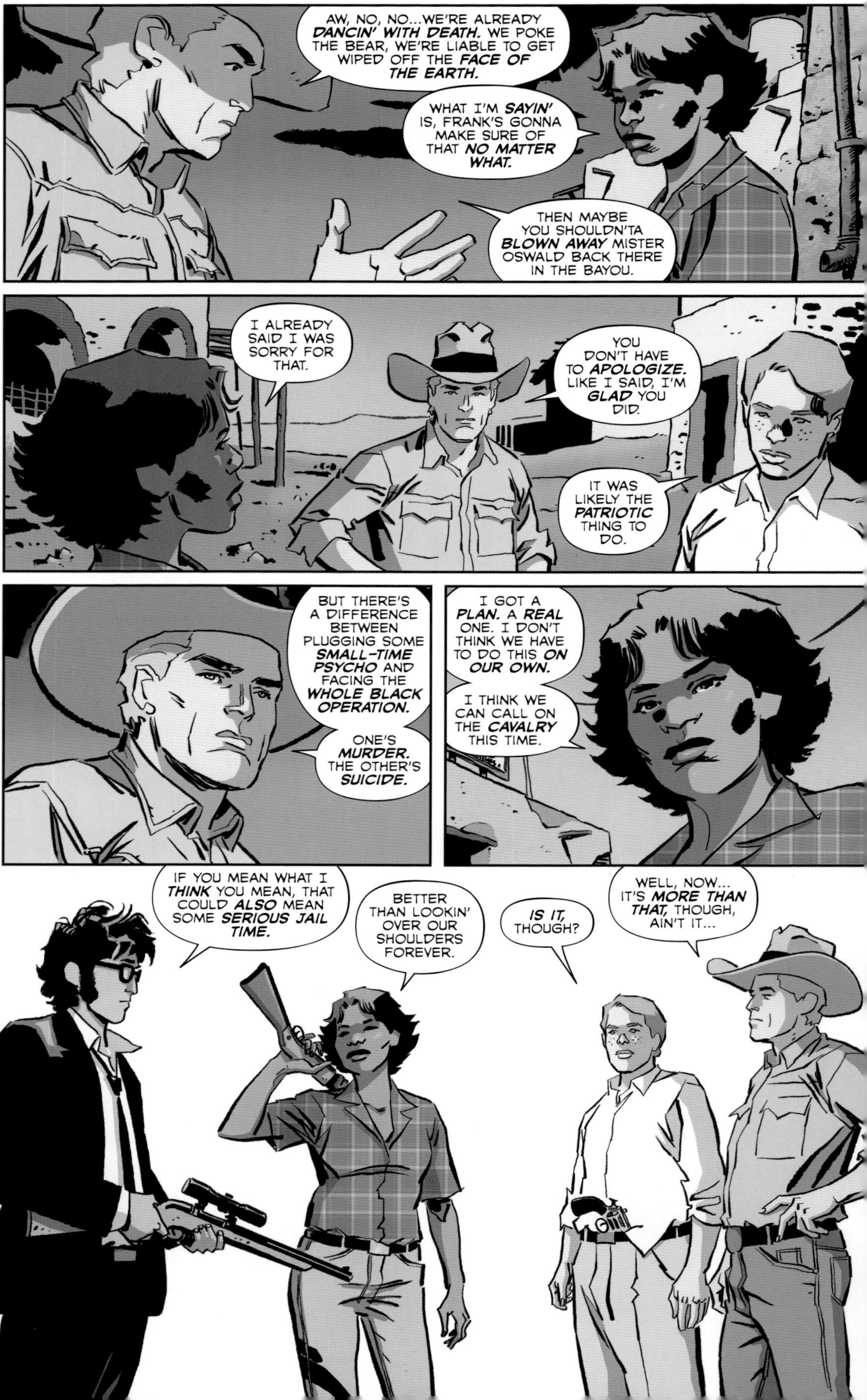
AW, NO, NO...WE'RE ALREADY DANCIN' WITH DEATH. WE POKE THE BEAR, WE'RE LIABLE TO GET WIPED OFF THE FACE OF THE EARTH.
WHAT I'M SAYIN' IS, FRANK'S GONNA MAKE SURE OF THAT NO MATTER WHAT.
THEN MAYBE YOU SHOULDN'TA BLOWN AWAY MISTER OSWALD BACK THERE IN THE BAYOU.
I ALREADY SAID I WAS SORRY FOR THAT.
YOU DON'T HAVE TO APOLOGIZE. LIKE I SAID, I'M GLAD YOU DID.
IT WAS LIKELY THE PATRIOTIC THING TO DO.
BUT THERE'S A DIFFERENCE BETWEEN PLUGGING SOME SMALL-TIME PSYCHO AND FACING THE WHOLE BLACK OPERATION.
ONE'S MURDER. THE OTHER'S SUICIDE.
I GOT A PLAN. A REAL ONE. I DON'T THINK WE HAVE TO DO THIS ON OUR OWN.
I THINK WE CAN CALL ON THE CAVALRY THIS TIME.
IF YOU MEAN WHAT I THINK YOU MEAN, THAT COULD ALSO MEAN SOME SERIOUS JAIL TIME.
BETTER THAN LOOKIN' OVER OUR SHOULDERS FOREVER.
IS IT, THOUGH?
WELL, NOW... IT'S MORE THAN THAT, THOUGH, AIN'T IT...

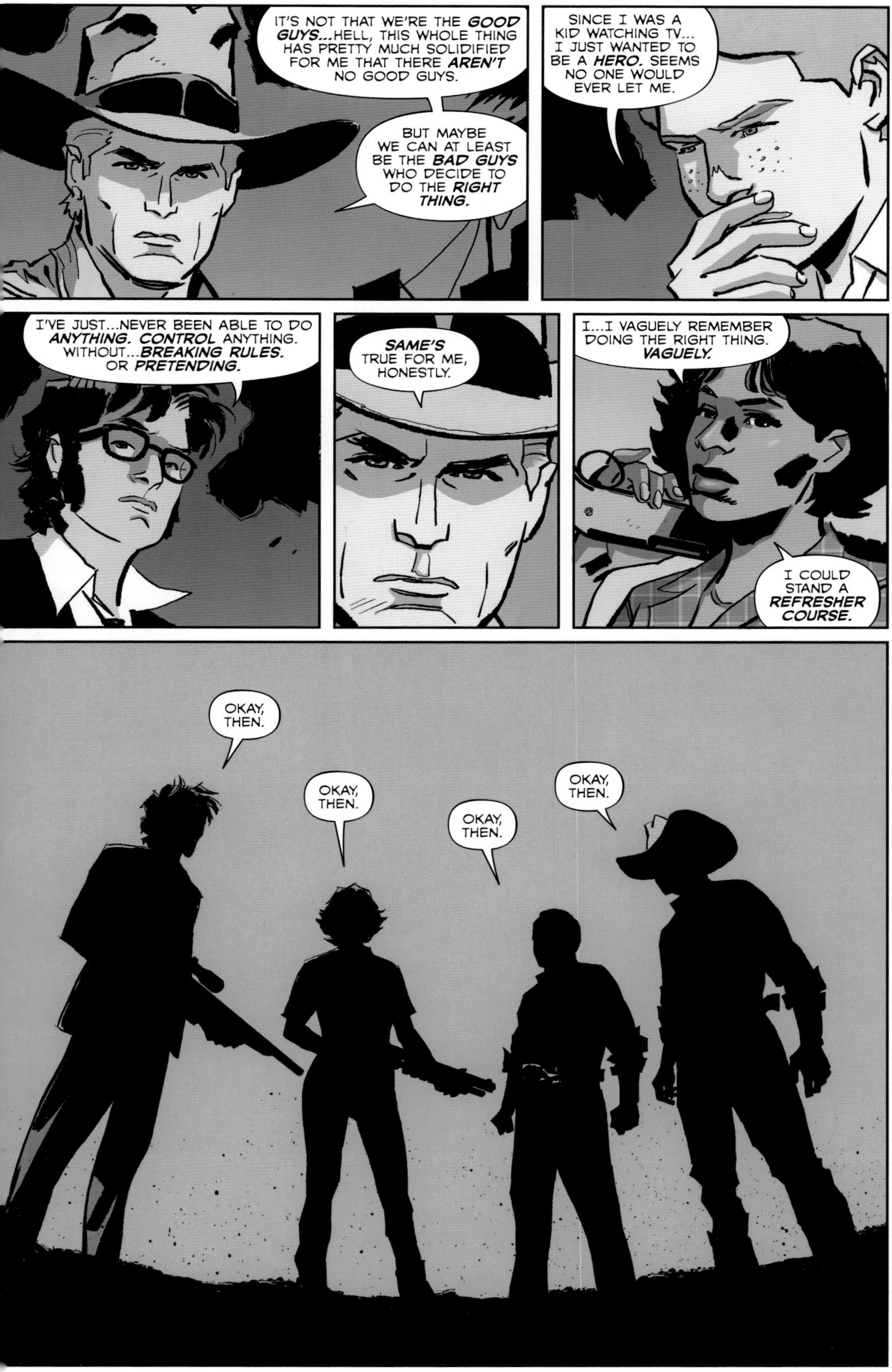
IT'S NOT THAT WE'RE THE GOOD GUYS...HELL, THIS WHOLE THING HAS PRETTY MUCH SOLIDIFIED FOR ME THAT THERE AREN'T NO GOOD GUYS.
BUT MAYBE WE CAN AT LEAST BE THE BAD GUYS WHO DECIDE TO DO THE RIGHT THING.
SINCE I WAS A KID WATCHING TV... I JUST WANTED TO BE A HERO. SEEMS NO ONE WOULD EVER LET ME.
I'VE JUST...NEVER BEEN ABLE TO DO ANYTHING. CONTROL ANYTHING. WITHOUT...BREAKING RULES. OR PRETENDING.
SAME'S TRUE FOR ME, HONESTLY.
I...I VAGUELY REMEMBER DOING THE RIGHT THING. VAGUELY.
I COULD STAND A REFRESHER COURSE.
OKAY, THEN.
OKAY, THEN.
OKAY, THEN.
OKAY, THEN.

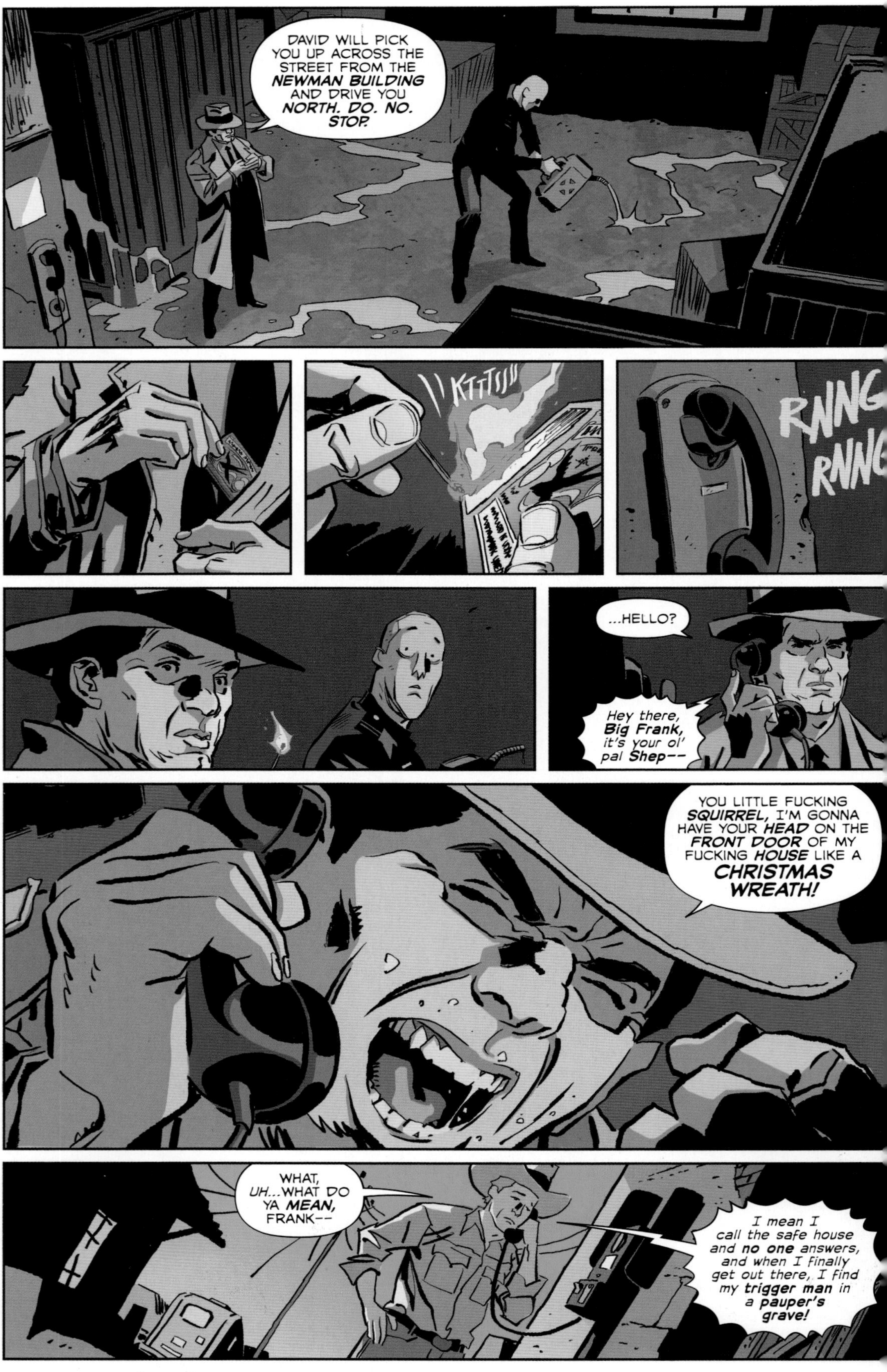
DAVID WILL PICK YOU UP ACROSS THE STREET FROM THE NEWMAN BUILDING AND DRIVE YOU NORTH. DO. NO. STOP.
KTTTSSS
RNNG RNNG
...HELLO?
Hey there, Big Frank, it's your ol' pal Shep--
YOU LITTLE FUCKING SQUIRREL, I'M GONNA HAVE YOUR HEAD ON THE FRONT DOOR OF MY FUCKING HOUSE LIKE A CHRISTMAS WREATH!
WHAT, UH...WHAT DO YA MEAN, FRANK--
I mean I call the safe house and no one answers, and when I finally get out there, I find my trigger man in a pauper's grave!

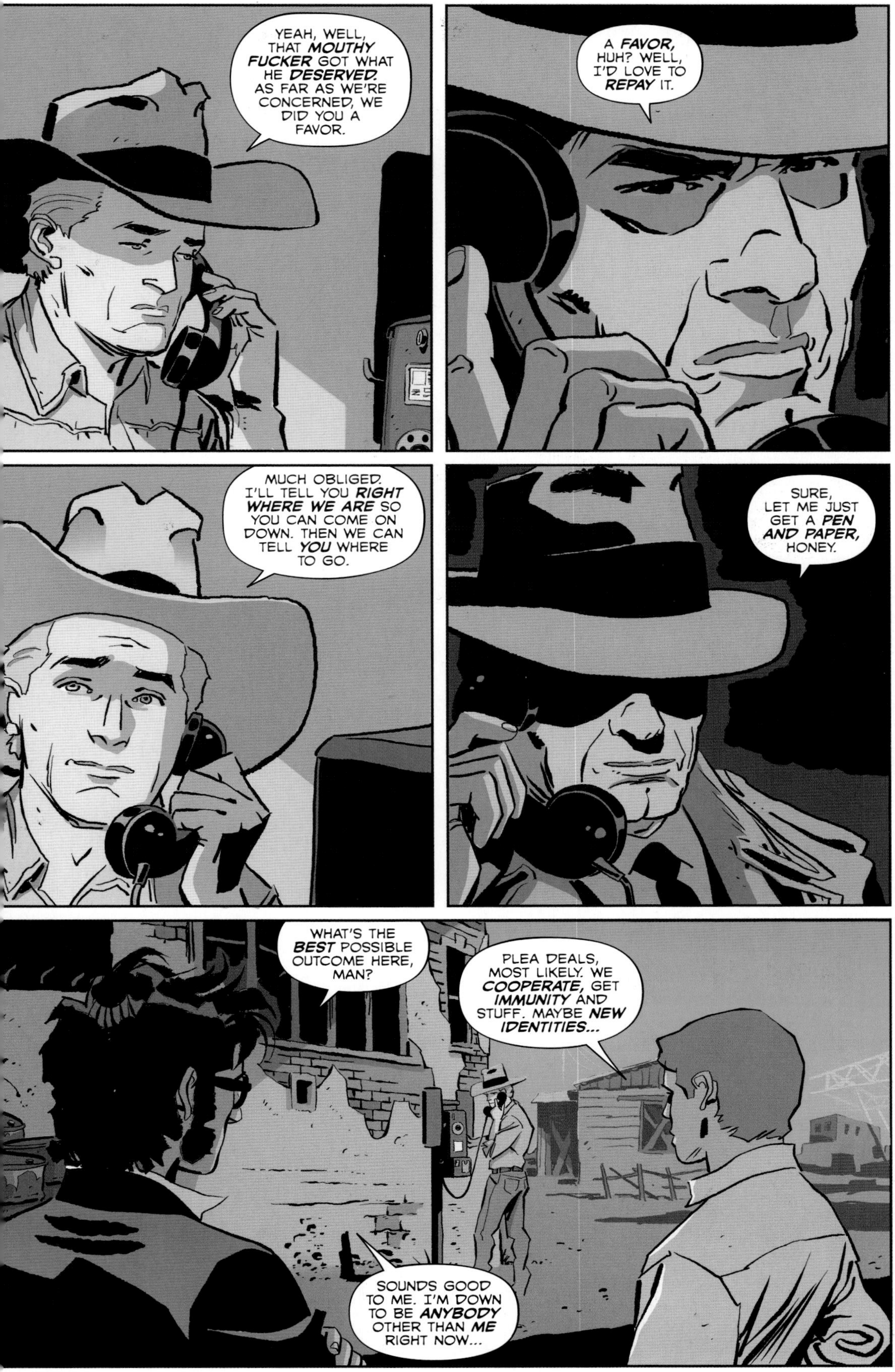
YEAH, WELL, THAT MOUTHY FUCKER GOT WHAT HE DESERVED. AS FAR AS WE'RE CONCERNED, WE DID YOU A FAVOR.
A FAVOR, HUH? WELL, I'D LOVE TO REPAY IT.
MUCH OBLIGED. I'LL TELL YOU RIGHT WHERE WE ARE SO YOU CAN COME ON DOWN. THEN WE CAN TELL YOU WHERE TO GO.
SURE, LET ME JUST GET A PEN AND PAPER, HONEY.
WHAT'S THE BEST POSSIBLE OUTCOME HERE, MAN?
PLEA DEALS, MOST LIKELY. WE COOPERATE, GET IMMUNITY AND STUFF. MAYBE NEW IDENTITIES...
SOUNDS GOOD TO ME. I'M DOWN TO BE ANYBODY OTHER THAN ME RIGHT NOW...

AGENT HOFFSTETTER.

I got something to share with you about the *murder of President Kennedy.*

MMMKAY...

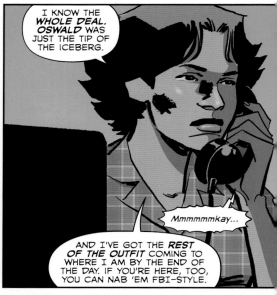

I KNOW THE *WHOLE DEAL. OSWALD* WAS JUST THE TIP OF THE ICEBERG.

Mmmmmmkay...

AND I'VE GOT THE *REST OF THE OUTFIT* COMING TO WHERE I AM BY THE END OF THE DAY. IF YOU'RE HERE, TOO, YOU CAN NAB 'EM FBI-STYLE.

WHAT'S YOUR NAME, MISS?

Just call me Yellow...um. Yellow...*Brick. Road.*

MMKAY, *MISS YELLOW BRICK ROAD,* WHERE ARE YOU EXACTLY?

LOOK, I KNOW YOU THINK I'M SOME *KOOK,* BUT THIS IS *LEGIT.* AND I'VE GOT *EVIDENCE* RIGHT HERE TO PROVE IT.

WHAT EVIDENCE DO YOU HAVE, MISS YELLOW BRICK ROAD?

I've got verifiable personal effects of one *Lee Harvey Oswald.* Shit that should be on his rotten body in the *dirt* right now.

IT'S IN *MY HANDS* BECAUSE THAT'S *NOT* LEE IN THAT DIRT. HE'S IN *DIFFERENT* DIRT...I MEAN...THE GUY *Y'ALL* BURIED... *FUCK.* JUST...

TERLINGUA, TEXAS. C'MON, G-MAN. MAKE YOUR CAREER TONIGHT.

HERE I COULDN'T WAIT TO GET OUTTA *MADISON*, AND NOW I'M GONNA *DIE* IN SOME FUCKIN' MEXICAN STANDOFF.

WHAT'S A *MEXICAN STANDOFF?*

IT'S WHEN EVERY PARTY IN A GIVEN SITUATION IS SIMULTANEOUSLY *BACKED UP AGAINST A WALL* BUT ALSO CAPABLE OF *VIOLENTLY THREATENING* THE OTHER PARTIES. *NOBODY* WINS.

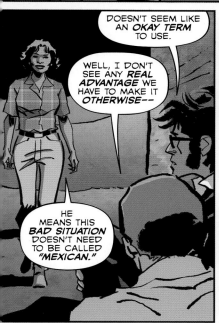

DOESN'T SEEM LIKE AN *OKAY TERM* TO USE.

WELL, I DON'T SEE ANY *REAL ADVANTAGE* WE HAVE TO MAKE IT *OTHERWISE--*

HE MEANS THIS *BAD SITUATION* DOESN'T NEED TO BE CALLED "MEXICAN."

WHAT'D THEY SAY?

THEY SAID THEY'RE COMING. WHAT ABOUT *FRANK?*

OH, BY GOLLY, HE SAID THE SAME.

NONE OF US IS GONNA SEE OUR FAMILY AGAIN. NO MATTER *WHAT* HAPPENS.

GOOD.

FINE.

NO, I DON'T THINK SO, BUCK...

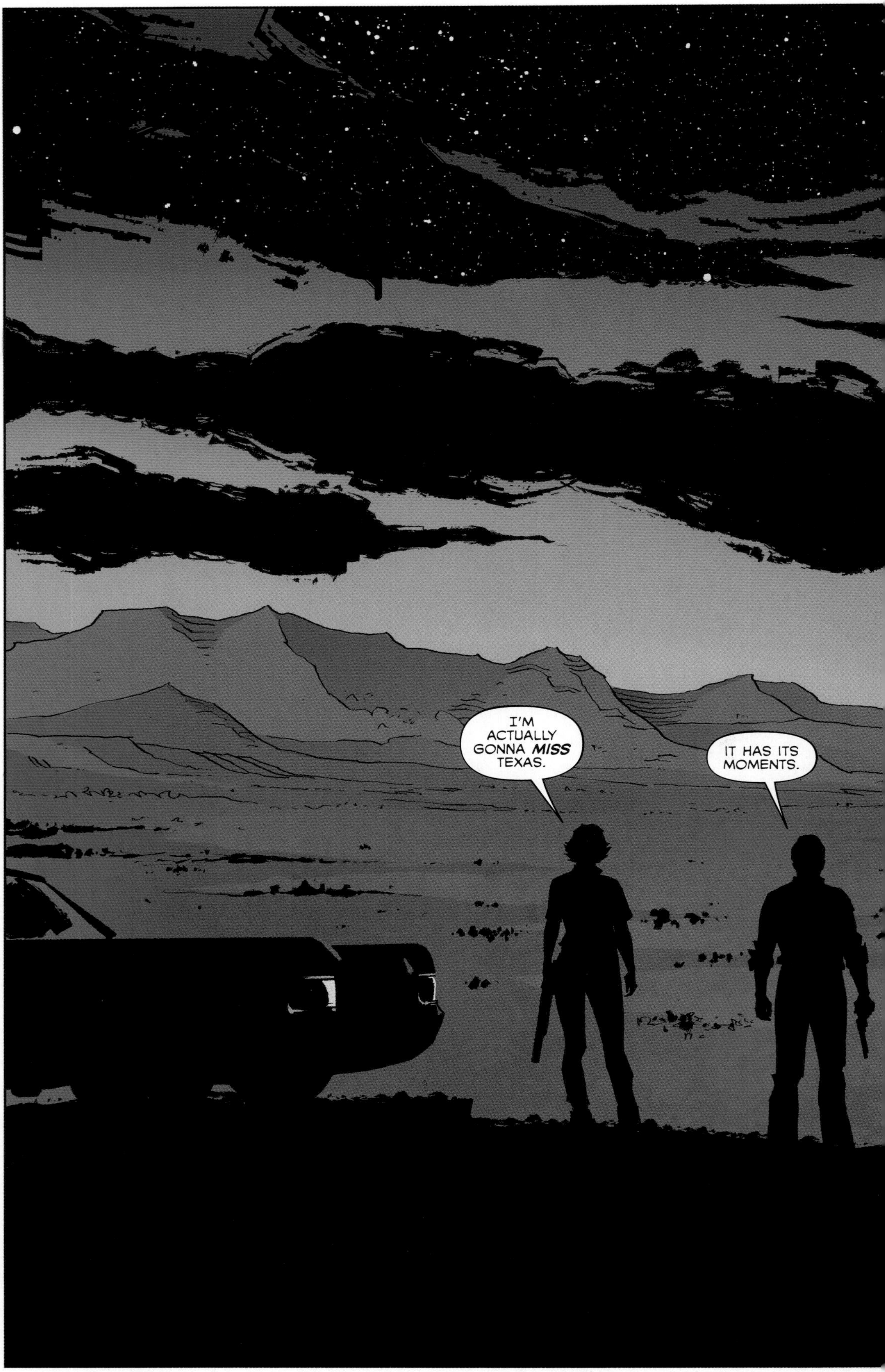
I'M ACTUALLY GONNA *MISS* TEXAS.
IT HAS ITS MOMENTS.

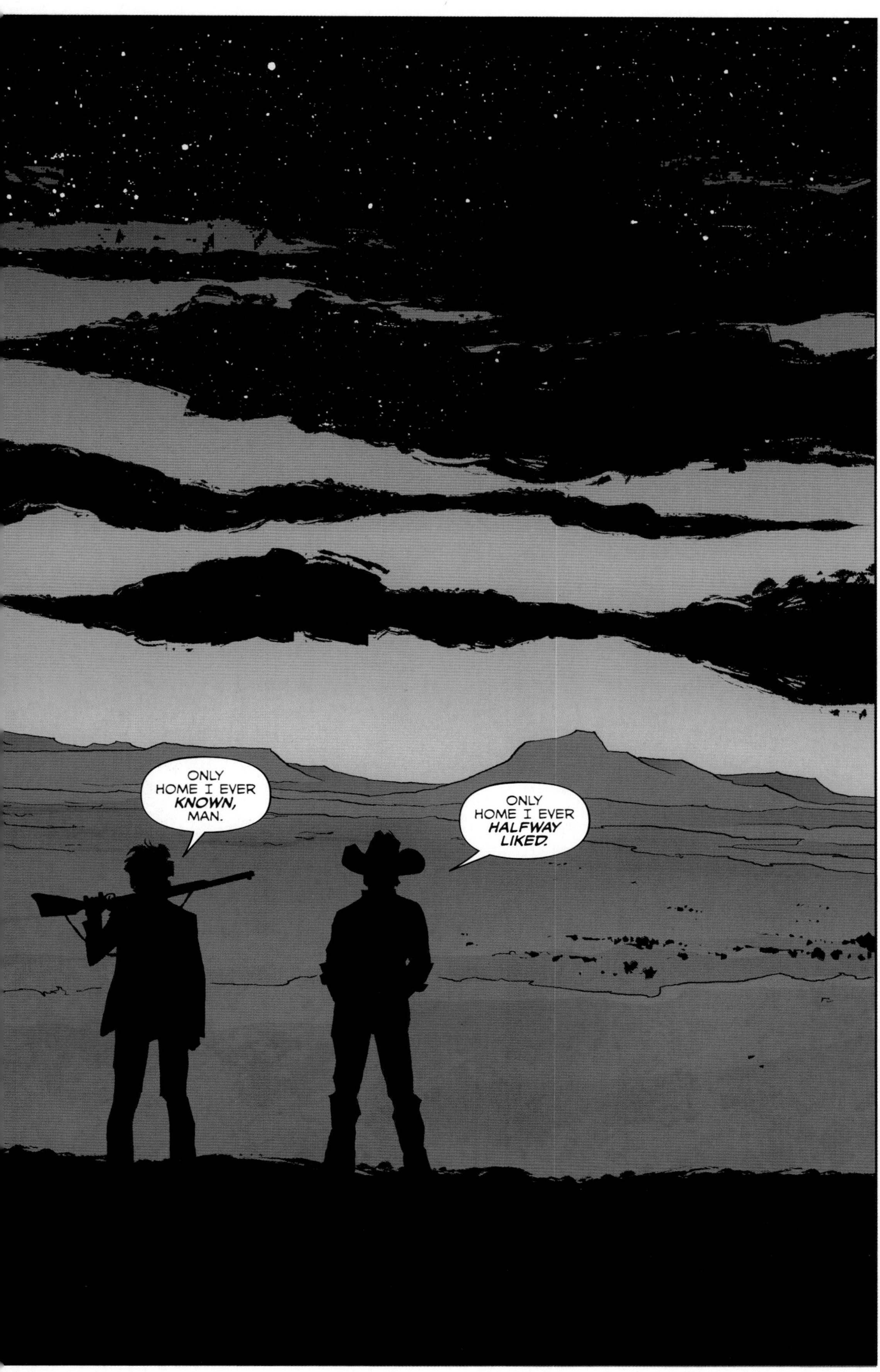
ONLY HOME I EVER KNOWN, MAN.
ONLY HOME I EVER HALFWAY LIKED.

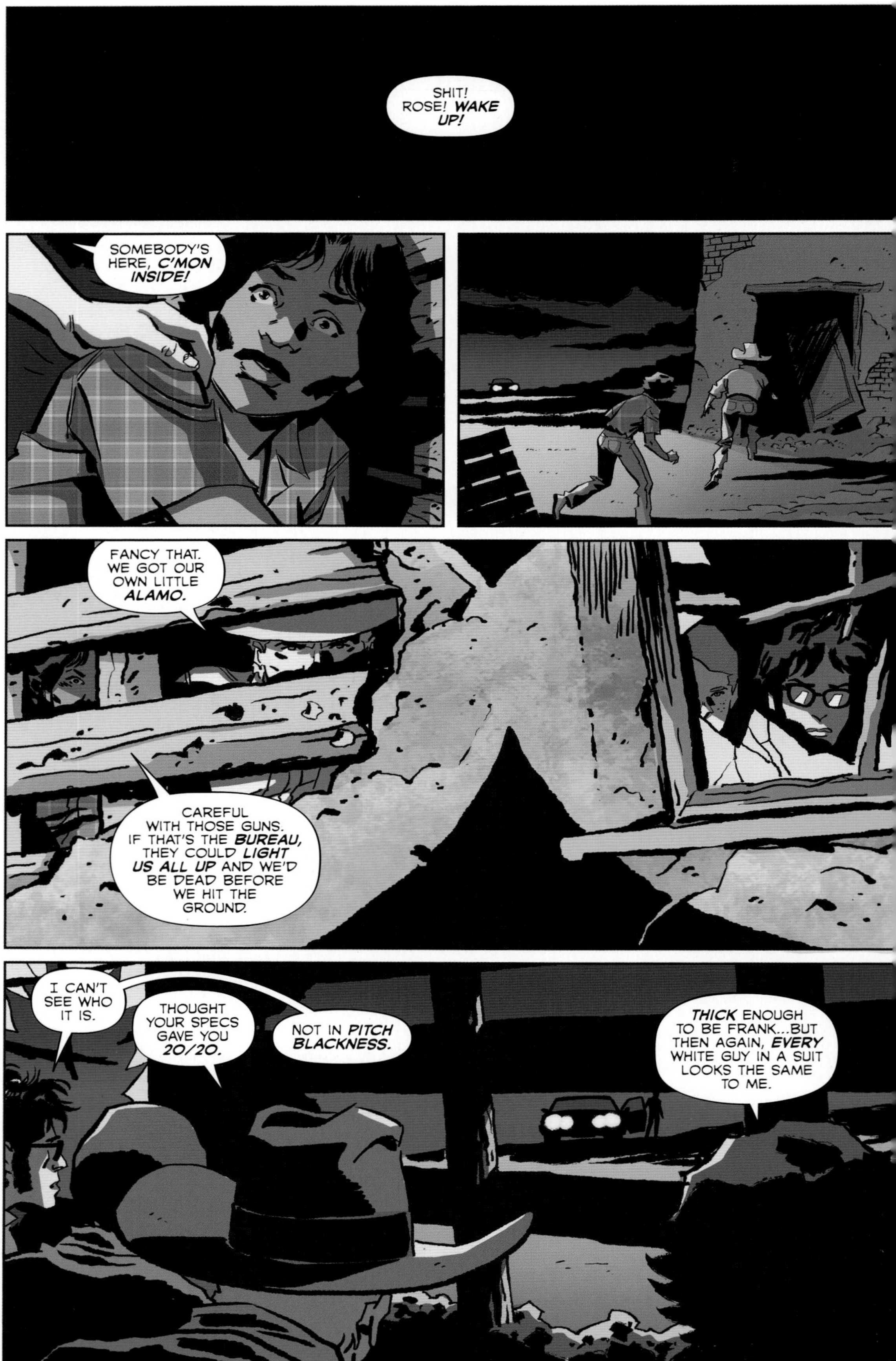
SHIT! ROSE! WAKE UP!
SOMEBODY'S HERE, C'MON INSIDE!
FANCY THAT. WE GOT OUR OWN LITTLE ALAMO.
CAREFUL WITH THOSE GUNS. IF THAT'S THE BUREAU, THEY COULD LIGHT US ALL UP AND WE'D BE DEAD BEFORE WE HIT THE GROUND.
I CAN'T SEE WHO IT IS.
THOUGHT YOUR SPECS GAVE YOU 20/20.
NOT IN PITCH BLACKNESS.
THICK ENOUGH TO BE FRANK...BUT THEN AGAIN, EVERY WHITE GUY IN A SUIT LOOKS THE SAME TO ME.

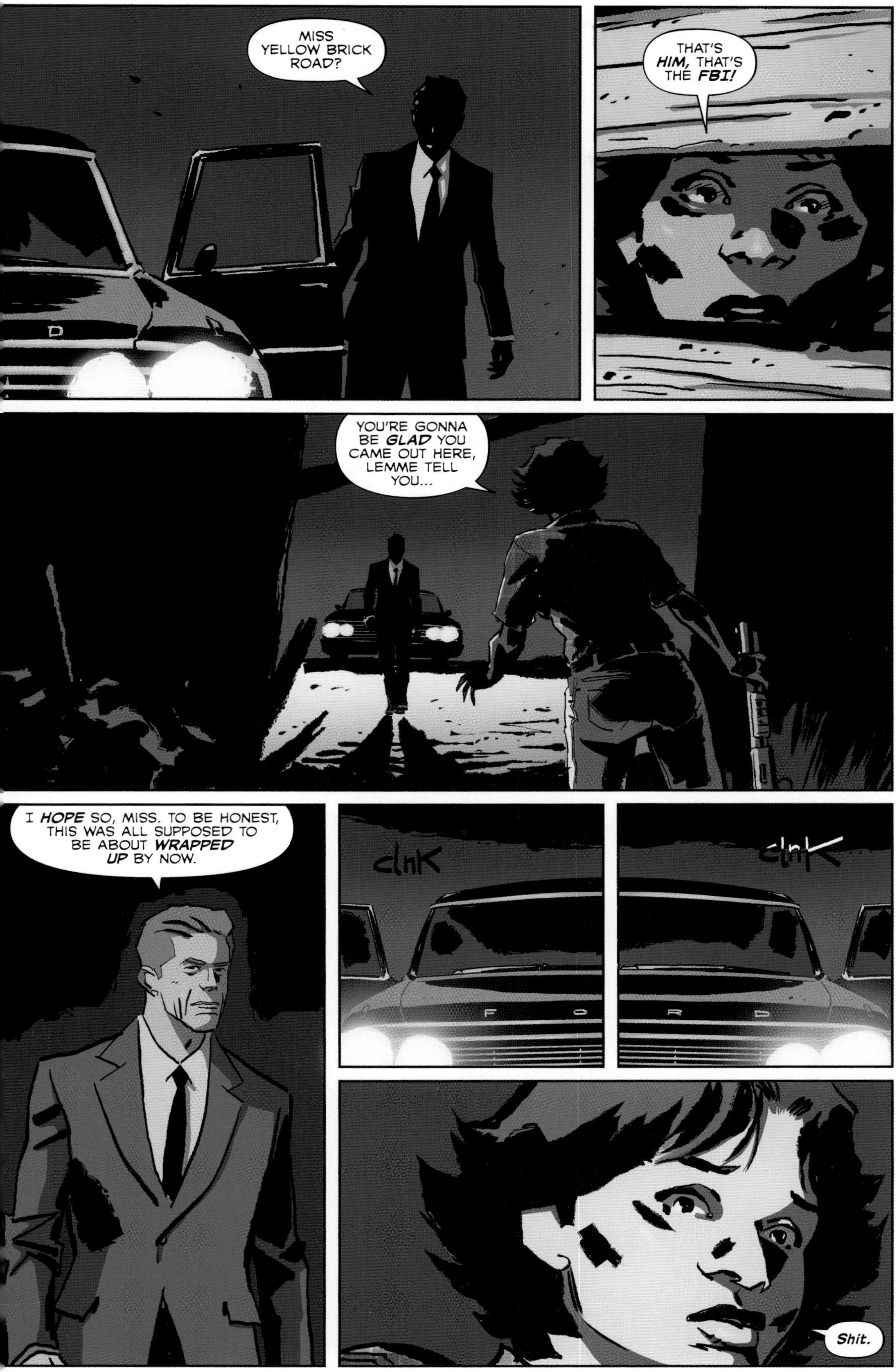
MISS YELLOW BRICK ROAD?
THAT'S HIM, THAT'S THE FBI!
YOU'RE GONNA BE GLAD YOU CAME OUT HERE, LEMME TELL YOU...
I HOPE SO, MISS. TO BE HONEST, THIS WAS ALL SUPPOSED TO BE ABOUT WRAPPED UP BY NOW.
clnk
FORD
clnk
Shit.

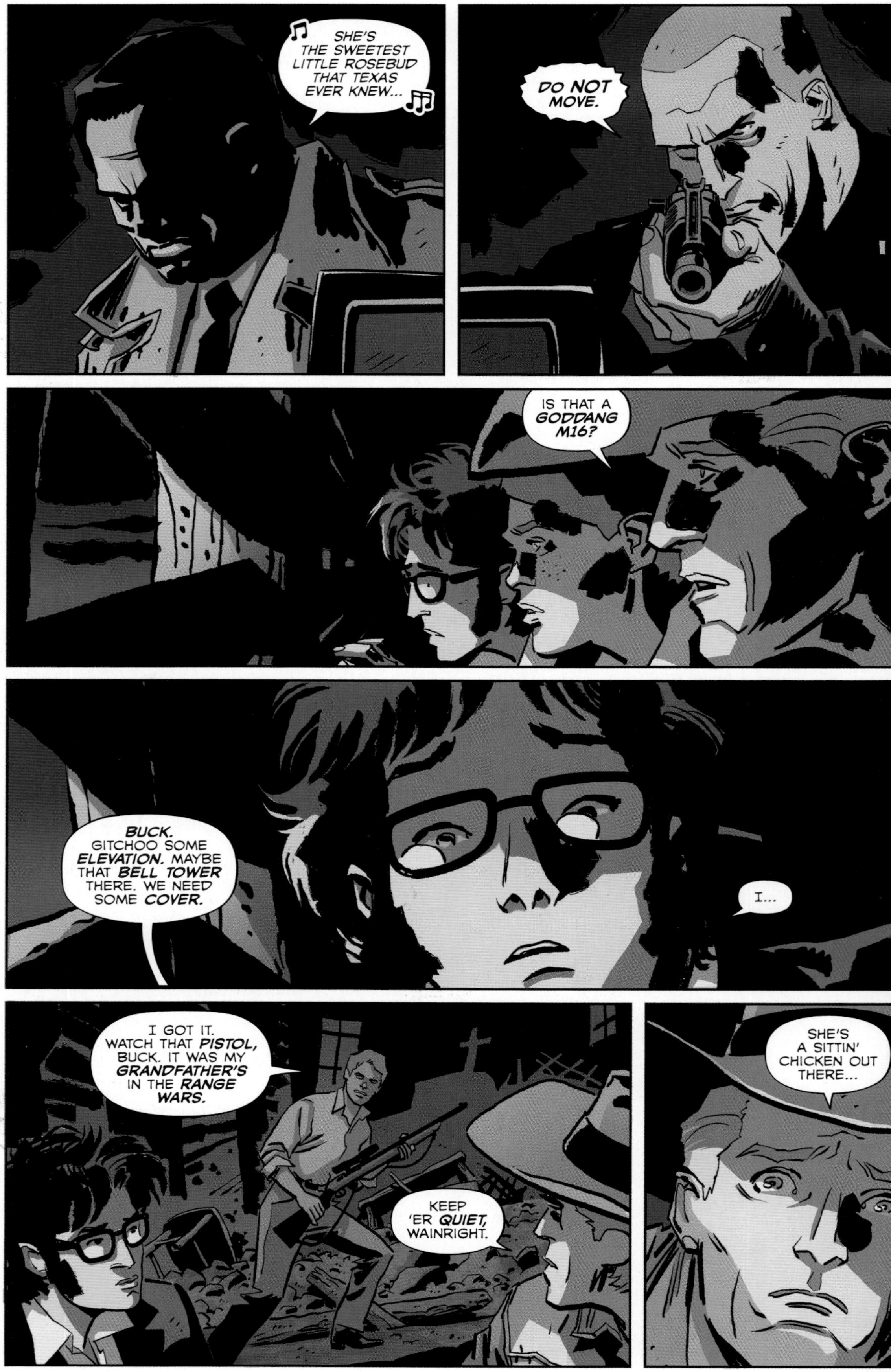
SHE'S THE SWEETEST LITTLE ROSEBUD THAT TEXAS EVER KNEW...
DO NOT MOVE.
IS THAT A GODDANG M16?
BUCK. GITCHOO SOME ELEVATION. MAYBE THAT BELL TOWER THERE. WE NEED SOME COVER.
I...
I GOT IT. WATCH THAT PISTOL, BUCK. IT WAS MY GRANDFATHER'S IN THE RANGE WARS.
KEEP 'ER QUIET, WAINRIGHT.
SHE'S A SITTIN' CHICKEN OUT THERE...

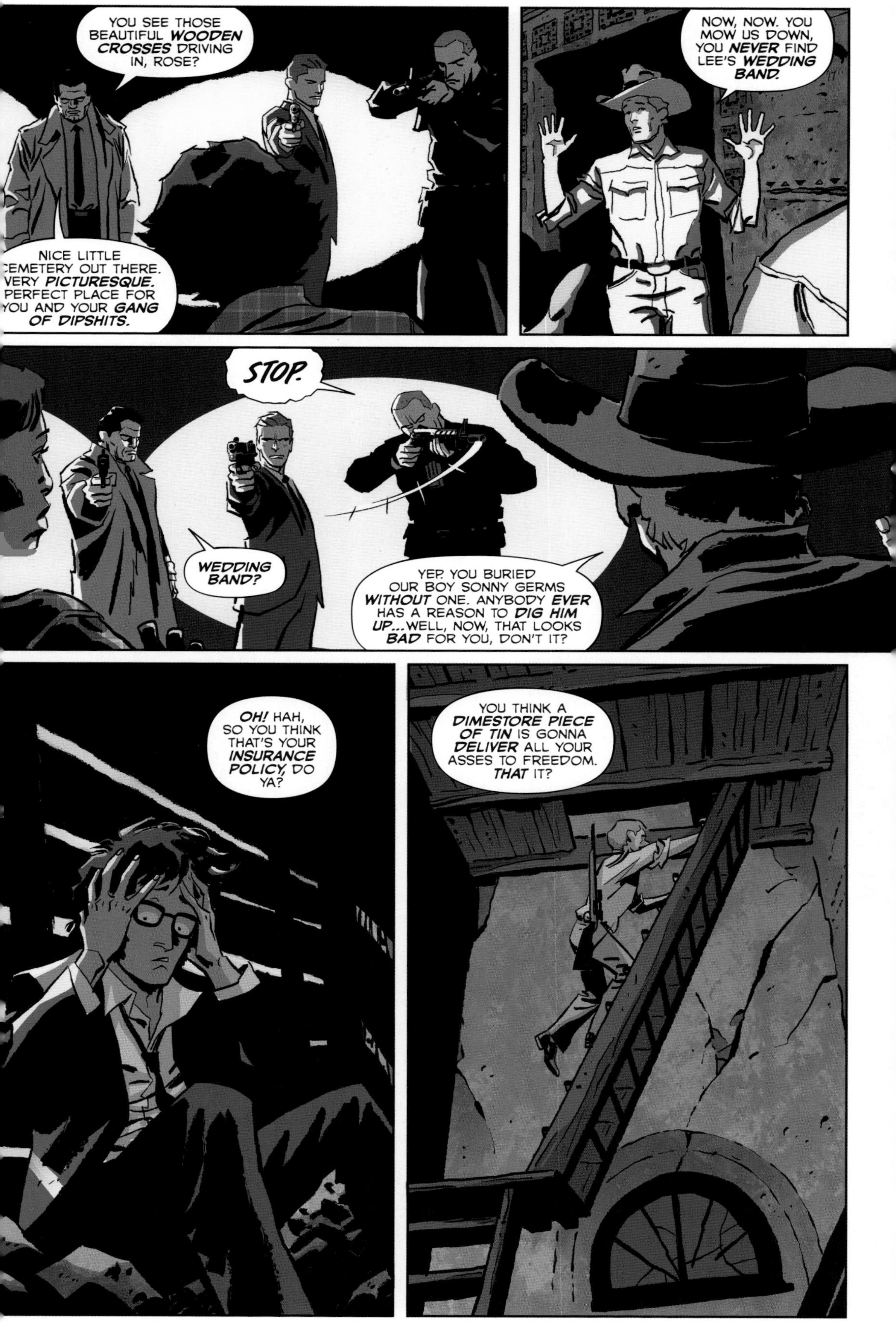
YOU SEE THOSE BEAUTIFUL WOODEN CROSSES DRIVING IN, ROSE?
NICE LITTLE CEMETERY OUT THERE. VERY PICTURESQUE. PERFECT PLACE FOR YOU AND YOUR GANG OF DIPSHITS.
NOW, NOW. YOU MOW US DOWN, YOU NEVER FIND LEE'S WEDDING BAND.
STOP.
WEDDING BAND?
YEP. YOU BURIED OUR BOY SONNY GERMS WITHOUT ONE. ANYBODY EVER HAS A REASON TO DIG HIM UP...WELL, NOW, THAT LOOKS BAD FOR YOU, DON'T IT?
OH! HAH, SO YOU THINK THAT'S YOUR INSURANCE POLICY, DO YA?
YOU THINK A DIMESTORE PIECE OF TIN IS GONNA DELIVER ALL YOUR ASSES TO FREEDOM. THAT IT?

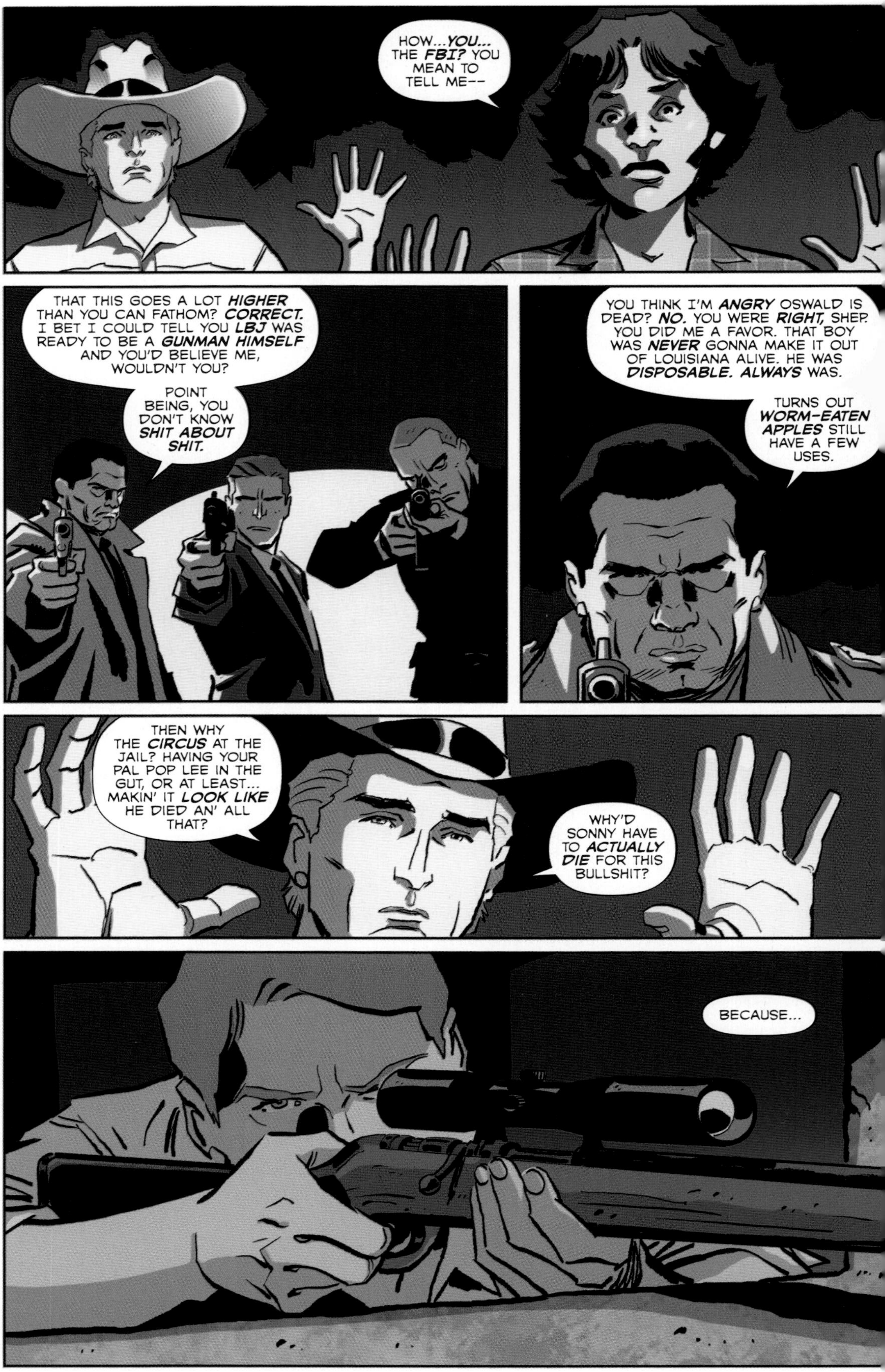
HOW...YOU... THE FBI? YOU MEAN TO TELL ME--
THAT THIS GOES A LOT HIGHER THAN YOU CAN FATHOM? CORRECT. I BET I COULD TELL YOU LBJ WAS READY TO BE A GUNMAN HIMSELF AND YOU'D BELIEVE ME, WOULDN'T YOU?
POINT BEING, YOU DON'T KNOW SHIT ABOUT SHIT.
YOU THINK I'M ANGRY OSWALD IS DEAD? NO. YOU WERE RIGHT, SHEP. YOU DID ME A FAVOR. THAT BOY WAS NEVER GONNA MAKE IT OUT OF LOUISIANA ALIVE. HE WAS DISPOSABLE. ALWAYS WAS.
TURNS OUT WORM-EATEN APPLES STILL HAVE A FEW USES.
THEN WHY THE CIRCUS AT THE JAIL? HAVING YOUR PAL POP LEE IN THE GUT, OR AT LEAST... MAKIN' IT LOOK LIKE HE DIED AN' ALL THAT?
WHY'D SONNY HAVE TO ACTUALLY DIE FOR THIS BULLSHIT?
BECAUSE...

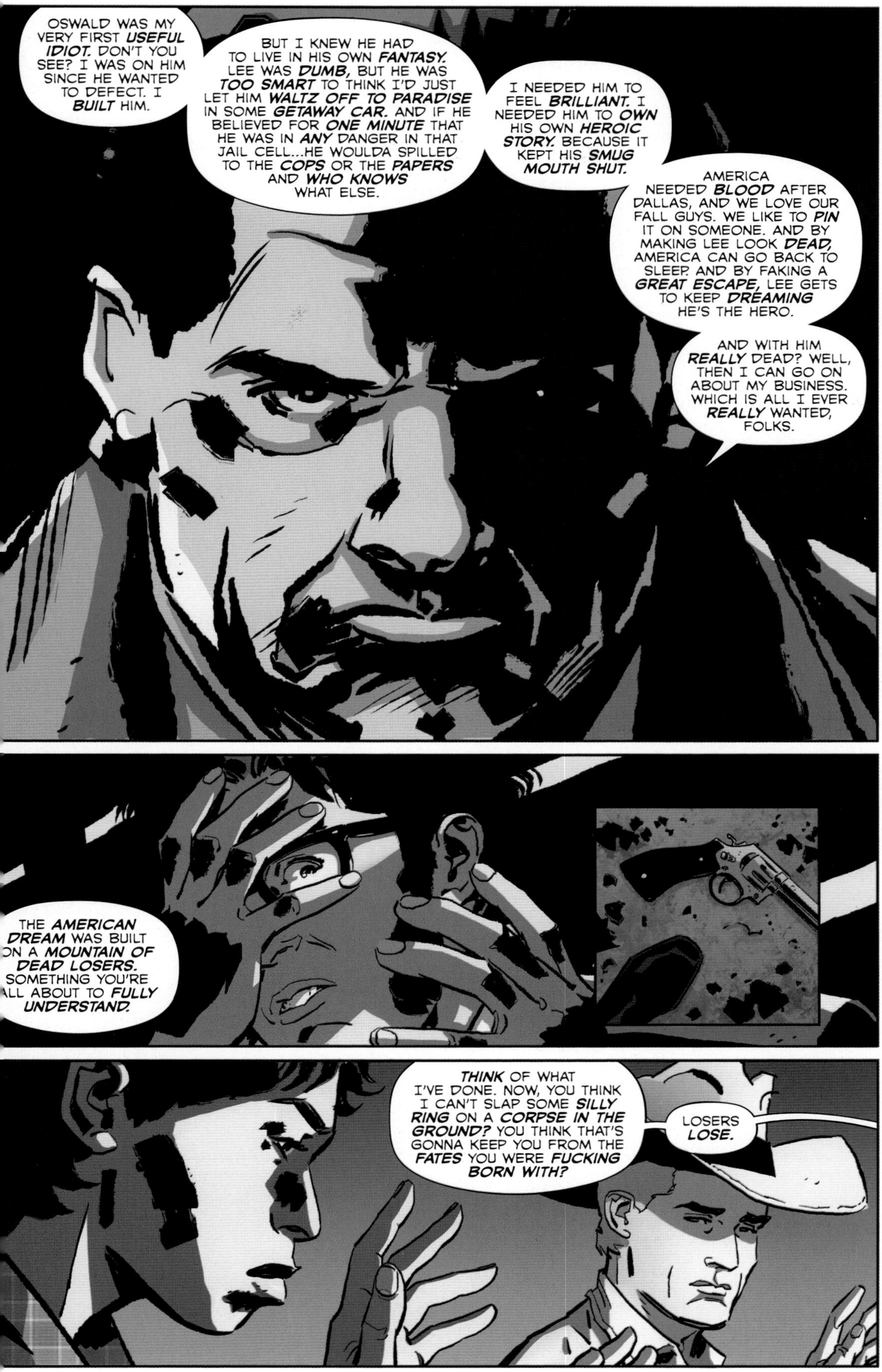
OSWALD WAS MY VERY FIRST *USEFUL IDIOT.* DON'T YOU SEE? I WAS ON HIM SINCE HE WANTED TO DEFECT. I *BUILT* HIM.
BUT I KNEW HE HAD TO LIVE IN HIS OWN *FANTASY.* LEE WAS *DUMB,* BUT HE WAS *TOO SMART* TO THINK I'D JUST LET HIM *WALTZ OFF TO PARADISE* IN SOME *GETAWAY CAR.* AND IF HE BELIEVED FOR *ONE MINUTE* THAT HE WAS IN *ANY* DANGER IN THAT JAIL CELL...HE WOULDA SPILLED TO THE *COPS* OR THE *PAPERS* AND *WHO KNOWS* WHAT ELSE.
I NEEDED HIM TO FEEL *BRILLIANT.* I NEEDED HIM TO *OWN* HIS OWN *HEROIC STORY.* BECAUSE IT KEPT HIS *SMUG MOUTH SHUT.*
AMERICA NEEDED *BLOOD* AFTER DALLAS, AND WE LOVE OUR FALL GUYS. WE LIKE TO *PIN* IT ON SOMEONE. AND BY MAKING LEE LOOK *DEAD,* AMERICA CAN GO BACK TO SLEEP. AND BY FAKING A *GREAT ESCAPE,* LEE GETS TO KEEP *DREAMING* HE'S THE HERO.
AND WITH HIM *REALLY* DEAD? WELL, THEN I CAN GO ON ABOUT MY BUSINESS. WHICH IS ALL I EVER *REALLY* WANTED, FOLKS.
THE *AMERICAN DREAM* WAS BUILT ON A *MOUNTAIN OF DEAD LOSERS.* SOMETHING YOU'RE ALL ABOUT TO *FULLY UNDERSTAND.*
THINK OF WHAT I'VE DONE. NOW, YOU THINK I CAN'T SLAP SOME *SILLY RING* ON A *CORPSE IN THE GROUND?* YOU THINK THAT'S GONNA KEEP YOU FROM THE *FATES* YOU WERE *FUCKING BORN WITH?*
LOSERS *LOSE.*

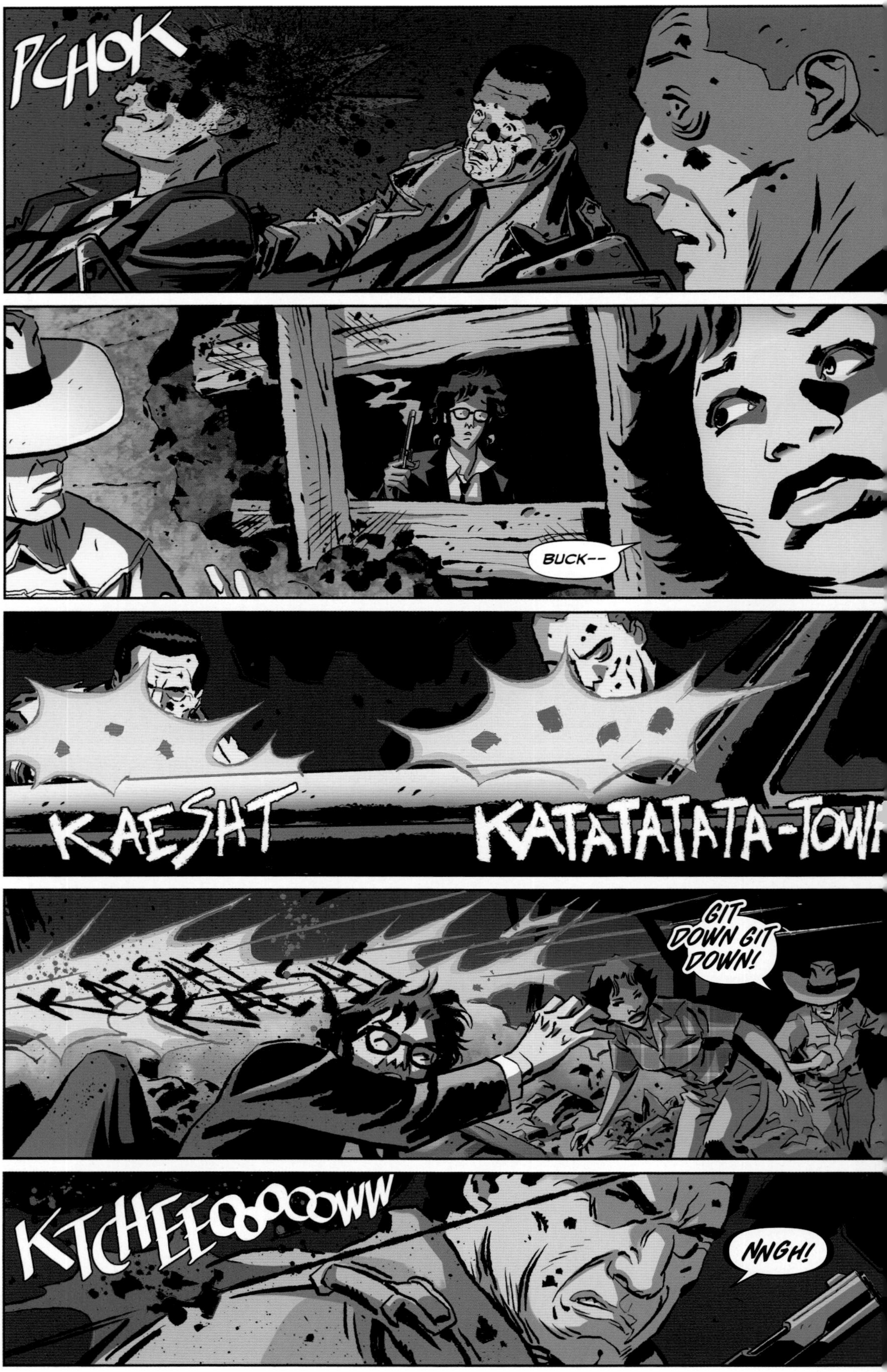
PCHOK
BUCK--
KAESHT
KATATATATA-TOW
GIT DOWN GIT DOWN!
KTCHEEOOOOOWW
NNGH!

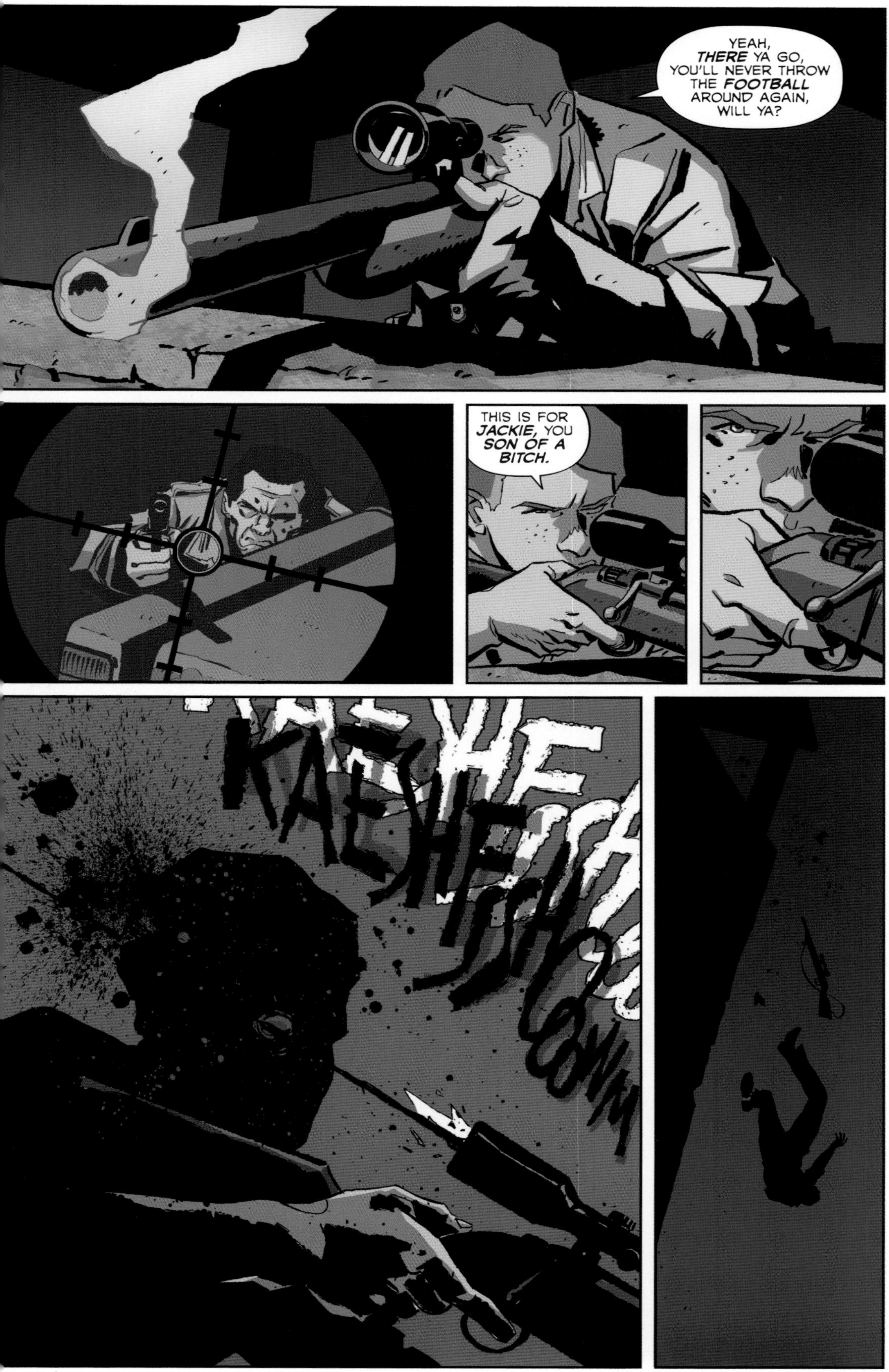
YEAH, THERE YA GO, YOU'LL NEVER THROW THE FOOTBALL AROUND AGAIN, WILL YA?
THIS IS FOR JACKIE, YOU SON OF A BITCH.

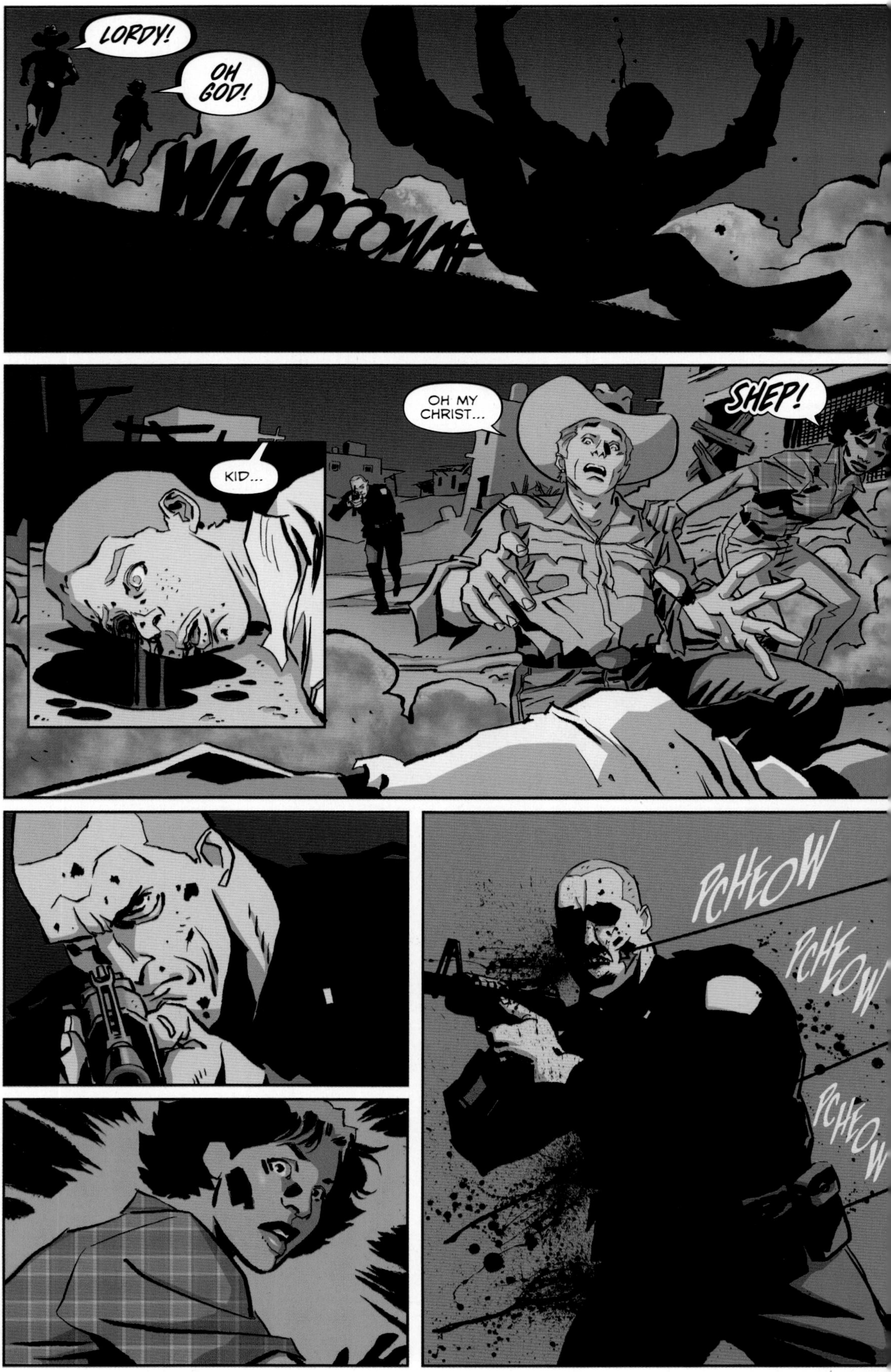
LORDY!
OH GOD!
WHOOOOOMF
KID...
OH MY CHRIST...
SHEP!
PCHEOW
PCHEOW
PCHEOW

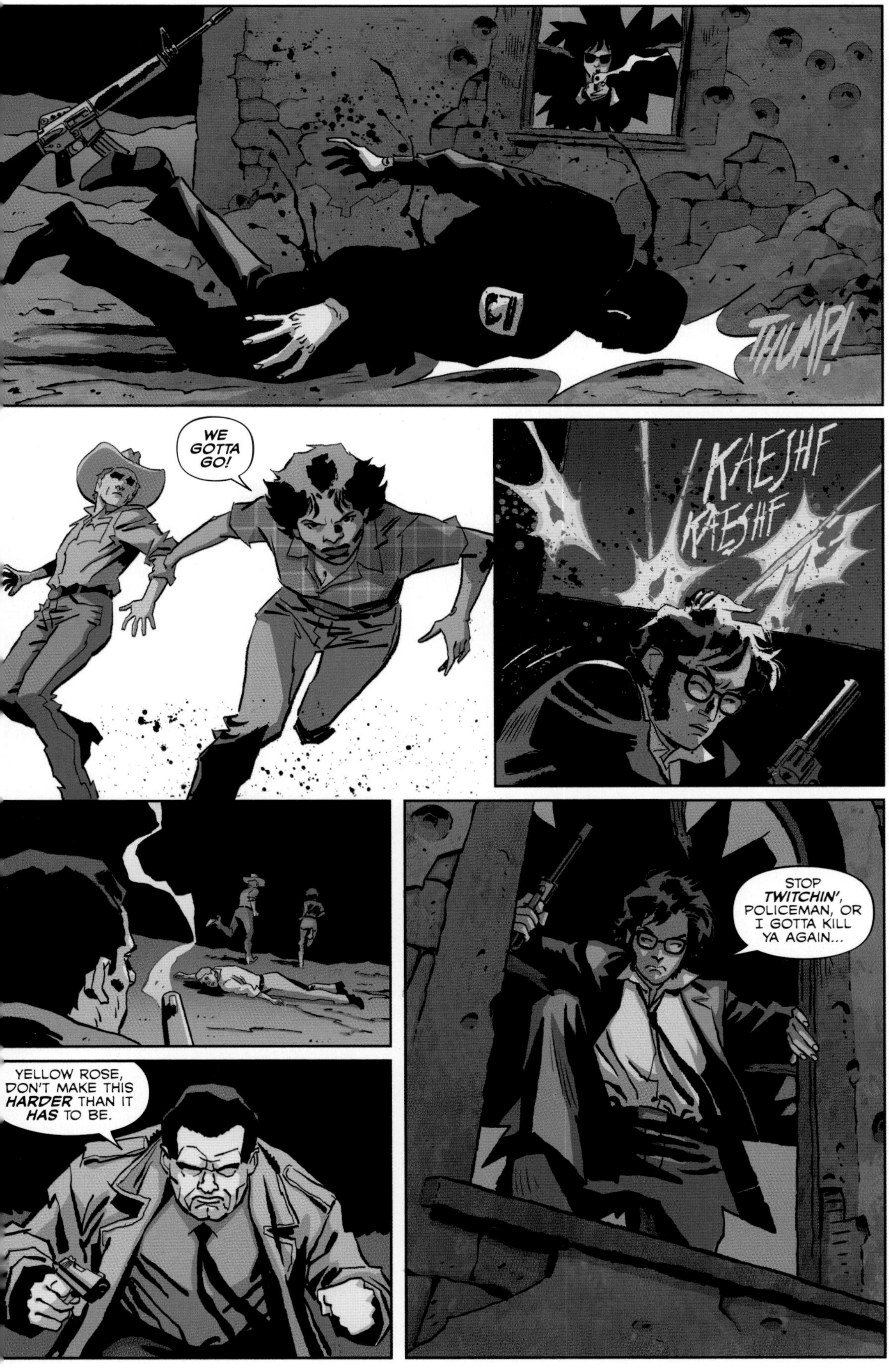
THUMP!
WE GOTTA GO!
KAESHF
KAESHF
STOP TWITCHIN', POLICEMAN, OR I GOTTA KILL YA AGAIN...
YELLOW ROSE, DON'T MAKE THIS HARDER THAN IT HAS TO BE.

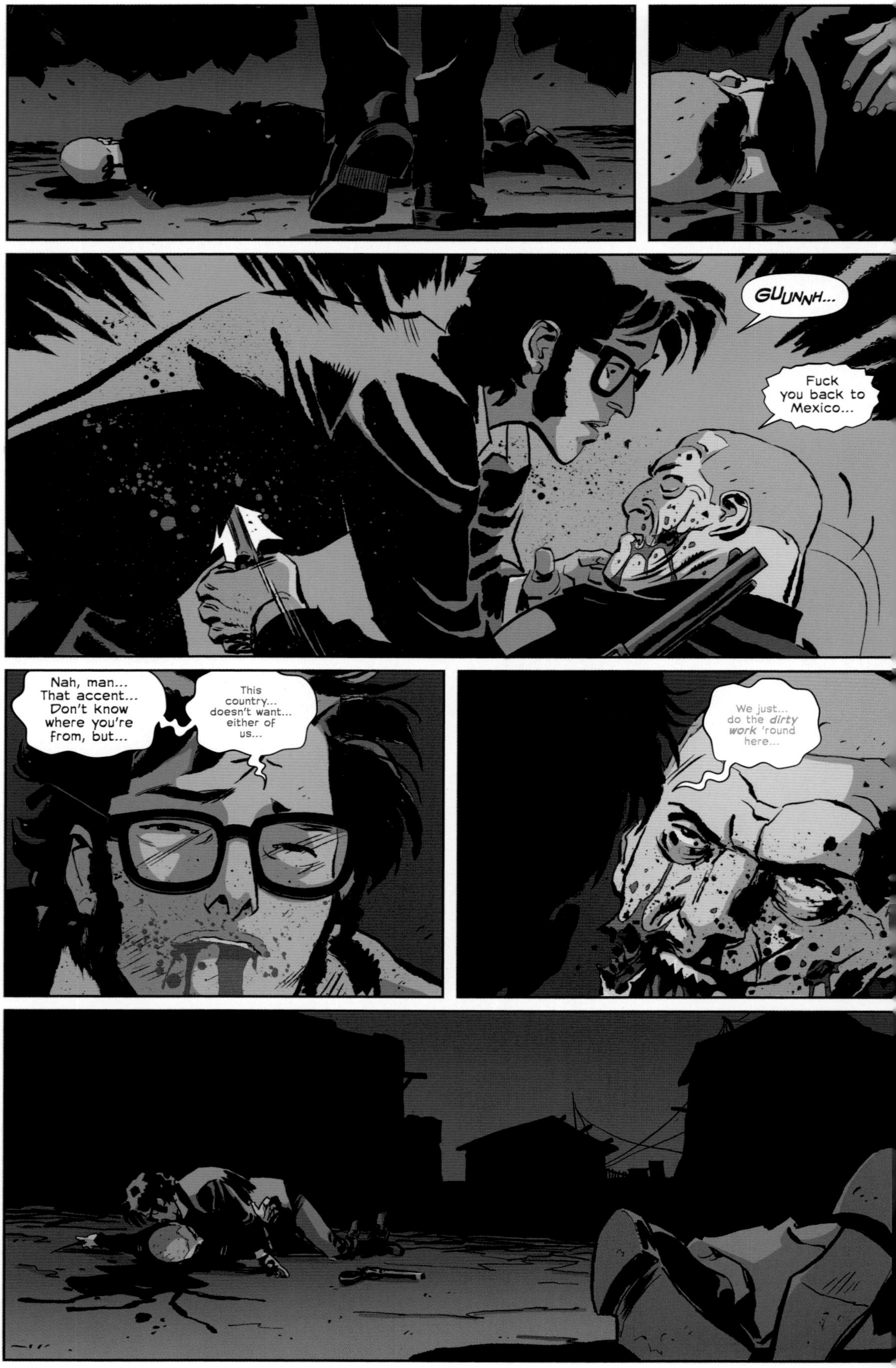
GUUNNH...
Fuck you back to Mexico...
Nah, man... That accent... Don't know where you're from, but...
This country... doesn't want... either of us...
We just... do the *dirty work* 'round here...

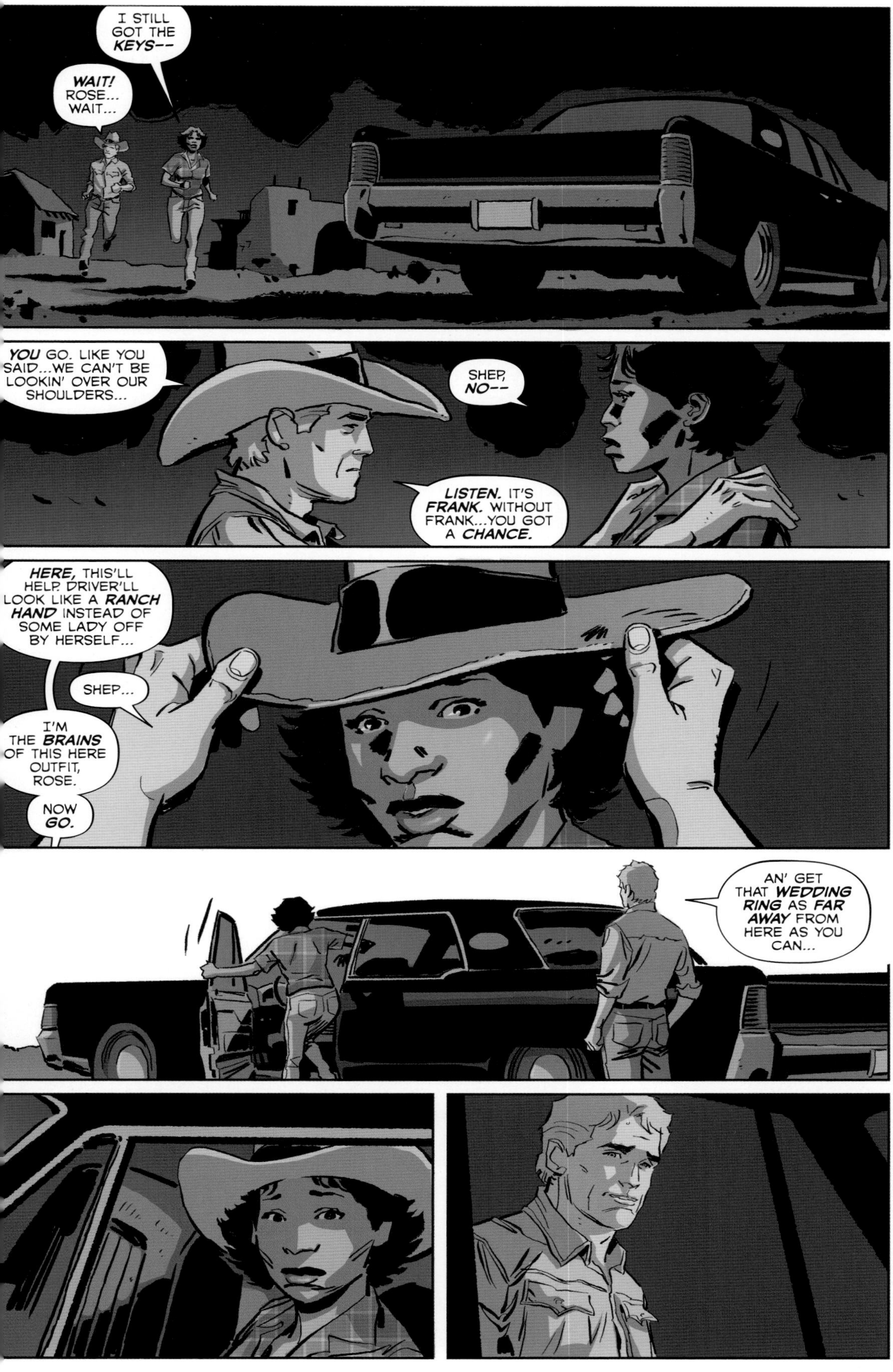

WAIT! ROSE... WAIT...
I STILL GOT THE KEYS--
YOU GO. LIKE YOU SAID...WE CAN'T BE LOOKIN' OVER OUR SHOULDERS...
SHEP, NO--
LISTEN. IT'S FRANK. WITHOUT FRANK...YOU GOT A CHANCE.
HERE, THIS'LL HELP. DRIVER'LL LOOK LIKE A RANCH HAND INSTEAD OF SOME LADY OFF BY HERSELF...
SHEP...
I'M THE BRAINS OF THIS HERE OUTFIT, ROSE.
NOW GO.
AN' GET THAT WEDDING RING AS FAR AWAY FROM HERE AS YOU CAN...

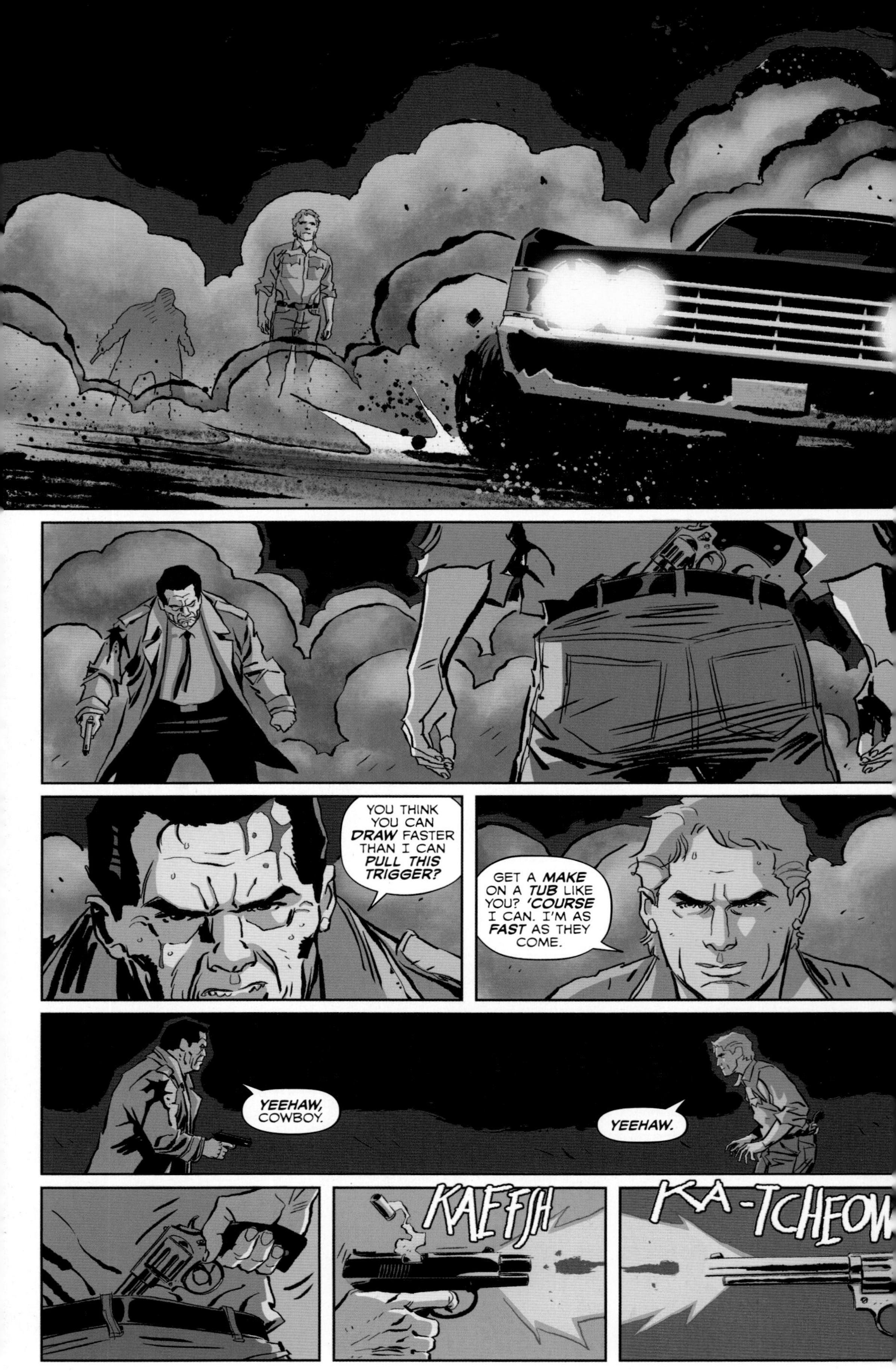
YOU THINK YOU CAN DRAW FASTER THAN I CAN PULL THIS TRIGGER?
GET A MAKE ON A TUB LIKE YOU? 'COURSE I CAN. I'M AS FAST AS THEY COME.
YEEHAW, COWBOY.
YEEHAW.
KAEFSH
KA-TCHEOW

WARREN COMMISSION CONVENES
Chief Justice to Preside Over Investigation of JFK's Death
December 1st, 1963

OSWALD ACTED ALONE

Lone Sniper Killed President, Commission Says

SEPTEMBER 27, 1964

RUBY DIES IN PRISON
Oswald's Assailant Victim of Cancer, Embolism
JANUARY 3RD, 1967

SHAW INNOCENT IN JFK CASE
D.A. Garrison Loses Big, Jury Decides in One Hour
MARCH 1ST, 1969

CONGRESS PROBES ASSASSINATIONS
House Select Committee to Investigate JFK, MLK
September 18th, 1976

SELECT COMMITTEE SAYS CONSPIRACY 'PROBABLE'
House Concludes Kennedy Killed by Unknown Parties
March 30, 1979

OSWALD TO BE EXHUMED

Autopsy Will Be Performed at Parkland,
Where **LHO** *and* **JFK** *Died*
October 4th, 1981

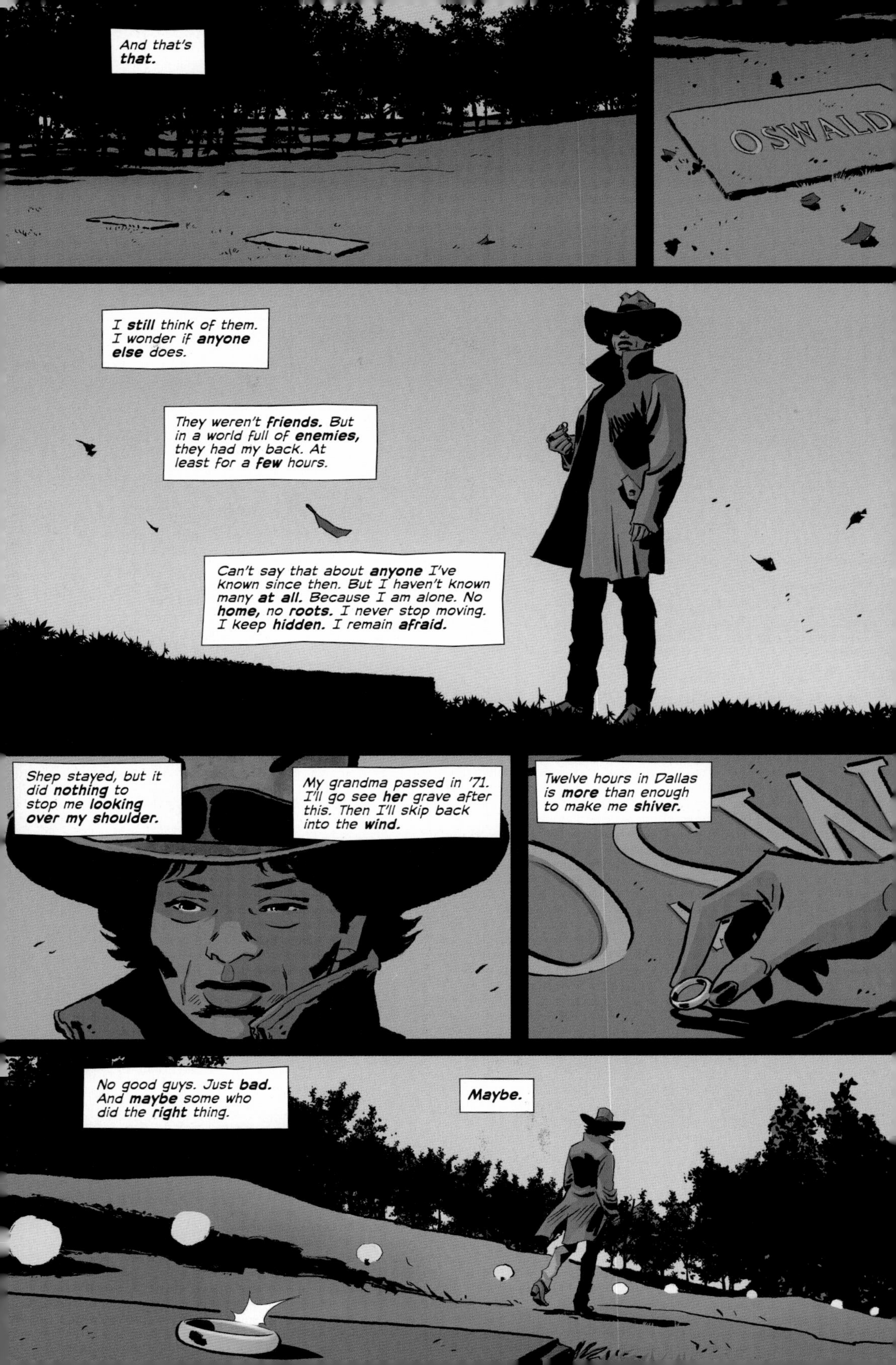

And that's **that.**
OSWALD
I **still** think of them. I wonder if **anyone else** does.
They weren't **friends.** But in a world full of **enemies,** they had my back. At least for a **few** hours.
Can't say that about **anyone** I've known since then. But I haven't known many **at all.** Because I am alone. No **home,** no **roots.** I never stop moving. I keep **hidden.** I remain **afraid.**
Shep stayed, but it did **nothing** to stop me **looking over my shoulder.**
My grandma passed in '71. I'll go see **her** grave after this. Then I'll skip back into the **wind.**
Twelve hours in Dallas is **more** than enough to make me **shiver.**
No good guys. Just **bad.** And **maybe** some who did the **right** thing.
Maybe.

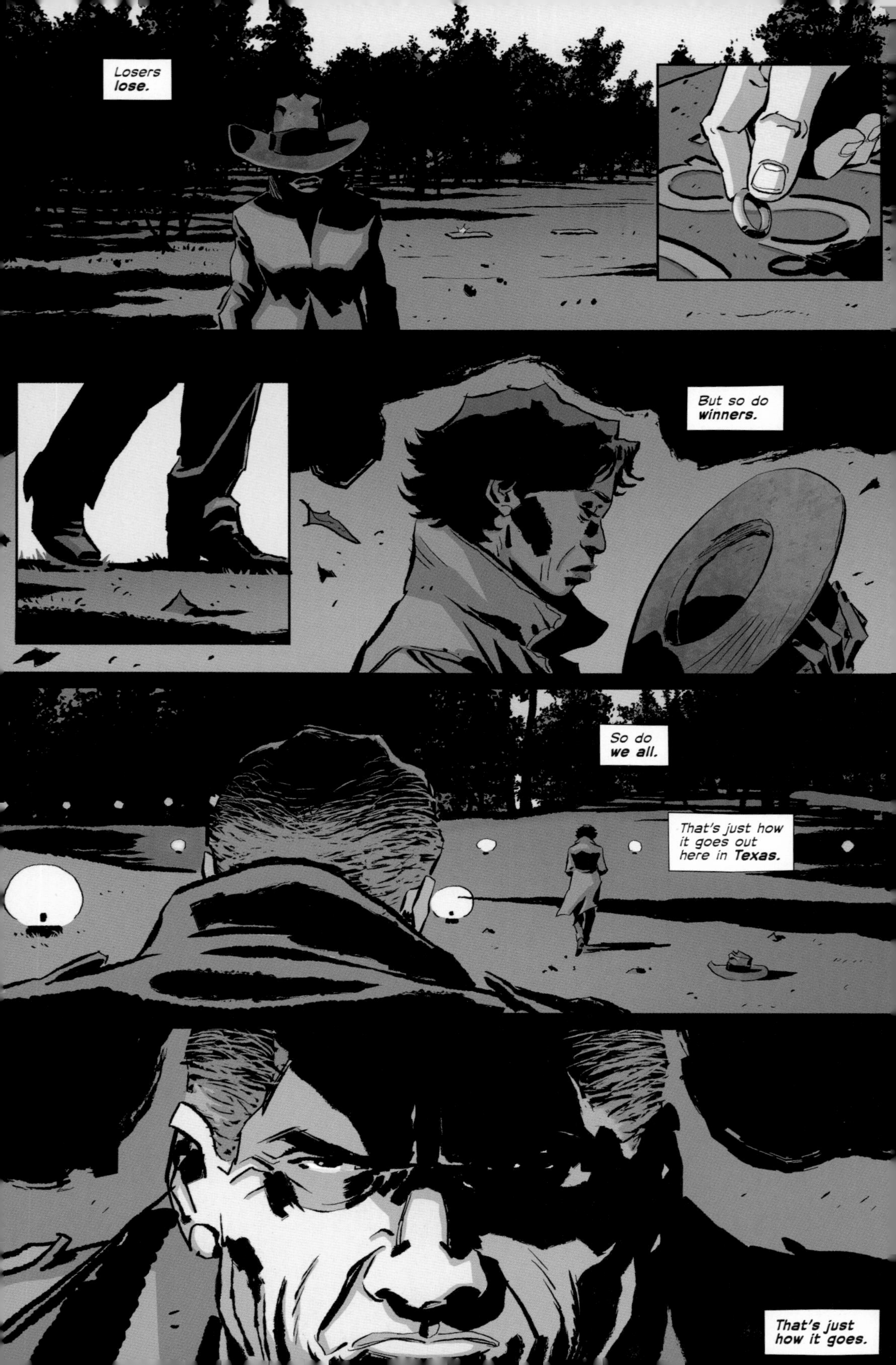
Losers lose.
But so do winners.
So do we all.
That's just how it goes out here in Texas.
That's just how it goes.

GROCER MISSING 30 YEARS ON:
Wooly's Manager Shepherd Walton Walked Out On Job In '61... And Never Came Back

SELECTED EGGS
40% OFF

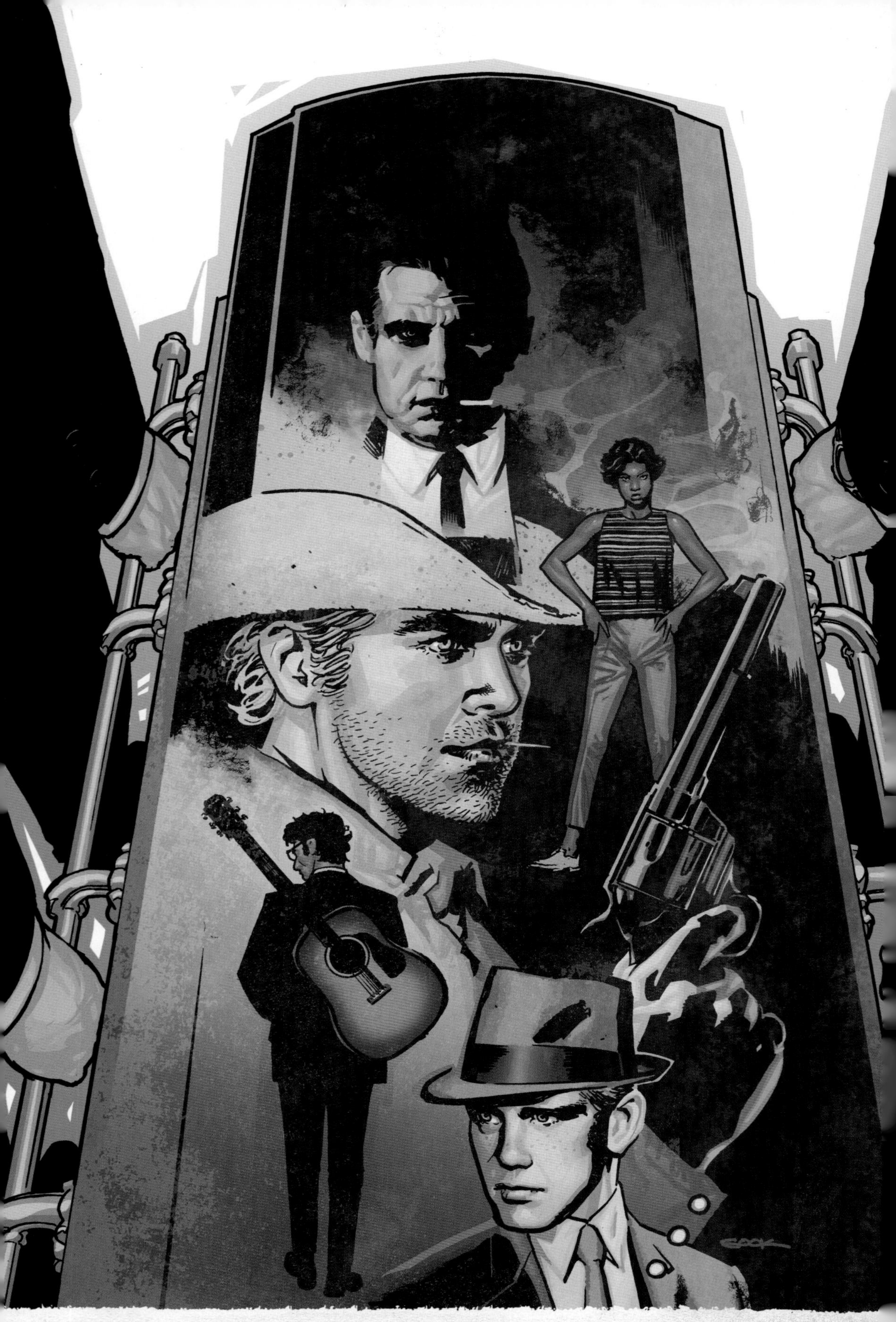

Additional Artwork by **Ryan Sook**

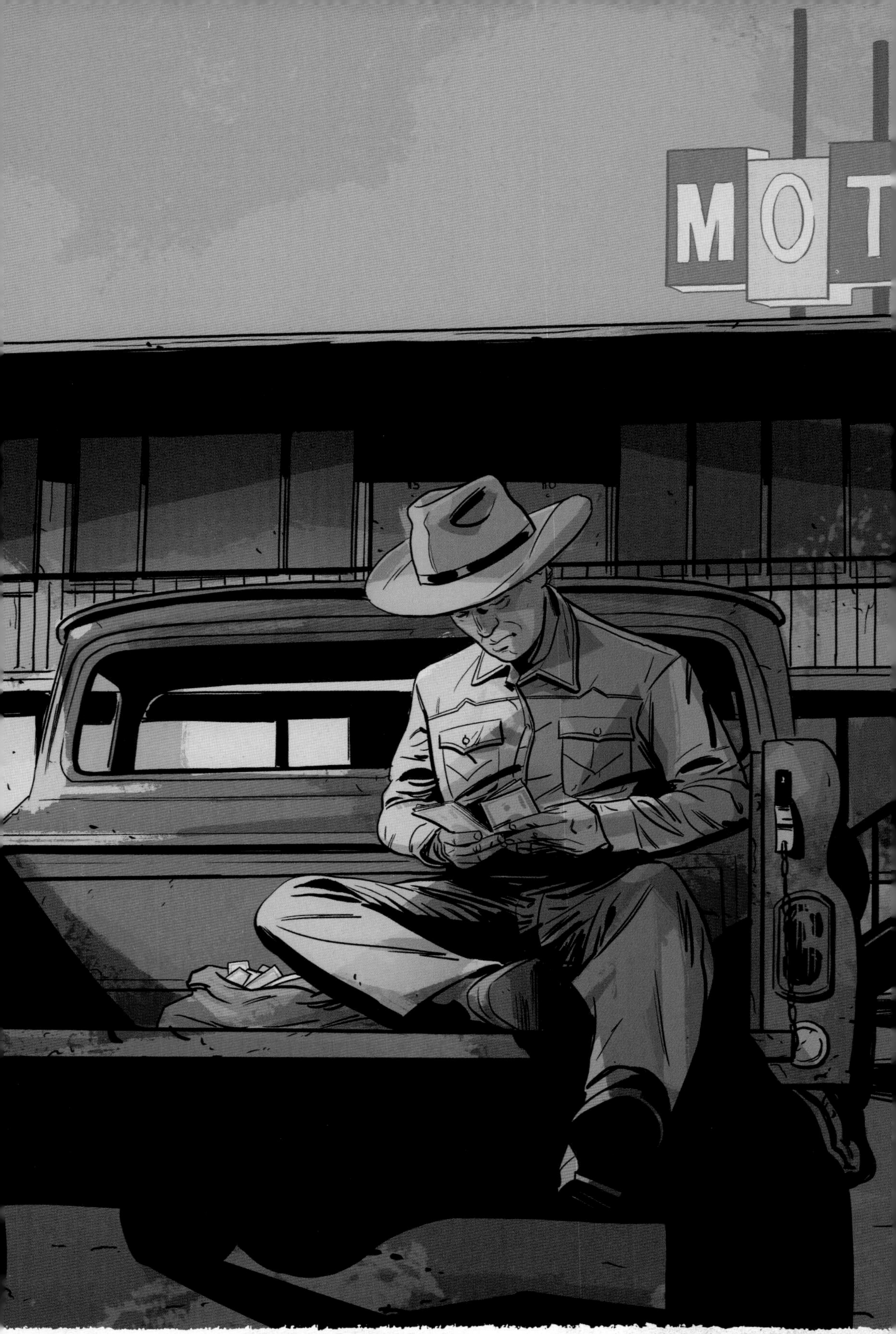
MOT

Additional Artwork by **Jacob Phillips**

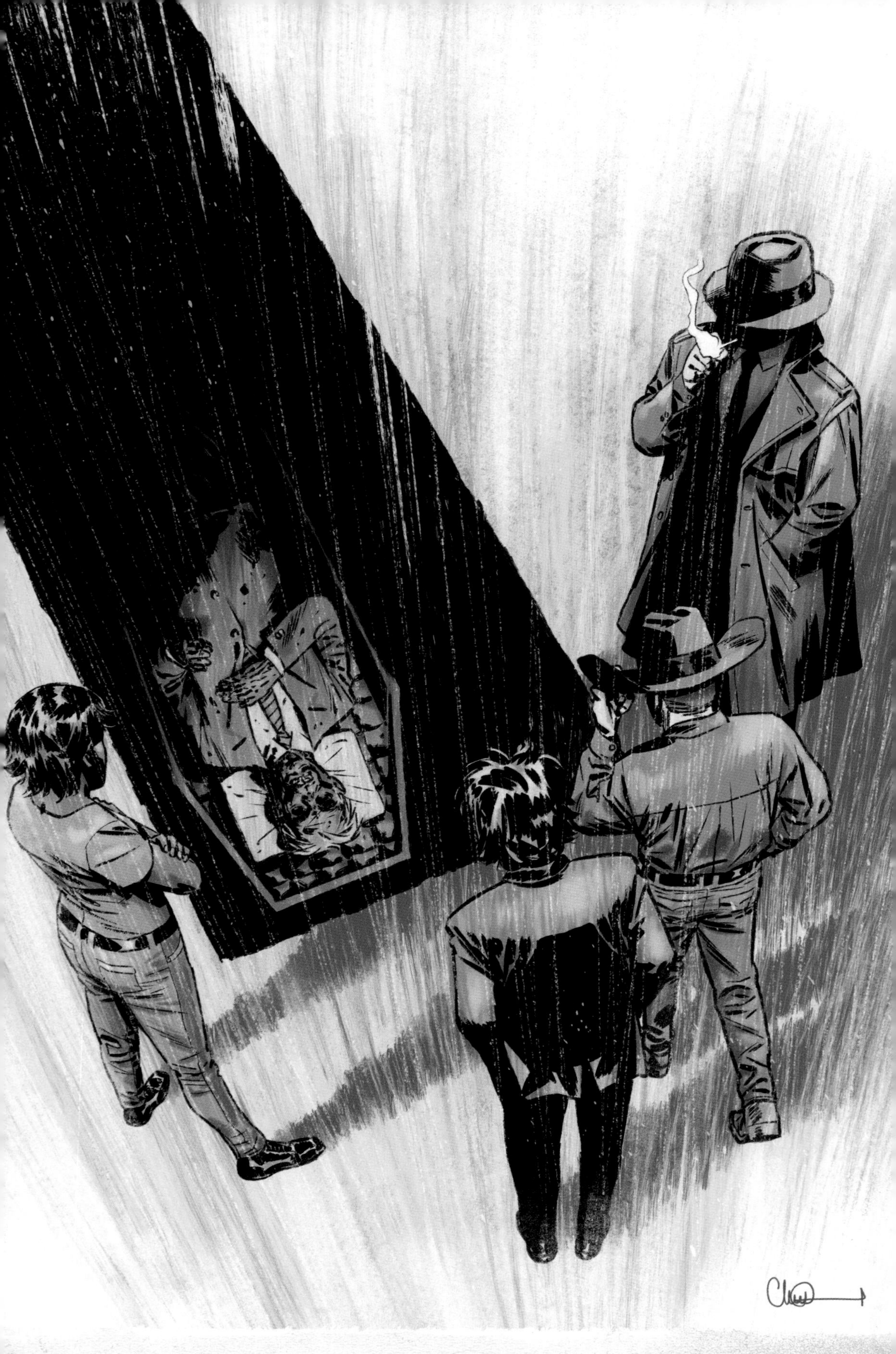

Additional Artwork by **Charlie Adlard**

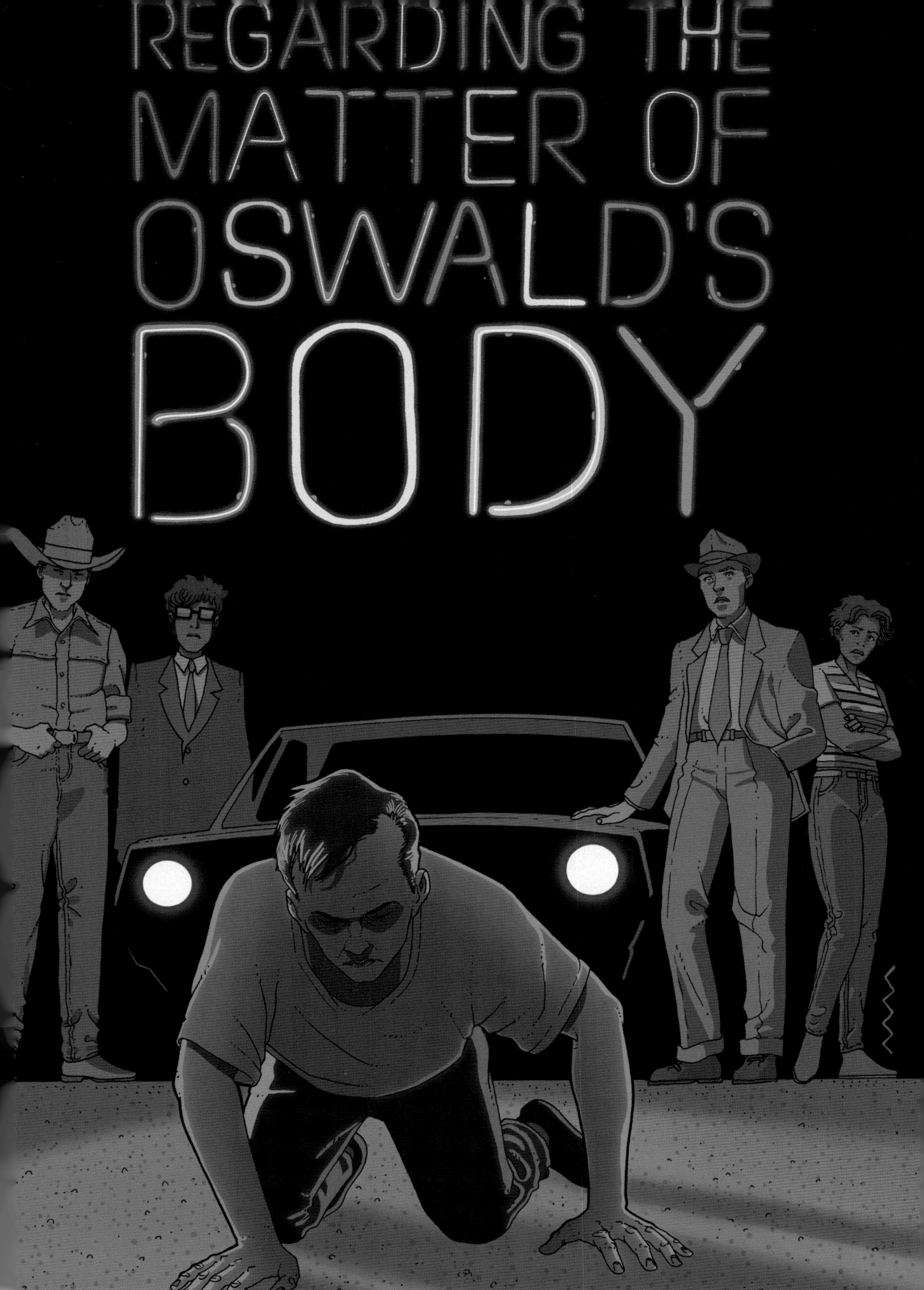
REGARDING THE
MATTER OF
OSWALD'S
BODY

Additional Artwork by **Martín Morazzo**

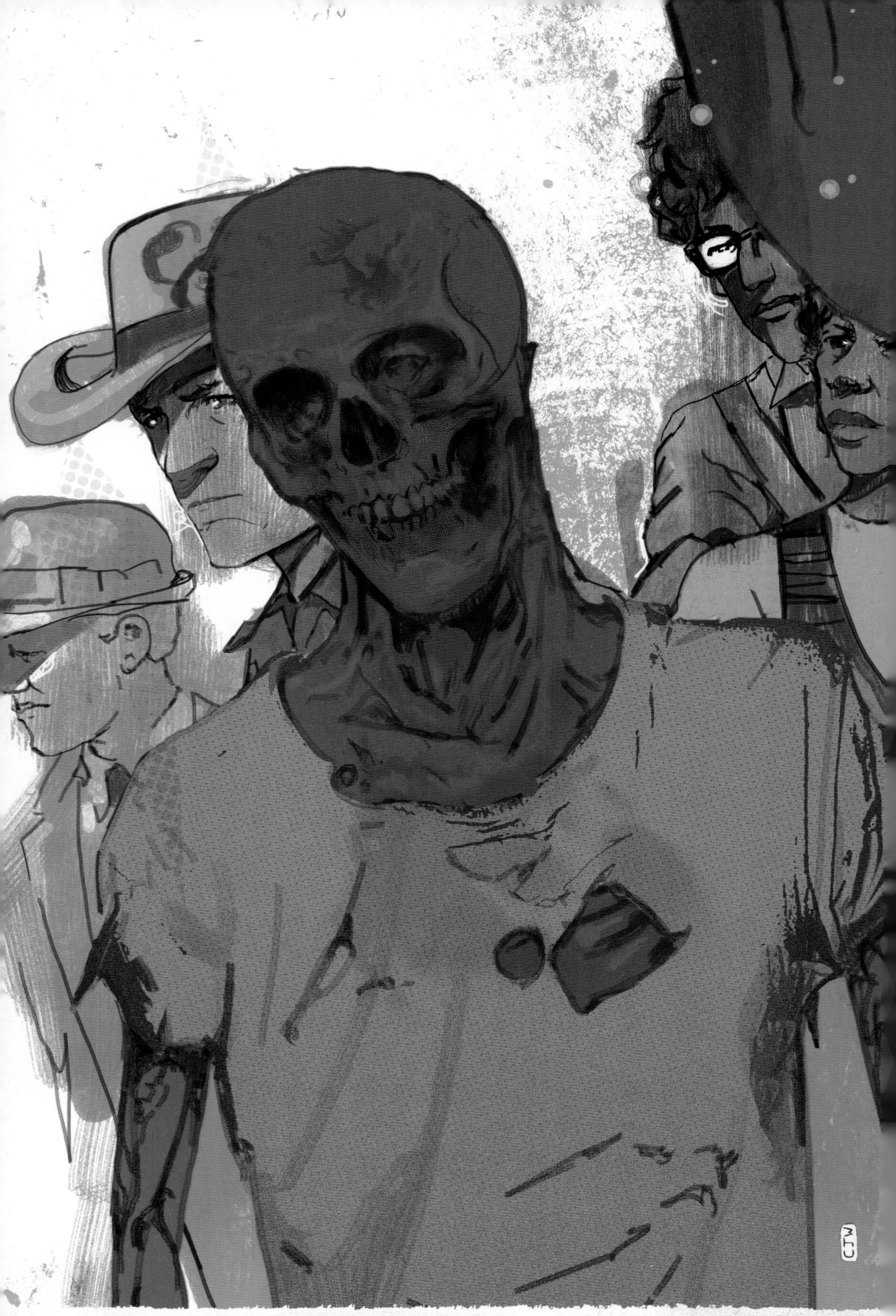
CJW

Additional Artwork by **Christian Ward**

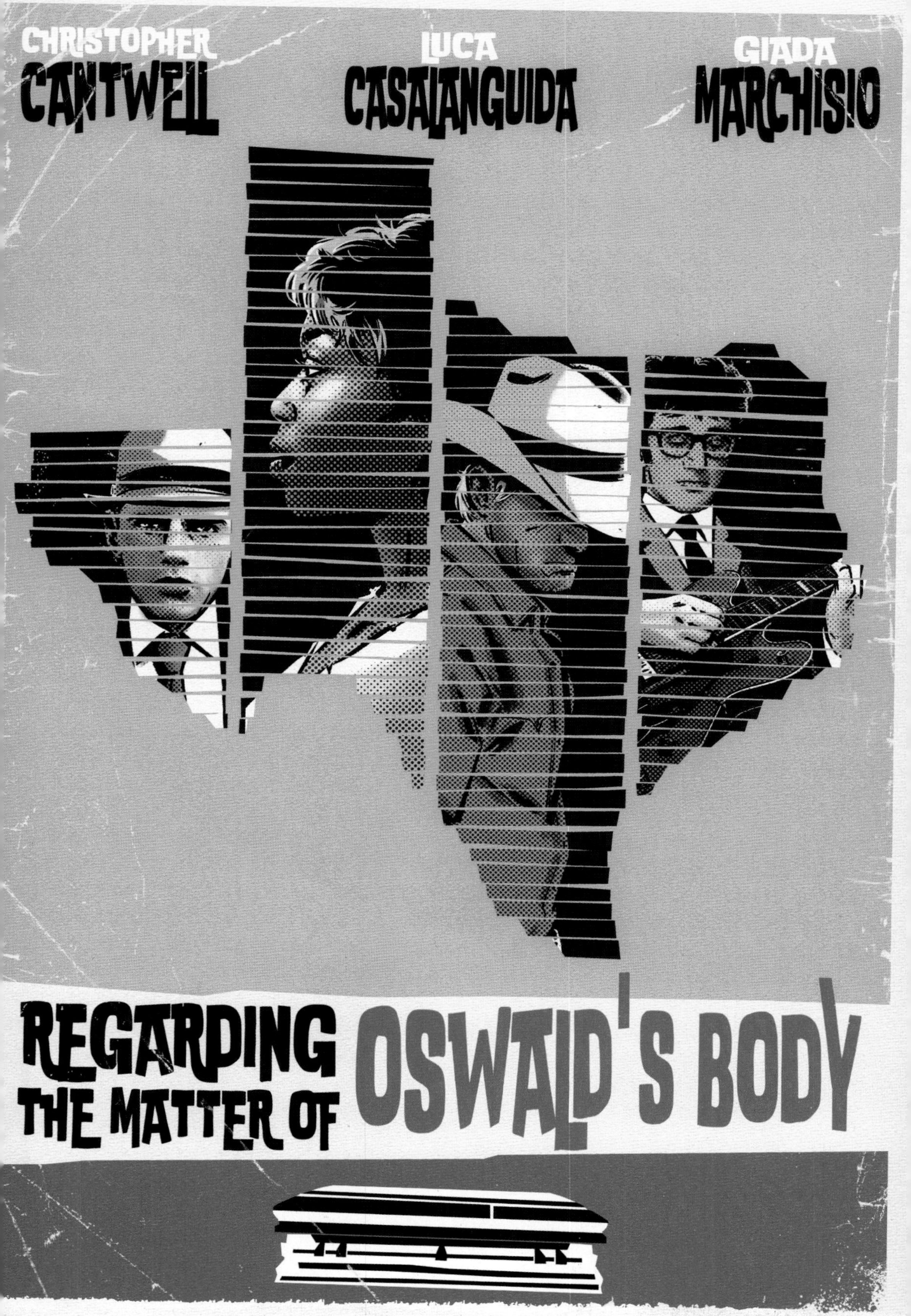
CHRISTOPHER CANTWELL
LUCA CASALANGUIDA
GIADA MARCHISIO
REGARDING THE MATTER OF OSWALD'S BODY

Additional Artwork by Jorge Fornés

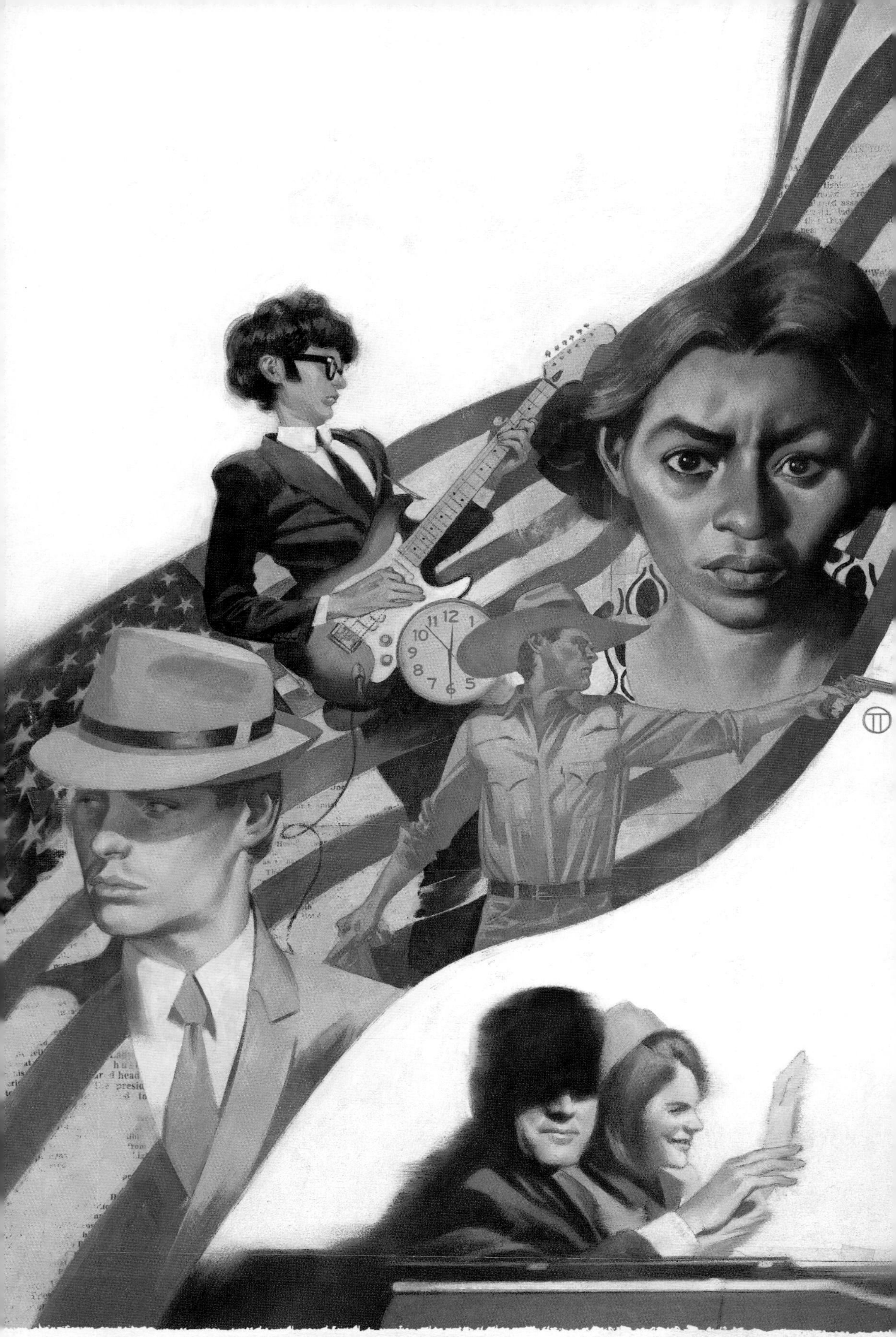

Additional Artwork by **Julian Totino Tedesco**

Regarding the Matter of OSWALD'S BODY

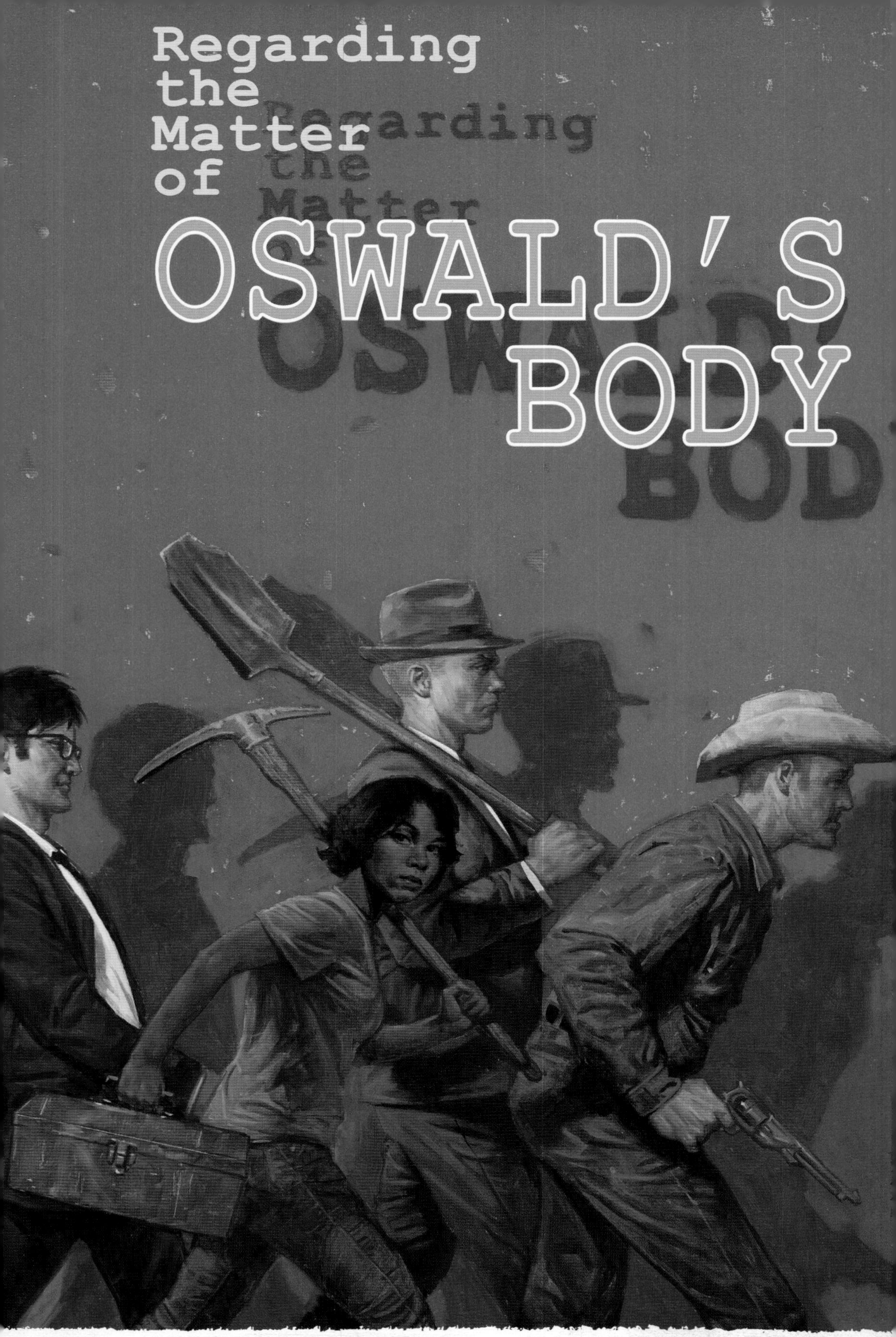

Additional Artwork by E.M. Gist

CHRISTOPHER CANTWELL

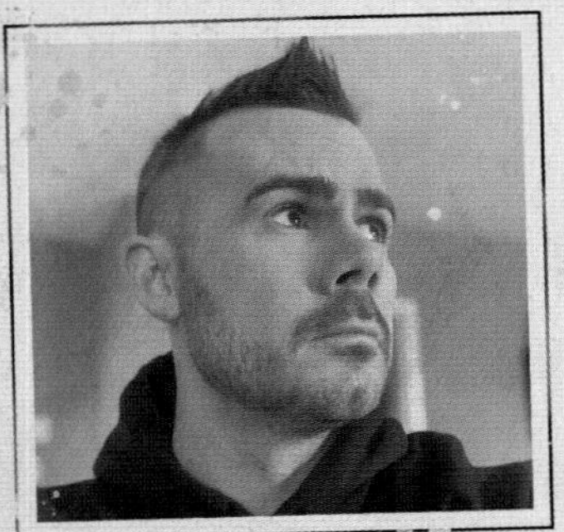

is the current writer of the ongoing *Iron Man* series for Marvel Entertainment. His other comics credits include *The United States of Captain America* and *Doctor Doom* for Marvel Entertainment, *The Blue Flame* for Vault Comics, and *She Could Fly* and *Everything* for Dark Horse's Berger Books. Cantwell is also a co-creator, executive producer, and showrunner of AMC's *Halt and Catch Fire* and additionally served as an executive producer on the first season of the upcoming TV adaptation of Brian K. Vaughan and Cliff Chiang's *Paper Girls*, coming soon to Amazon Prime.

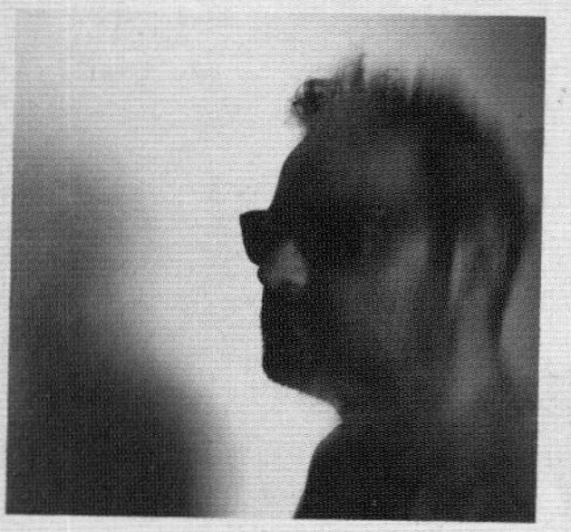

LUCA CASALANGUIDA

is a comic book artist from San Vito Marina, Italy. He has worked as an artist on comic book series published by Image Comics, Dark Horse, Top Cow, Aftershock, Dynamite and more. He also works in France for Delcourt and in Italy for Sergio Bonelli Editore on releases such as *Dylan Dog*.

GIADA MARCHISIO

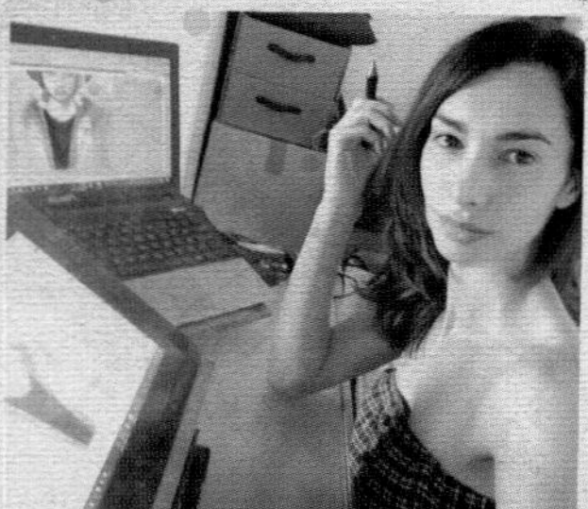

is an Italian colorist. After completing her studies at the International School of Comics and iMasterArt, she began working as an illustrator for Rizzoli, and in animation as a 2D artist. She entered the world of comics in 2017 as a colorist for Sergio Bonellli Editore. Since then, she was worked with Marvel, coloring *Astonishing X-Men*, *Cloak and Dagger*, *Avengers #700*, *The Spectacular Spider- Man*, *Marvel Comics #1000*, covers for *The Platoon: The Origins of the Punisher*, and more. She has also colored *Hit-Girl* with Goran Parlov for Mark Millar. She is currently working on *Star Wars: The High Republic: Trail of Shadows*.